MANAGEMENT OF ADP SYSTEMS

MANAGEMENT OF ADP SYSTEMS

BY

Dr. MARVIN M. WOFSEY

PROFESSOR OF MANAGEMENT

THE GEORGE WASHINGTON UNIVERSITY, WASHINGTON, D.C.

FIRST EDITION

AUERBACH®
publishers

philadelphia
new york
london

AUERBACH Publishers Inc., *Philadelphia, 1973*

Library of Congress Cataloging in Publication Data
Wofsey, Marvin M.
    Management of ADP systems.
    (Auerbach computer science series)
    Bibliography: p.
    1. Electronic data processing—Business.
    2. Electronic data processing departments—Management.
    I. Title.   II. Series.
HF5548.2.W62 -973   658'05'4   73-3042
ISBN 0-87769-155-X

To Erna and Avrom

◀ CONTENTS

◀ LIST OF ILLUSTRATIONS

◀ LIST OF TABLES

◀ FOREWORD

In the relatively short span of 22 years since computers first were used for business purposes, the equipment has gone through several generations. Programming languages have progressed from machine language to assembly languages to higher-level languages. In contrast, the development of systems using the capabilities of computers has not kept pace. Information on how to manage computers and the computer-based systems has lagged even further.

The forward-thinking manager of data processing can profit from this book by comparing his operations, procedures, and relationships with those espoused in the text. Its exceptional value as a textbook and study guide for college-level courses becomes apparent when the questions provided at the end of each chapter are reviewed, together with the well-detailed illustrative material contained throughout the book and its appendices. Wofsey has culled through virtually everything available on these subjects, and has distilled that which he considers worthwhile. To this he has added some provocative ideas.

Readers may not agree with all of Dr. Wofsey's definitions, ideas, methods, and suggestions. If they are prudent, however, they will try the recommendations, evaluate the results, and modify them to fit particular situations.

Dr. Wofsey's introduction to the educational field began when he joined forces with Dr. Lowell H. Hattery at The American University in 1960. The collaboration of Drs. Hattery and Wofsey has been a fruitful one. From it came not only added courses, but also the Center for Technology and Administration, with Dr. Hattery its first director and Dr. Wofsey the assistant director.

Dr. Wofsey is a professor of management at the School of Government and Business Administration at The George Washington University, where he is chairman of the doctoral committee. He has assisted there in the development and implementation of bachelors, masters, and doctors degrees, with major fields in data processing and information technology.

Dr. Wofsey is a lifetime member of the Data Processing Management Association, and is a holder of the Certificate in Data Processing. His activities with the association include member of the Certificate Advisory Council, International Director; General Chairman of the 1968 International Data Processing Conference; and lecturer on computer management subjects.

R. Calvin Elliot, Executive Director
Data Processing Management Association

◀ PREFACE

Although the first computer was accepted by the federal government in 1946, it wasn't until five years later that one was used for business-type operations. UNIVAC 1, Serial 1, was first used by the Bureau of the Census in 1951, where it assisted in processing 1950 census data. It is quite appropriate that the Bureau of the Census be involved in the first governmental use of a computer for processing business-type data. In the latter part of the nineteenth century both Hollerith and Powers developed their models of electric accounting machines, which were conceived and used primarily as data-handling devices to assist in preparing census tabulations. Although the use of these predecessors of computers spread throughout government and business, their application generally was restricted to accounting and tabulating.

Comparatively few people recognized the importance of the computer in the early 1950s. If the impact it would have on business was recognized, few wrote or did anything noteworthy to foster its development. It was not until the latter part of the decade that the potential of the computer as a powerful tool of management was accepted generally. Coupled with advances in the technology of communications media, the computer became the means of assisting centralized control of large, geographically decentralized government and business organizations. Paradoxically, the computer permitted the decentralization of certain decision making and yet centralized control of large organizational complexes.

A new generation of phrases entered the management field: integrated data processing, management information systems, total systems, command and control systems, data base management systems, information storage and retrieval systems, and virtual memory systems. Unfortunately, however, to date they have denoted more theory than accomplishment. True, some advances have been made, but the surface has only been scratched. New hardware and software developments have opened the gate more widely for significant advancement in the design and implementation of management information systems.

The Industrial Revolution, during which facilities for physical production were expanded and improved, is waning. On the other hand, computers have become a dynamic force in a cybernetic revolution. A deterrent to large integrated systems has been the inability of the human mind to bring to bear the many relevant details encompassed in a large enterprise. Prior to the computer, so much time was consumed in distilling facts from nonrelevant information that it usually was too late to initiate optimum actions. The computer, however, makes it possible to store data and then to recover it in time and in the form needed to take appropriate actions. The computer is an extension of the human brain. As such, it is the primary factor in the cybernetic revolution now in progress. An analysis concerning how well this powerful tool is being managed, therefore, appears to be justified.

Two terms often mentioned with regard to data processing are electronic data processing (EDP) and automatic data processing (ADP). Sometimes they are used loosely to mean the same thing. Throughout this book they have specific meanings. EDP refers to the computer and the peripherals attached to the computer. ADP, on the other hand, includes all automatic data processing equipment, including electric accounting machines and other nonelectronic equipment.

This book is based primarily on a doctoral dissertation at The School of Government and Public Administration of The American University, Washington, D. C. The author wishes to express particularly his appreciation of the assistance furnished him by Dr. Lowell H. Hattery, chairman of his dissertation committee, who provided guidance throughout the periods of research and writing. Without the stimulus he furnished, it is doubtful that the dissertation and this book would have been completed.

The material upon which this book is based has resulted from the author's consulting and teaching experiences in North America, Europe, and Asia. His avocation is helping developing countries use computers effectively. The results of this research have been amplified by the current literature. The author is especially indebted to Captain John O. Bachert, U.S. Navy, who wrote Chapter 2—Organization.

Finally, appreciation is expressed to the hundreds of data processing managers who discussed frankly the problems they had and the decisions they made, so that others may profit by their mistakes and corrective actions be taken. Every effort has been made to keep these managers anonymous, although each example cited is based upon an actual happening.

MANAGEMENT OF ADP SYSTEMS

1 ◀ PLANNING

An important primary step in the planning process is the establishment of goals, or objectives, followed successively by more and more detailed specifics concerning how these goals are to be accomplished. If one were planning to take a trip, the objective might be to travel to a particular location. The policy would be to go by a specific method, such as an automobile. The procedure would involve the selection of the vehicle to be used, the routes to be traveled, and other details concerning how the trip was to be made.

There are many possible ways of characterizing types of planning—by function, by organizational level doing the planning, and by the time frame encompassed in the planning. In a time framework the three levels might well be characterized as objectives, long-range plans, and short-range plans. Accordingly, this chapter, as applied to managing data processing, will be divided into three sections: objectives, long-range plans, and short-range plans.

OBJECTIVES

Trends

In the early 1950s, when computers first were applied to the problems of business, the primary objective was the reduction of clerical cost. As late as 1960 a study of 20 companies by the United States Department of Labor showed this to be the most prevalent data processing objective. Savings of equipment and space were next in order of importance, followed by the expectation that greater accuracy and new information ultimately would result in more efficient management and cost reduction. In 1971 a study of about 100 of the top 500 corporations in the United States indicated that savings were still the major objective.

Although during the 1950s the most important objective of data processing was the reduction of clerical cost, some managers recognized the tremendous potential of the computer as a tool of management. An early 1950

1

article, for example, considered the computer to be a challenge to management's capability limitations. It suggested strongly that the computer be used as a tool to accomplish management objectives.

Discussions of the subject of data processing objectives with managers of 13 computer installations in private industry and 3 in government in the middle 1960s showed that only half of them knew of written objectives for their installations. These computer installations ranged in size from a small card computer to a large computer with 10 magnetic tape drives, together with a smaller computer with 4 tape drives.

If anything, the foregoing shows a higher level of use of objectives than actually existed. One reply classified as having written objectives was:

> My objective is listed in my mission: "Accomplish all data processing requirements of the company."

Another respondent, answering the question in the affirmative, wrote:

> Our objective is to do what the company should do—make profit. The feasibility study lists what needs to be accomplished, and provides yardsticks for measuring the degree of accomplishment.

Further questions elicited the information that the feasibility study mentioned was four years old at the time.

Although most data processing organizations by 1967 or 1968 appeared to have written objectives or missions, either in organization manuals or in feasibility studies, these objectives were seldom consulted. Data processing managers more often were confining themselves to seeing that reports got out on time and that they were accurate. The managers also solved personnel problems, responded to crises, and considered the possible advantages of new equipment. In such an atmosphere many decisions were based on the pressures of the situation—management by crisis. The decisions were cures for current emergencies rather than mature considered judgment based on long or short-term objectives. Although the managers might not have understood all details or ramifications of the objectives they were trying to accomplish, they did show a general understanding of at least the major objectives.

It wasn't until the middle 1960s that many data processing managers were asking such questions as:

> What are the objectives of the overall system of which data processing is a part?
> What role does data processing play in achieving these goals?
> Do the objectives of data processing reflect that role?

What possible alternatives are available which will enable the better completion of these objectives?

Despite the fact that the incidence of such penetrating system-evaluation by data processing managers was increasing, the growth of goal analysis at first was painfully slow. Its overall impact on data processing management was not especially significant. There were perceptible movements in this direction, particularly in large governmental systems where the emphasis was on program management. Objectives appeared in industrial organizations such as chemical processors, oil companies, large manufacturers, and railroads. By the early 1970s, written data processing objectives were evident in most areas of industry and government.

Establishment

Much of the pertinent literature indicates that managers should establish objectives. The level of management to do this, however, is not clear. One theory is that top management should use an overall plan to direct all major moves in the right direction. Since data processing crosses all units and functions of an organization, it is felt that senior management should set the original goals. Then it should maintain an active interest in data processing. A management consulting firm advised that management must set the automatic data processing goals to provide a frame of reference for guidance. A management bulletin stated that the success in any job is measured by a set of criteria. A manager should try to identify the criteria used by his superiors or, if appropriate, should help establish them. He should identify his own criteria and, in turn, provide criteria for his subordinates.

If it is assumed that top management, senior management, and management are at the same level of management, it would appear that there is complete agreement. Even within top management, however, there is a distribution of responsibility, and executives in these areas raise questions as to which group or person is to establish data processing objectives.

Both in government and in business it appears that the objectives of the system that data processing serves are established by top management. Often this is done in consultation with upper levels of management. The objectives of data processing, however, seldom originate at top management level. Instead, the first objectives generally are written by the management department or by the team that completed the feasibility study and designed the system. These objectives are then amended and/or later approved by top management. With the emergence of assistant bureau or corporate directors for management information, the establishment of such objectives tends to concentrate at that level. Ultimately, top management approves these objectives.

When data processing objectives derive from the experiences of the company, or are developed by data processing managers rather than by top management, they tend to lose the comprehensive and broad view that normally would be exhibited by top management. For example, a director of data processing suggested the following data processing objectives:

1. Develop policies for systems, programming, and operating.
2. Direct data processing and ensure prompt and continuous implementation of policies.
3. Develop data processing personnel through training and on-the-job opportunities.
4. Maintain an active recruitment policy.
5. Maintain close liaison with customers.
6. Develop liaison with potential customers.
7. Develop training programs for actual and potential users.
8. Consider the potential values of data processing for the organization.
9. Inform management of new potential benefits, both within and outside the organization.
10. Develop a comprehensive and understandable flow of information to actual and potential users.
11. Report failures, problems, successes, costs, and savings to management.
12. Develop data processing budgets and plans for personnel, equipment, supplies, and space.
13. Schedule priorities and placate users.
14. Develop a sympathetic and cooperative attitude among data processing personnel toward the needs of customers.
15. Develop a conscious drive for accuracy.

A survey indicated that, generally, technicians rather than top management set the goals for computer organizations. This is cited as a primary reason for the failure to realize the true potential of data processing. The failure of top management to set objectives is a primary reason for ineffective use of computer systems.

Since top management has not formulated objectives for data processing, and objectives devised by technicians generally lead to failure, is there another alternative? The setting of such objectives by a steering or coordinating committee has been successful in several companies. In these cases the committee was composed of a representative from top management and a representative from each of the major operating departments. These representatives were managers, not technicians. They were high enough in the organizational hierarchy of their departments to understand priorities, goals, and policies that were in effect. Some knowledge of computers and their potential use helped. In one company surveyed, the original function of the committee was to determine priorities and to judge the merits of contending applications. As time passed, this committee established a viable set of objectives for data processing. While many people may question the effectiveness of a committee for such purposes, it has an indisputable advantage. It opens the lines of communication between data processing and the operating departments and between the departments themselves.

One of the most frequent and recurring complaints of data processing managers is that they cannot get top management to establish objectives for them. Instead of complaining, they should take the initiative themselves. To the best of their abilities, they should select objectives for data processing that will support the overall purposes of the company as they understand them. After these objectives have been formulated, they can be submitted to management for approval or amendment.

Objectives are needed to clarify the interests and aims of management before action is taken. A definition by management of the objectives to be attained is probably the single factor most important to successful computer operations. These statements typify a belief that data processing objectives should be established "in the beginning." Policy, however, often emerges from experience. Although objectives should be promulgated when a new organization is established, these should change in accordance with experience.

In a data processing division the policies should be sufficiently stable to assure the other divisions of the organization that the data processing division will fulfill its commitments to furnish reports at specific times. It is felt that objectives should be dynamic, not static, and that these objectives should be revised as conditions change. Three events that might indicate need for a review of objectives are a shift in top management personnel, a change in organization, and a change in the product line. Even when conditions do not change, a review of objectives is indicated if, as frequently happens, the original objectives are too ambiguous or too general.

Although practically all data processing installations visited by the author had objectives, in most cases these objectives were effected when data processing was established or when the computer was added. Occasionally, the objectives of all elements of a company were reviewed and updated. At that time the objectives of the data processing division were updated together with those of other divisions.

It is suggested that the objectives of data processing be reviewed approximately once a year, unless conditions make it evident that such a review is needed earlier. If the review is premature, this will be readily apparent, and the review may be aborted. Waiting until it is clear that a change in objectives is needed may be too great a delay. Gradual changes in organization and product line may not stand out until the total change is well past the time when objectives should be revised. Furthermore, regular review will reveal that objectives may have been faulty when promulgated.

Documentation

It is fairly evident that objectives should be written, not only to prevent their distortion as time passes, but also to furnish guides that the manager of data processing can use in making decisions. Although, in an ideal situation, the essential parts of the objectives should be in writing, there are circumstances where this would be either unwise or impossible. In an emergency situation there may not be time to write up the objectives. In a large company it may take months to analyze the situation. This is also true in controversial situations. Furthermore, security, business, or political reasons may make it unwise to write the policy formally.

As previously mentioned, half of the managers of computer installations interviewed stated that they had written objectives. It is not contended that this survey will withstand rigorous tests of randomness, or that it is representative of data processing installations in general. The significant elements, however, are that one data processing manager did not know that he had specific objectives to fulfill, and that half of them were not aware of any written objectives. Since many of them did not know of any written objectives, the processing decisions made were quite often based only on a general understanding of the major objectives rather than with consideration of specific written objectives.

Characteristics

More and more people desire to give their best efforts for a purpose, a direction, a goal. This purpose, or policy, must be one that commands respect and that seems to be worthwhile.

Meaningful Goals. Failure to establish broad, meaningful objectives can impair the effectiveness of data processing. A survey rated the data processing operations of large corporations into three categories: high effectiveness, average effectiveness and low effectiveness. In the more effective category, 61 percent had broad goals, as contrasted with 26 percent in the middle group and 12 percent in the less effective category. Stated another way, 88 percent of the less effective data processing installations had either narrow goals or no goals. Some electronic data processing failures were traced directly to the failure of management to define its needs. The study concluded that until management used the computer as a tool to increase profits, really significant gains would not be realized. Examples of applications cited as being in the profit-making category included: forecasting sales, determining optimum inventory, and planning material requirements.

Specific Goals. The desirability of broad goals, however, should not be carried to the extreme view that only broad goals are good goals. Specific goals in terms of time, cost, quality of information, end use, etc., are needed to permit the exact placement of responsibility.

Objectives should be sufficiently detailed to provide a firm basis for selecting application areas, for determining sequence of conversion, and for deciding the extent to which existing methods and procedures should be revised. The first objectives established for data processing are frequently over-ambitious and too general. The basic goal of increasing profit, referred to earlier in this chapter, is too general an objective. It might, however, be replaced by such long-range goals as improved competitive position and increased share of the market. Examples of operating requirements that the computer might have the objective to correct are difficulty in obtaining personnel, volume increases, and shortages of space.

An examination of the written objectives for the data processing departments in several governmental bureaus indicated a tendency to delineate areas of cognizance—offices for which data processing services were to be performed and systems for which work would be done. These, of course, are not objectives toward which data processing divisions can aspire. For example:

Accomplish data processing requirements of the Bureau of _____ _____, the _____ Office, and the _____ Office.

Control drivers in the State of _____.

Perform complex calculations otherwise impractical due to manpower shortage.

Provide a centralized data bank for all existing facilities.

Designs, develops, programs, tests, monitors, and maintains the Manpower and Personnel Management System at the Headquarters, Department of the _____ level, except that support rendered by _____ in the Manpower Authorizations area.

Measurable Goals. Objectives should be in sufficient detail to measure the results after the new system is in operation in each application area. If clerical cost reduction is the only goal, a logical measurement is the difference between the costs of the most efficient system without automatic data processing and the costs of people and functions under automatic data processing. Objectives, however, are often less tangible than clerical cost reduction. It is not easy, but nonetheless necessary, that management should set some criterion of cost increase that will justify the achievement of the objective. Management executives are the only ones with sufficient knowledge and experience to estimate the value of these intangibles. There are, however, certain items that might help management in placing these values:

1. It is advisable to try to be realistic and not overestimate the advantages of automatic data processing.
2. If automatic data processing results in fewer employees, savings will be generated in lower payroll expense, lower training costs, savings from more available space, and savings from providing other personnel support functions.
3. If use of the computer results in a lower inventory, there will be savings in the amount of money invested in inventory and in the cost of maintenance of inventory. It will also result in making more space available for other purposes. This space has value.
4. Faster service and fewer errors will result in customer satisfaction, and this in turn will generate increased sales. This certainly has value.

An examination of the preceding items shows that some of them are relatively easy to measure. Others, however, are far more difficult. Comparison of dollar investment in inventory held prior to computer implementation of inventory control with investment at later periods may not be indicative of actual savings. Changes in product line and/or increases or decreases in sales volume probably would result in inventory changes, whether or not the application was on the computer. This problem might be overcome by calculating the ratio of dollar inventory to dollar value of sales, and multiplying it by the dollar value of sales prior to putting the application on the computer. Similar statistical techniques might be employed to calculate savings due to more rapid payment of accounts receivable.

If the objective were to lower customer irritation, a measurement of their actual dissatisfaction would be rather difficult. On the other hand, the ratio of the sum of the "not-in-stocks" and the erroneous deliveries to the total orders might be a fairly good indicator of how well the objective of lower customer irritation is met. This ratio might also be a pretty good measure of the effectiveness of the inventory-control system. Objectives such as greater customer satisfaction, greater prestige, and enhanced competitive position seem to be too general for an accurate measure of the degree to which they are met.

The more general an objective, the more difficult it is to measure how well it is fulfilled. Before deciding that it is impossible to measure the degree to which each objective is met, ingenuity and determination should be used until it is clear that no reliable measure can be devised.

Lack of engineered data processing standards is an indication of the rather general failure of data processing installations to estimate how well they are fulfilling their objectives. In a survey of 16 data processing installations only 3 had specific, established methods of approximating the degree to which they met their objectives. Only one claimed methods that precisely determined the degree to which each and every one of these objectives was achieved.

Consistency. A company decided to put the current electric accounting machine applications on a computer with little or no change in procedures. The data processing personnel were to get experience in computer programming and operation, and then were to design and convert to an integrated system. The full effort of the data processing installation was required to revise the programs to take into account the changes required in procedure, form, and information collection. Eleven years later no integrated system had been designed for the company, to say nothing of implementing it.

Although written secondary objectives may be consistent with the primary objectives and the short-range objectives consistent with long-range aims, quite often the primary long-range objective is eliminated completely from consideration in order to fulfill the short-range objective. The problems of the moment clearly overshadow any aim for achievement not projected to the immediate future.

Devising Worthwhile Objectives. One might say that the objective of an inventory system is to furnish material when needed, where needed, and in the quantity needed. It is almost impossible, however, to measure how well such an objective is met. What does the word "needed" mean? Are all needs equal? How can meaningful objectives be devised for such a system? The important elements in an inventory system are how many items can be filled from stock, how fast each order is filled, and how many errors are made. One wouldn't want to be able to fill every order from stock, because it would be necessary to double the stock on hand to go, for example, from 98 percent to 100 percent. It might cost twice as much to fill every order the day it is received, as contrasted with allowing two or three days, or even a week. It is desirable to eliminate errors completely, but this would involve checking and rechecking, with the attendant extra cost and loss of time. The effects of errors in an emergency order normally would be far greater than those in routine or deferred requirements.

In almost any inventory system, orders are classified into four categories: emergency, priority, routine, and deferred. For each category, specific, meaningful, measurable, and consistent objectives can be devised. Table 1.1 is an example of how such objectives can be quantified. It is not contended that any specific figure in the table is a valid objective. Only the management of a company can establish such goals, and these goals will differ between companies.

TABLE 1.1

OBJECTIVES FOR INVENTORY-CONTROL SYSTEM

	Category of Material			
	Emergency	Priority	Routine	Deferred
Orders to be filled, %	98	90	80	50
Maximum time between receipt of order and shipment of material, days	1	2	7	30
Errors, %	0	1	2	2

LONG-RANGE GOALS

The purpose of planning is to make the best possible use of available resources to achieve company objectives. Long-range plans are an orderly arrangement of things that must be done to accomplish these objectives. Available resources, exigencies of the moment, and limitations in capabilities or resources may temporarily cause a detour from their direct achievement. Long-range plans, however, constitute a beacon, so that, as soon as possible, efforts can be exerted toward the accomplishment of company objectives.

The environment in which the company operates is complex. Social aims change. With new technological developments, production facilities and markets change. Business firms are faced by so many imponderables that they must turn to planning as a means of coping with uncertainty.

Two developments are evident. As the manager moves up in the organization, he spends a greater percentage of his time in planning. Furthermore, of the time spent in planning, more and more is spent in long-range planning, as contrasted with short-range planning. Therefore, top management spends a great amount of its time in long-range planning. It considers developments expected in the future, and relates company policies to them. A long-range plan, then, is an expression of how the organization intends to cope with the vagaries of the future in accomplishing its objectives.

It should not be inferred from this that top management is the only level at which long-range plans are developed. On the contrary, top management must involve all in the organization who can contribute to the long-range planning process. This not only improves the planning but also contributes to the participatory gratification of many people in the organization who will feel that they have a share in deciding which way the efforts of the company will be directed. This motivates them to greater efforts and at the same time lessens the probability of their leaving for other positions. The function of top management becomes one of arranging for needed inputs from those who can supply the information and of integrating these inputs with top management's contribution in developing a viable plan for the future. Since this plan will be the basis for decision making until at least the next year, it must be explicit, expressing not only what is to be accomplished, but also how it is to be done. All managers will know the objectives of the company and their decisions can be directed toward their accomplishment.

Five-year Dynamic Plans

The difficulties in planning increase geometrically as the length of time covered by a plan increases arithmetically. The various echelons of management rarely object to short-range planning, since they consider such planning to be a function of the position. As requests for plans cover longer periods of time, however, resistance increases markedly. Managers feel a greater degree of uncertainty. They are hesitant about predicting the future. A plan for the next month, the next quarter, or even the next year is relatively easy. The manager knows where he stands today; he has a pretty good idea of which employees will stay or leave in the near future. He knows the strong points and the weak points of each person. He knows what he intends to accomplish. Since he has a lot of information about what he intends to do and the resources available, he is not reluctant to develop a plan. As the plan extends to longer periods of time, technological changes and possible social and/or political developments intrude. Employees considered to be stable may leave for higher wages elsewhere or for other reasons. A change in the economic status of the community or of the country could alter the labor market considerably. The manager becomes less confident, both about what he intends to do and the resources he will use. He is reluctant, therefore, to estimate under these circumstances.

Many companies and government organizations have found that five years is about the longest period of time for which plans can be made and still retain any semblance of relationship with what actually occurs. Managers often object to estimating for such a long period of time, pointing out that they are not sure what is going to happen in the next year, to say nothing of what is going to happen in the next five years. Top management must let them know that it recognizes that estimates for the fifth year will not be as accurate as those for the first year. These managers, however, are in the best positions to make the estimates. The projections must be made, if a plan of action for the period is to be completed. At the end of the first year the managers will be asked to develop a new five-year plan. At that time, the former fifth year, of which they were so uncertain, will become the fourth year. They will have more information at that time, and can revise their plans in the light of this new information.

Companies that work on an annual budget often integrate these five-year estimates into budget requests for the next year. They include in this budget request what is intended to be done in each of the next five years and the resources needed—personnel, funds, and equipment—to do the job. Top management can consolidate these requests and consider them from a companywide standpoint. If there are not enough resources to accomplish all requests, or if some are deemed not vital to company purposes, enough information is available to make a rational decision regarding which to approve, which to change, and which to reject. Figure 1.1 is a five-year plan that can be used either as the first step in developing computer requirements in a feasibility study or as a component of the annual budget request. It will be noted that the illustration is limited to information-processing requirements. In this particular case, data or information processing is funded separately. If this had not been the practice, the illustration would include all elements of cost for the budget activity.

SHORT-RANGE PLANS

As stated in the preceding section, long-range plans are an expression of the company's objectives in terms of a general statement of its intended means of achievement. Such statements constitute a means of evaluating the problems of the moment in terms of what ultimately is to be done. Since they often cover a period of five years, the margin of error grows with each succeeding year. Furthermore, they normally deal in more general terms of what is to be done.

Short-range plans, on the other hand, are expected to be more accurate than long-range plans. They usually cover only the next operating period, be it a day, a week, a month, a quarter, or a year. The imponderables of a long-range projection, for the most part, do not impinge on decisions to be made. Priorities of competing applications for a share of the resources have been evaluated generally in the budget process. What is to be done and the resources available for its accomplishment have, for the most part, been determined. The short-range plan then becomes a fairly precise statement of how the application is to be executed and what resources will be used.

System Analysis, Design, and Programming

Despite all that has been written, the most important factor in allocating priorities to individual systems is savings. Savings constitute an element that can be measured quantitatively, one that management cannot miss. Since savings are the most important factor to top management, it should also be the most important element in deciding the order in which applications are to be put on the computer. If the company will grow, applications

DATA PROCESSING WORK LOAD PROJECTIONS MAY 1972 – 77

1. Originating Dept.	2. Project Name	3. Current Computer Activity ☐
		Replaces Manual Activity ☐
		New Activity ☐

4. Purpose of Project

5. Input:	a. Source	b. Volume in terms of data or pieces of information	c. Frequency (daily, weekly, monthly, etc.)	d. Method (card, tape, etc.)

6. Output	a. Form (regular printout, special format, galleys, CRT, terminal print, charts, etc.)		b. Frequency (daily, weekly, monthly, etc.)	

7. Special Equipment or Program Package

Remote Terminal ☐   Visual Display Console ☐   Plotter ☐   Permanent Disk ☐   Other _____

8. Expected Timetable (starting date: Month/Year)

a. Feasibility Study: b. Project Development: c. Project Testing: d. Production:

9. Resource Input:	EDP Manpower (manweeks)	Input (number of cards)	Computer Time (hours)	Internal Storage (characters)
Feasibility Study		-0-	-0-	-0-
Project Development				
Project Testing				
Regular Production				
Maintenance				

10. Describe: use by other departments or outside the Fund (Actual/Potential)

11. Other remarks

13

that forestall future costs should be given second priority. Systems that eliminate bottlenecks or chronic problem areas are next. Although this author would like to see this area rated higher, potential profit-making computer applications follow.

The real potential capability of the computer is in facilitating better decisions, resulting in a better competitive position, customer satisfaction, a greater share of the market, and greater profits. Management would like to have all these advantages, but it is not sure that the applications for those purposes will be successful—that the benefits will be achieved. One cannot find much fault with management's position. Too often, computer managers and system designers have predicted rosy futures, only to fail completely or to make only modest advances. Too often, the additional costs have exceeded the value of the benefits. Even when the value was more than the costs, the difference often was so slight that the resources could have been used for another application, more modest in promise but surer of success.

New computer installations should start small and gather experience and confidence before attempting the large, high payoff applications. Almost invariably, applications such as payroll, customer accounts, or inventory accounting should be tried first. There may be some clerical savings, although the costs of the new system frequently exceed those of the old one. The major gain is experience in using the computer. Those within the data processing department develop more confidence in their ability to make the computer do what they want it to do. More important, however, is that those not working in data processing will have greater confidence in the ability of the data processing people to do a job successfully. They see that the department has been successful in putting a fairly important job on the computer. Everyone in the organization is affected by the payroll application. Everyone gets his check and can recognize that the check is printed on the computer, that it is on time (possibly earlier than before), and that it is accurate. Furthermore, income tax statements of amount earned and amounts deducted usually are received earlier than those processed manually or by an electric accounting machine.

Plans can be made for the implementation of more ambitious systems after some success has been achieved. These systems need much planning. They are larger, development costs are high, and there will be a longer period between the plan and its fulfillment. It has long been recognized that although there are many analysts who can plan and implement routine applications, relatively few of them have success with complex new applications. The risks are greater in designing and implementing more sophisticated systems, but the potential gains are also greater. This process might be likened to a person who starts his gambling in a low-limit poker game where he develops his skills and confidence. After surviving such apprenticeship, if he has sufficient capital, he is ready to play for higher stakes.

In order to make a better decision concerning which system to implement first, the decision maker needs reliable information concerning the benefits, the purposes, and the cost. Figure 1.1 is an example of the means of providing such information. In this case the project-manager method of managing systems development (discussed in detail in Chapter 2) has resulted in a statement of the job to be done, the resources to be used, the times when certain milestones and the project are to be completed, and what the final product should be. For all essential purposes, it constitutes a contract between an employee and his supervisor. The employee is promising to produce a specific product within a certain time, using particular amounts of resources such as personnel, keypunch and clerical help, computer time, and possibly contractual assistance.

Operations

Many articles discuss the day-to-day scheduling of computers. This part of the chapter, therefore, will concentrate on planning for such operational problems as additional computer capacity. The moving five-year annual projections discussed earlier in this chapter are a primary vehicle for predicting when more computer capacity will be needed. Secondary tools are analyses of programs and measurements of the use of individual components of the computer.

If a program does not use the available computer facilities efficiently, a great deal of computing time can be lost. On the other hand, time of programmer and analyst to detect inefficient programs and then make modifications to improve their operation can be quite expensive. It becomes evident very quickly that a program that takes little time and is not run very often should not be modified to increase its speed. In planning the priority of programs that are to be examined, the analyst arranges them in order of the total computer time each uses annually. Those with the most computer time are likely candidates for major savings.

Analysis of the use of individual computer components, until recently, has been a combination of experience, knowledge, intuition, and luck. Operating and logging systems rarely provide enough information for analysis. Probably the greatest aids in configuring a computer are probes, which are attached to specific parts of the computer. Information on the use of each component is gathered on tape as various programs are run on the computer. The resulting data is analyzed so that appropriate reconfiguring action can be taken. In one instance, with which this author is familiar, a very large computer installation reported that the use of these tools resulted in realignment of peripherals on individual channels. Some changes in components were also made. The net result was a significant increase in throughput with less monthly computer rental.

The purpose of this discussion is to point out that adding more core or peripherals, or installing a larger computer, is not the only way of getting more computer capacity. Before planning for such additional physical facilities, the computer manager should make use of all possible available tools. He should ensure that his large programs are efficient and that his computer is configured properly. Then, if his dynamic five-year plan indicates a future need for greater computer capacity, he should start planning what he needs and develop a time schedule for implementation.

SUMMARY

Objectives

Trends. The early incentive at the top management level for installing a computer was frequently savings. The emphasis, although still primarily for savings, has shifted to some degree toward profit and better fulfillment of organizational purposes. At the data processing department level, objectives for that department have not for the most part played a major role until quite recently. Whether this resulted from the comparatively minor organizational importance of many such departments, from the lack of managerial background in a large number of managers of data processing, or from other causes has not been determined. Along with the trends that have been moving the data processing department to a higher location in the company hierarchy has been the attraction of this area for a higher proportion of well-educated and intelligent managers. The tendency to consider system objectives in making data processing decisions is increasing. This increase, however, is far more visible in large industrial and governmental complexes. It is anticipated that the tremendous potential of communications-oriented real time and time-sharing systems will enhance the establishment of objectives oriented to profit rather than to savings.

Establishment. Ideally, data processing objectives are established by top management. With the emergence of assistant directors for management information, these persons are the appropriate developers of such objectives. Another good source is a steering committee, including representatives from the major operating departments. In the absence of objectives being furnished for data processing, the manager of the department should propose them, and then have them amended and/or approved by top management. These objectives should be formulated early and revised whenever major changes in the systems are to be supported by data processing. Even if there are no such major changes, an annual review of data processing objectives is a worthwhile practice. In general, objectives should be documented and promulgated. It is recognized, however, that in certain circumstances it may be necessary to proceed without the formality of such documentation and promulgation.

Characteristics. The objectives of data processing may be stated best in terms of their impact upon the system the processes serve. Data processing is not an end in itself. Its sole purpose is to permit the system of which it is a part to function more effectively. Thus, in order to evaluate the success or failure of the data processing installation, its objectives should be defined in terms of the effects to be achieved in the system supported. Thus, objectives should be broad enough to be meaningful, but at the same time should be specific enough so that the degree of fulfillment will be measurable. Furthermore, they should be consistent, not only in their internal formulation, but also with the goals of the system they support.

Long-Range Plans

Long-range plans are expressions of what an organization intends to accomplish and how it plans to cope with the uncertainties of the future. Top management not only spends much of its time in planning for the future, but must also develop means for ensuring that the lower echelons of management participate in the planning effort.

A five-year annual plan has been found to be an effective means of long-range planning. The plan can be updated yearly, dropping the first year, which by then is mostly history, and projecting a new fifth year. At the same time, each of the other four years is revised in accordance with the latest information. Such dynamic five-year plans often can be combined effectively with the annual budgetary process.

Short-Range Plans

Short-range plans are specific statements of what is to be done and what resources are to be used. In planning for system analysis, design, and programming, savings constitute the most important consideration to management. Savings, therefore, should be the most important element in assigning priorities to individual projects. New computer installations should concentrate first on normal applications such as payroll. This will help increase their ability and confidence, and the confidence placed in them by the rest of the company. After that, they can consider the high payoff areas. The project-manager method of planning and controlling the development and implementation of systems has often been quite successful. Before planning for possible additional components on a computer, other elements should be considered—making large programs more efficient and reconfiguring the current computer.

EXERCISES

1. Trace the types of objectives established for data processing organizations during the past 10 years. Project them for the next
   5 years. Defend your projection.
2. It is fairly well agreed that top management should set the objectives for a computer organization. If top management fails to set
   such objectives, what tactics can be used to establish valid objectives? How might these tactics differ between small and large
   companies?
3. Discuss the desirable characteristics of information-processing
   objectives. Use specific examples to illustrate your discussion.
4. Assume that the objective of a company manufacturing household
   electrical products is to increase company sales 10 percent per
   year. This is to be accomplished by
   a. the development of at least one new major product each year,
   b. improvements in products now manufactured and sold,
   c. better service to products already sold, and
   d. quicker and more accurate responses to orders and requests
      from dealers.
   What objectives would you establish for data processing to further
   these company goals? How would each of your data processing
   objectives contribute to the attainment of company goals?
5. Five-year plans can be primary vehicles for long-range planning.
   Discuss the advantages and disadvantages of such plans. How
   would you implement the preparation of such a plan?
6. Discuss the relationships between long-range and short-range
   plans. Use examples from data processing to illustrate your points.

2 ◀ ORGANIZATION

The objective of this chapter is to examine the organizational implications of automatic data processing. This examination may be segregated into four areas, which constitute the framework around which the chapter has been organized:

1. If feasibility and applications studies are to be made, to whom should the teams report, and what should be their relationship to other parts of the organization?
2. When should data processing be centralized or decentralized in a company?
3. Where in the organizational hierarchy should the data processing department or division be placed? What will be its relationships with the other divisions of the company? What other organizational changes will be needed?
4. What functions of data processing will be accomplished by the data processing department or division? To which sections of the department or division will the individual elements of the processes be assigned for optimum completion?

FEASIBILITY AND APPLICATION STUDIES

Definition

When computers were first used for business-type data processing, the term "feasibility study" was applied to the entire analysis, including the selection of a computer. In today's approach, what was formerly considered an entity has been broken down into separate analyses and study of feasibility, application, equipment selection, and equipment acquisition resources. As a result, a feasibility study is considered to be a relatively short one, usually under three months in duration. However, there are situations where no feasibility study has been conducted or where inversion of order has taken place. This latter occurs when top management wants a computer for power or prestige, for its connotation of progress, or for some other reason. In any event, the primary purpose of a feasibility study is to determine whether the value of the applications will exceed their cost. The application study, on the other hand, is intended to design the system and to recommend the organization that can implement the new system.

Trends

In general, the evolution of studies and study groups has paralleled the development path taken by computers. There has been a transition from involvement with the controller of a firm to the office manager, and from the manager to a point where top and general management are emphasized. When the controller was responsible for accounting, the computer was used as a sophisticated tabulator, and study groups often reported directly to him. Then, as computers were used for reports and personnel records as well as for accounting, many firms placed the data processing function under the office manager, who was responsible for systems and procedures. Finally, when experience and applications software permitted expansion into a broad range of business problems, top management became actively involved.

Controller

In the early 1950s, the computer was conceptualized as an ultra-high-speed tabulator. Hence, almost invariably, industrial corporations placed the study under the chief financial officer. This approach was effective in governmental agencies or in private companies such as financial institutions and insurance companies, which primarily produced documents. In many firms this practice still exists, and for good reason. Placing the study under the controller is a sound practice for financial companies where the primary emphasis is almost entirely financial management. Where production and process control are of primary importance, however, it might seem more logical to place the study under the process managers. In the latter case, however, heavy influence of the controller will still be expected. In a soft-goods department chain, the controller and the marketing manager might share the responsibility for the study.

The foregoing review helps to highlight an intrinsic danger—that a team reporting directly to the controller might not consider a system study covering the entire company. Instead, it might limit conversion to accounting applications. On the other hand, the same might be said of any department's preference for conversion to applications peculiar to that department. If heads of operating departments feel that data processing is a function of the controller, they might resist investigation of their areas. Furthermore, through lack of knowledge, the controller could be oblivious to the opportunities of integrating a variety of functions to be put on the computer.

There are many instances where controllers have been successful in the conduct of studies. This takes in not only automation of paper work, but also the financial management and ratio analysis necessary for profit-center operations and cost-effectiveness studies of the firm. Accounting, although not minor in nature, has become standardized, and studies often are not required for this area. As a matter of fact, applications packages for many accounting functions can be purchased. Thus, studies placed under the controller tend to be broad in scope and to encompass the entire company. The primary emphasis, however, probably would be on financial management.

Office Manager

Placing data processing under an office manager has created similar, but more pronounced, difficulties than those encountered with the controller. Essentially, this occurs because office managers have had little, if any, data processing experience. This was true in the past and is still true. In government, as in industry, there has been a serious lag in this area. Studies placed under office managers or administrators have failed in many instances because of resistance and fear that the computer would replace personnel. On the other hand, technology has provided techniques for information storage and retrieval that are of great value to any company of even moderate size. Because his responsibilities are of such a different nature, however, an administrator is not likely to have the necessary knowledge for conducting the types of studies in question. Consultants may prove helpful where lack of expertise in this area is likely to be inhibiting.

General Management

It is in the area of general management that increasing emphasis and responsibility for studies have been placed. New techniques, technological changes, improved hardware, and both improved and greater quantity of software packages have permitted a more integrated approach.

One large computer installation in the Department of Defense (DOD) provides support to the Office of the Secretary of Defense (OSD). The primary user in OSD decided that it might be less expensive to own and lease a computer of its own, so a feasibility study was conducted. Several deficiencies of the study were identified as contributors to its failure. First was the fact that it was based on a predetermined conclusion that could not be justified to top management. Second, the study group comprised only two or three individuals and did not represent the necessary spectrum of users. Third, top management was not directly involved. Instead, the group reported directly to its immediate superior, who lacked sufficient status to influence acceptance of the study by general management at the apex of the government, which in turn lacked proper perspective. In industry, as in government, however, many studies have been successful when conducted under some general management scheme.

A long-time common practice has been to assign many different types of studies to steering committees. Practices used and committee composition have affected success, which in most cases depended upon the cooperation of the members and that of the people with whom they dealt. In general, a steering committee is made up of representatives from several departments, and therefore will have a balanced companywide point of view.

Such committees may be established in organizational structures as a means of guiding major projects, or in government and large, multilevel industrial firms for the purpose of coordinating departmental operations. But progress made by any committee is often slowed because individual members are involved in other responsibilities that take priority. Decisions are few and stalemates not uncommon. This is also true of a steering committee that has not been formed specifically for the purpose of a feasibility study that will furnish a balanced view in coordinating the actions necessary for converting from one computer to another. These negative effects are worth noting in order to understand points that will be made in the following example.

At a large government installation a conversion is being made from the present computers to those purchased through the decisions of WWMCCS (World Wide Military Command and Control System). All operating departments are represented in the WWMCCS by either the head or his deputy as members. Each member has a veto power over decisions taken or actions proposed if he feels that the decision would vitally affect the efficiency of his organization. In the event of a veto, the problem must be referred to higher authority. One result is that integrity of objectives is maintained. In cases of policy or management questions, too, the veto power prevents preempting the prerogatives of higher authority.

The committee does not have a policy-making authority, nor can it take action that would affect overall organizational efficiency. Its ostensible role, however, is one of coordination and review, as well as monitoring progress. Basic problems arise from a need for department heads to be engaged actively in the everyday business of many projects and routine supervision. Another restrictive factor is the need for decisions to be made at a much higher level than the organization itself, but which directly affect the progress of the conversion effort. These two factors produce a critical lag in the rate of progress. Target dates are not being met, and it is doubtful that the completion date of the projected conversion can be met. This is a case where both internal and external pressures are rendering a steering committee somewhat ineffective. On the other hand, committees have been used effectively in feasibility studies, if not in applications studies. Their effectiveness is in the role of sounding boards for the development of computer-based data processing systems and as a reporting channel to management.

Although a steering committee of operating heads should have the functions of advice, evaluation, and review, the actual work of the study group should be under the direct authority of the head of the company. The committee could be effective in evaluating team efforts of the study group, since it would be informed about the team's progress. Such a committee should include all departments affected, and it should help in the overall survey planning. It should not, however, have the responsibility for the day-to-day work of the group. The department heads or their representatives could help to plan broad objectives and to review results. They should meet approximately twice a month for a progress report and to settle policy matters. Knowing the detailed plans of the study group, the members will be able to ensure that their respective departments can aid the team. The exact form of the committee depends upon the company structure and the type of personnel available.

During the initial stages, when ready access to top management is considered by many to be a necessity, this access often is achieved through the committee. Representation on such a committee tends to enhance the interest of top management. Furthermore, one way to facilitate interdepartmental analysis of potential applications is to bring into the committee all department heads concerned with the impact of the new system on their operations.

An advantage of a top-management committee is that it can solve major organizational problems that arise because the data processing system cuts across departmental lines. The best method of processing data under the new system might necessitate new policy decisions, which a committee of this type can facilitate. Unless such decisions are made quickly and with authority, the entire study may be slowed down considerably.

The study group should be under the direct authority of a single person, since it is not reasonable for a committee to report to a committee. Top management, however, should be represented in the form of an advisory or steering committee, the functions of which are to advise on present policy and on changes as they occur, to review progress, and to provide overall direction. This committee should be representative of management levels high enough to make or to obtain decisions quickly and easily.

In the final analysis one cannot state conclusively that a steering committee should be appointed. Data processing systems that have been developed where there was a steering committee have been no better or no worse than those in which there was no steering committee. The size of the company, internal and external pressures, need for a balanced company-wide view, etc., are all determining factors in the decision. If a study group is formed, considerations such as charter, personnel attributes, administrative assistance, and the cooperation of those affected are primary concerns for top management.

Study Group Charter

Top management is in a position to effect a successful study by giving the team the strength and independence to make a well-rounded approach. This is needed especially in the design and installation of an integrated system, which crosses departmental lines and requires considerable time, effort, and study.

It is recommended that top management define the objectives and scope of the study in its declaration of purpose, or charter. The committee needs the authority to suggest possible changes in procedures, forms, reports, and/or organizations. Even though there are changes in top management during the necessarily long period needed for the design of a complex data processing system, the study can proceed constantly in the direction planned with a minimal diversion of effort. The charter should fix responsibility firmly and provide for adequate authority, people, and resources. Also needed is a time-phased schedule so that progress can be evaluated and goals and priorities ascertained.

Examples of feasibility- and applications-study charters are included in Appendixes A and B. They are based on actual charters and can be used as a standard guide for adaptation. Of interest is the fact that, although originally published several years ago, they were recently adapted for a group formed in a large organization, requiring extensive coordination between internal and external elements.

The charters are signed by the president of the company and addressed to all offices and divisions. After furnishing background information, a full-time working committee is established on a specific date, with headquarters assigned. The steering committee is composed of division directors and has the functions of review, evaluation, and advice. A chain of command over the working committee is prescribed, and all operating and staff management are directed to assist the study groups. Provisions are made for consulting and technical assistance, funds, and clerical help. The group is directed to consider an integrated data processing system and to study the equipment of different manufacturers. They are to make monthly written progress reports and to develop a long-range program. Specific dates are established for completion of both the feasibility and the applications studies.

Attributes of Study Group Members

The responsibility and authority for all initial study should be assigned to a person with practical background and adequate education and training. He should be able to state the problem clearly, analyze it intelligently, and devise clear and practical objectives. The study group should be composed of top-level personnel with knowledge of the major functional areas, skill in systems, and an understanding of the methods, techniques, and equipment for data processing. Members of the team should be mature, coordinated, and expert in the subject matter, and should include at least one person with a technical knowledge of computers. Personnel selected should be those who plan to remain with the company.

The chairman of the study group should be just below the top levels of the organizational hierarchy, and he should be well educated and knowledgeable in systems theory. Above all, however, he must have the confidence of top management. Within the team, which normally is composed of middle-management personnel, there should be a knowledge of the formal and informal organization, the flow of information, data processing, and associated equipment, as well as of systems analysis and design techniques. Specialized knowledge (such as auditing, legal, and operations research) can be solicited on an ad hoc basis.

Vendors and Consultants

In the feasibility-study stage, assistance of the vendor almost invariably results in an analysis of how the vendor's equipment can be used. In the applications-study phase, the vendor's help often results in designing systems to fit the equipment rather than in designing optimal systems and selecting appropriate equipment. The assistance of manufacturers has been helpful to system designers, especially those with little background in computers, but this assistance is most valuable when sought after the system has been designed.

The principal advantage of using consultants is to make use of the knowledge they have acquired through broad experience. The disadvantage is that, when the consultants leave, they take with them much of the knowledge required for continued successful operation. It is preferable, therefore, to use people who will remain with the company. Since communications among the vendor, customer, programmer, and applications expert are difficult, it appears to be a good field for consultants. Those experienced in data processing often advise that the study be conducted with company personnel, but with some guidance from experts. If the company does not have anyone who is familiar with automatic data processing and does not want to involve its personnel in a long and detailed study, a consulting firm can be used advantageously.

It is not economical for a firm to keep a consultant on the payroll only for special occasions. Furthermore, his influence on others tends to degenerate after he has been with the company over a period of time. Company personnel are inclined to consider him as another employee rather than as a consultant. Therefore, it is preferable that he be engaged when needed. A good consultant should see to it that company workers participate in the planning and that these workers understand each step. When the changeover is complete, the employees will be trained to operate the new system at maximal efficiency.

Analyses of cases in which consultants have been used show they are helpful if used correctly. The most effective arrangement is to have in-house talent do the study and consultants act in an advisory capacity, on a part-time basis.

CENTRALIZATION VERSUS DECENTRALIZATION

There is probably no best way to handle a discussion of the issue of centralization versus decentralization. So much has been written on this issue that almost anything said here would be redundant and repetitive. It is a two-sided argument for which there seems to be no middle ground. The proponents for each side seem to enjoy the argument and have tended to perpetuate and extend the debate over a long period of time. One would suppose some compromise could have been reached with the passage of time. If all organizations were alike, however, perhaps an end to the argument would emerge. The following quote from Berman[1] may highlight the nature of the argument and some of the issues involved. Italics have been added for emphasis.

> When I wrote the Forum . . . with a negative view of Dr. Solomon's . . . article on the economics of scale, there was no intention to get into a long term debate on the subject of centralization versus decentralization. However, with Dr. Solomon's rebuttal some answer is due. *I doubt in the end whether I will change his interpretation of management principles as applied to EDP organizations nor will he change mine.* However, we agree on very many of the more important conceptual aspects of EDP organization although we disagree on many of the conclusions on how to apply these broad principles in actual practice.[1]

The questions raised by the article are:

1. Is centralized data processing a giant monolithic structure?
2. Does centralization ignore the needs of the users?
3. Does centralization impede automation of applications and evaluation of project proposals?

1. Peter Berman, "Decentralization Again," *Datamation* (Oct. 15, 1970), pp. 141-142.

4. How are analysts and programmers assigned in centralized and decentralized organizations?
5. In terms of system development under decentralization, is there less chance of failure than under larger and more massive EDP units, and can management be held solely responsible regardless of the size?
6. Is there a relationship between the size of the system staff and job satisfaction on one hand, and competitive salary levels and high standards on the other?
7. Are proper standards maintained better under a centralized or a decentralized organization?
8. Does decentralization invalidate the concept of central control?

Berman went on to say:

> There have been too few rational decisions regarding the organization of the computer. Too often EDP organization just happens without analysis as to how best to fit the power of the computer to serve the corporation. When this happens, chaos is just around the corner.

Discussion of centralization versus decentralization is basically a process of tuning to organizational structures and a decision-making process. On a corporation basis there are many more factors to consider than just organizational structure and a decision-making process. For an EDP organization, the factors to consider are in reality of a different nature than those pertaining to an entire corporation.

One of the advantages of centralization attributed to control of the computer is power and prestige. Power and prestige have also been accorded those who control information. A natural conclusion might be that centralization has to take place in order to maintain the necessary control over the direction of the firm. The problem is that the issues of where the computer is to be, the degree of centralization, and who is to control it become political problems. Often, because of their intensity, they must be treated as such in a political atmosphere.

Developing nations exhibit most clearly the drive for prestige and status attendant on ownership of a computer. An example of this is typified by a small Latin American country that had a problem relating to approximately 40,000 accounts, for which it sent out bills quarterly. Only about 4000 of these bills were based on meter readings, the remaining 36,000 were for the same amount each quarter. The problem was that arrears were increasing and errors were occurring in the bills. Despite the fact that labor was cheap and there was little money for the purchase of equipment, a computer was installed. Such commitments primarily for the sake of prestige are self-defeating and will do little to solve the existing problem. Actually, in a case such as this, the lack of computer background would probably cause a higher error rate. Even more ominous would be the implementation problems.

Computer-related problems in developing countries, other than lack of technical skills, are insufficient usage, language barriers, and air-conditioning needed for high-speed electronic equipment. This is not to say that the urge toward prestige is confined to developing nations. There still remain in the United States today those who believe in the computer as a symbol of power, prestige, and advanced management practice. Their devotion extracts a price in the many problems they suffer privately.

For the sake of historical perspective, an article previously cited will be amplified by more recent events. The article, mentioning a strong trend in the centralization of computers, noted that the federal government

> . . . has run two to four years ahead of business in trends and computer applications is becoming increasingly disillusioned with . . . the centralized computer system approach.

The problems of span of control, getting information to customers, and the shortage of programmers contributed to this disillusionment. As the system increased in size, system analysis difficulties, problems resulting from poor input data, and turnaround time increased. The last item was one in which the problems appeared to grow at a geometrical rate as the length of time grew arithmetically. In order for large systems to work, flexibility and innovation could not be tolerated to any extent. Control systems sometimes resulted in elaborate records, which cost more than the value of their contributions to the system. Despite government's disillusionment, the article anticipated an increased centralization and a trend to multiprogramming.[2]

Other observers, however, have not been able to detect an increased disillusionment in centralized data processing in the federal government. In fact, standardized logistics systems with centralized programming, decentralized partial processing, and centralized compilaton of manpower information are being developed in the Air Force and in the Navy. They appear to herald a concept of centralization with many of the advantages of both centralization and decentralization. Decisions concerning such items as reorder points, amounts to be purchased, and vendor selection can be made on local computers throughout the system, with full knowledge that each decision will be in accordance with the overall plan as it was programmed.

The comments expressed in the preceding two paragraphs appeared in the literature cited and are as topical today as when they were first written.

2. Harwood G. Kolsky, "Centralization: Good or Bad," *Journal of Data Management* (November 1963), pp. 14-18.

However, at this juncture a new dimension, called command and control, has been added to the centralization or decentralization issue within the government. This dimension is one of paramount importance. Before examining its import, however, it might be prudent to discuss two areas: centralization of hardware and centralization of systems.

Centralization of Hardware

Herbert Grosch's law states that computing power tends to increase in accordance with the square of the cost. Test after test has validated this law. It has, however, been misapplied quite often. If the computer is to be used for computing, there is substantial agreement that the formula in the law is approximately correct. If, however, the computer is to be used for the usual business applications and/or is input/output bound, Grosch's law does not necessarily apply. Centralization, therefore, although it is usually the better recommendation for computing, is not the only answer for business applications; nor is decentralization the only alternative. One must consider the entire spectrum between the two extremes. What are the advantages of centralization versus those of decentralization?

Advantages of Centralization

The first advantage of a centralized computer installation is that normally it will be more economical than a decentralized one. Fewer operators will be needed, since the numbers of people needed to run a large computer or several computers in one location are fewer than those needed to run several computers in different locations. Furthermore, programming effort will be decreased because certain common programs will be written once, instead of being written for each location. Also, less space is needed for one large installation than for several smaller ones.

Another advantage of the larger sized computer is that peripheral gear may be added. Work involving such calculation as the inversion of a large matrix can be accomplished more rapidly. It is also possible to have direct output from such devices as plotters and cathode-ray tubes, which normally are not available on small computers.

Shared use of centralized computers is a factor that permits a higher utilization of the computer. A large manufacturer of automobiles in the United States recently reported 95 percent utilization of a centralized computer center operating three shifts a day, six days a week. The term "utilization," however, can be very misleading. Does it mean that the computer is running 95 percent of the time, or does it mean that the computer is on productive runs 95 percent of the time? Another survey indicated that about 40 percent of the time of computer installations was devoted to such things as rerun time and idle time. Owing to scheduling difficulties, more time was lost in the large installations than in the smaller ones. A question arises that concerns the value of what was produced on the computer. A computer in Asia that ran for 110 hours a month resulted in criticism of its management for not using the 176 hours for which rent was paid. From then on it was run over 170 hours a month, even going as high as 204 hours in one month. The increase in time run, however, could not be attributed to increased workload or production.

An advantage of a larger installation is that it will attract and hold better computer technicians. The smaller, decentralized installations normally cannot offer the challenging positions, higher pay, and stimulation of working with high-caliber computer professionals. For this reason the competent, ambitious computer technicians tend to gravitate toward the larger computer centers.

The final advantage of a centralized computer installation is that of coordination. It is much simpler to coordinate the data processing effort when such effort is in one place than it would be to coordinate the efforts of several individual computer installations.

Advantages of Decentralization

The advantages of decentralized installations start with such items as responsiveness, flexibility, and turnaround time. An installation that is located in, and controlled by, a department or division should be completely responsive to the needs of that organization. Any large installation has standards, rules, and regulations. In order to use that installation, one must comply with them. He must adjust to the computer installation rather than expect the installation to adjust to him. Furthermore, to get maximum use, a computer normally requires scheduling and the running of particular types of jobs concurrently. This, combined with the necessity to use various communications media to get data into the computer and to transmit the results to the user, takes time, resulting in a longer turnaround time.

Examples of people who, over a period of time, have been promoted to one level above their capabilities (the Peter principle), are much more evident in large installations than in small ones. Thus, although decentralized installations have difficulty in attracting and holding capable computer professionals, they find it easier to get rid of incompetents.

Another advantage of decentralization is the area of budgeting and cost accounting. It is much simpler to budget for and to charge the costs of a smaller, decentralized computer than for a large computer running in a multiprogramming mode.

The perfect computer installation, of course, would combine the advantages of decentralization with those of centralization. Examination of the advantages of centralization indicates that such advantages disappear, leaving little or no possibility of recovery, if decentralization is elected. The major advantages of decentralization are responsiveness, flexibility, and lower turnaround time. It is possible, even with a centralized computer, to be responsive, flexible, and to give rapid turnaround time. This can be done through such devices as time sharing, remote terminals, and high-speed printers in the hands of users. It is responsive because the user has access to the computer whenever he desires, and for any purpose. It is flexible because time-sharing programs can be written that adjust to the experience level of the user. Turnaround time, unless the computer is saturated with work, tends to be rapid in time-sharing installations.

The key problem here is the percentage of total time taken by the time-sharing and the operating systems. In a 1969 talk in England, Dr. Grace Hopper[3] first put forth a very interesting thesis for eliminating operating systems ultimately. She would replace the large computer with minicomputers. Incoming data with accompanying identification would be accepted by the message-switching minicomputer and stored. The message switcher would notify the appropriate minicomputer where the data were stored, and then would go on to the next piece of data. The minicomputer would then process the data and store the results. Minicomputers are quite cheap and fast. The problems of backup diminish because, if one minicomputer is down, another can take its place.

Such a system, at first glance, is untenable to many computer specialists. It would take a lot of planning but, if successful, would combine the advantages of both centralization and decentralization. Minicomputers could be connected by telecommunications from various locations. There would no large overhead cost for the operating system. One cannot say that this is the solution, but one should leave his mind open to consider it. This may not be the best solution today, but it may be in the future.

Guidelines

If one is trying to decide whether to install computers in centralized or decentralized locations, certain guidelines may help. If the relative volume of computing, as contrasted with data processing, is high, the answer almost has to be to centralize. If the volume of data processing is high, there is a much better possibility of decentralization. But even here, one is led by economic and personnel reasons to a centralized computer installation. From either standpoint, computer power should be centralized.

3. *For example*: Grace Hopper, only recipient of both The Data Processing Management Association Data Processing Man of the Year award and the American Federation of Information Processing Society Harry Goode Memorial award.

Centralization of Software

The term "software," as used here, includes both systems and programming effort. Although the hardware, for economic and personnel reasons, almost always should be centralized, the answer is not anywhere near so clear with regard to software. Again the problem is a highly political one, where often the decision depends on expediency rather than on economics and the results sought.

Recently a consultant was called into a large organization that had decided to get a computer. There was no disagreement concerning where the computer was to be physically, nor was there much problem about supervisory control. Three of the four departments involved wanted to continue doing their own analysis and programming, whereas the fourth wanted completely centralized operations. Even though a solution from a mechanistic standpoint was to centralize software production, such an answer was not politically acceptable. It was decided that the three departments would continue to do their own analysis and programming, and that a central group would be formed. This group would supply assistance for departments that did not have their own software staff.

Any corporation or agency, in deciding whether to centralize or decentralize software preparation, should consider the advantages and disadvantages of each and then select the degree of centralization most desirable for it. What are the advantages of centralization over those of decentralization?

Advantages of Centralization

One of the most important advantages of centralization is the ability to attract and hold highly motivated systems and programming professionals. It is possible for such people to advance both within and outside the systems field. This is, of course, much more evident for the systems people than for programmers. Since the software cadre is larger, there tend to be more highly paid positions at the top. Furthermore, the centralized organization gives the analyst much more opportunity to cut across organizational lines in developing systems. Additionally, there are many more chances of moving directly into administrative positions outside the software organization. Analysts get more diversified experience in a centralized software group. A centralized group is where the "action" is. Unless each of the decentralized groups is large enough to furnish ample opportunity for advancement, sooner or later requests for transfer to the central group will emerge.

The software man has a much greater chance of achieving an identity or status in a centralized group. Regardless of his ability (if, for example, he is not an accountant but is an employee in a decentralized software group for accounting), he is considered to be a specialist. He has little or no opportunity for real acceptance or advancement. His only chance to supervise is within the software function, for in other areas his organizational status is staff rather than line—and a very specialized staff at that.

Standardization of documentation, programming techniques, instructions to computer operators, and similar items are much more easily enforced with a centralized group than with a decentralized one. Members in decentralized operations tend to resent and feel imposed upon when standards are issued by a centralized group. Much less resentment is felt when the standards group and those designing systems and writing programs are part of the same organizational segment. However, this psychological problem is not so serious as the possibility that similar systems will be designed and implemented for individual departments—each "inventing the wheel" again, and thus compounding the problem of coordination. A single system may cover two or more departments.

In a centralized systems area the systems people have access to information in many different areas of the country instead of being restricted to data arising in their own organizations. Decentralized operations, on the other hand, although they do not automatically preclude one segment from using the data of others, make this difficult in actual practice. The outside group either must arrange to get data as a by-product or as complete information concerning such things as file structure, and must get permission to access the desired data.

If an integrated data base is desired, it is much more easily achieved with centralized control than with decentralized operations. Such an organization maximizes the ability to retrieve data, and simultaneously minimizes redundancy—that is, the same data appearing more than once in the files of a company.

In a centralized organization the top systems man is likely to be of higher caliber and more highly paid than if the systems talent were spread into many different departments. As such, top management will have direct access to a systems man with the ability to plan and implement a fairly effective information system.

Finally, a centralized information system will not be affected greatly by reorganizations. The usual person who is not a computer professional does not recognize the inherent inflexibility of a computerized management-information system. It is much more easy to reorganize the departments of a company than it is to reorganize a large, computerized, management-information system. If the system is built for one department, and that department is merged with another, the necessary changes in the information system may take years to implement.

Advantages of Decentralization

The primary advantages of decentralization of systems work and programming all relate to the fact that the user has his own people to do what he wants them to do. Politically, it maximizes satisfaction in the greatest number of people. The managers of individual departments have access to systems analysts who are completely responsive to their needs. Furthermore, operations people are more likely to be involved in the design of systems and, in turn, are more likely to make use of the resultant output. The difficult barrier of gaining acceptance, so often encountered in centralized systems, is obviated. In turn, systems analysts will have little or no difficulty in relating to functional management and will have ready access to information and data needed.

Another advantage is that there will not be a software conglomerate so large that other departments feel threatened. With smaller individual groups, other corporate internal organizations will not feel that the systems people are trying to take over their operations.

Decentralized groups are likely to get a job done faster and less formally. There are fewer problems of semantics, since words tend to have the same meaning within individual areas.

The difficult problems of designing systems to serve multiple users disappear. Systems for the use of one functional area are more likely to be less expensive, easier to develop, and easier to manage.

Degree of Centralization

In discussing systems, one often hears the term "total system." A total system is usually defined as a system integrated to the nth degree. One picks up magazine after magazine, each having articles describing, in glowing terms, total system after total system. When one examines these systems one by one in the clear light of reality, he finds that the so-called total system is total, but only for a specific segment of the company's operations. Possibly, one shouldn't talk about total systems, but instead about the degree to which a corporation's systems are integrated. This author has visited more than 200 computer installations during the past 18 years, but never has he seen a system that, by any stretch of the imagination, is 100 percent integrated.

Similarly, isn't it possible that organizational structures do not have to be completely centralized or decentralized? Possibly some combination of centralization or decentralization might be optimal for a specific corporation. Computers do not cause centralization or decentralization. They merely enable a manager to choose his manner of operation. The degree of centralization that might succeed in one organization might fail disastrously in another. One reads reports of success with partial decentralization in some cases, a degree of success in some others, and outright failure in others.

Some organizational guidelines were proposed in interviews with various companies:

1. A systems organization is too decentralized if
    (a) the systems groups are too small to attract good people.
    (b) there is substantial duplication of files and computer programs.
    (c) the top management of an integrated organizational complex does not have close access to a responsive systems leader, who in turn has ready access to all information resources.
2. An organization may be too centralized if
    (a) the systems organization is not becoming intimately involved in the major opportunities within the line organization.
    (b) management of major line components do not have ready access to responsive systems groups.
    (c) the systems organization has become an unresponsive bureaucracy.
    (d) the systems organization has weak political support from line management.
    (e) the perception of costs and benefits associated with systems functions has become blurred.[4]

Examination of the above guidelines with respect to a company's system may suggest increased or decreased degrees of centralization.

Approaches to partial decentralization depend on the size of the company.

Large Companies. Centralize the hardware in a single computer facility. Economics indicate that the hardware should be centralized unless the corporation is extremely large and geographically decentralized. In these companies, higher costs of communications may more than offset lower hardware costs. The individual systems groups in big companies may well be large enough to attract and hold competent systems personnel. Establish an Electronic Data Processing Coordinating Committee (EDPCC) made up of senior individuals representing the major departments of the corporation. Examples of the functions of such a committee follow:

1. Establish priorities for different departmental systems-development plans.
2. Examine proposed systems annually for each department, and

---

4. Mayford L. Ruark, "Centralization versus Decentralization of the MIS Effort." Paper presented at the Annual Conference of the Society for Management Information Systems, Washington, D.C., Sept. 14, 1970.

suggest a distribution of the company systems-development budget by department.

3. Provide a focal point for ensuring minimal duplication of the development of common systems by individual departments.
4. Provide top management with a coordinated plan of systems development that considers the entire corporation rather than the provincial needs of individual departments.
5. Enhance the cooperation of individual departments.

Establish an Electronic Data Processing Technical Committee (EDPTC) made up of senior technical representatives from each of the individual systems groups. Examples of the functions of this committee follow:

1. Furnish technical information to the EDPCC to facilitate their making policy recommendations.
2. Facilitate the establishment of and adherence to standard approaches and methods, such as documentation, data elements and codes, programming practices and conventions, and compatibility of applications.
3. Settle such disputes as those that arise when the practices of one department tend to monopolize critical computer facilities to the detriment of other departments.

Establish a centralized systems group headed by a competent professional. The problem is to establish a group with a measure of power commensurate with line authority set by the corporation involved. It should not be so strong that it poses a threat to the individual groups, but it needs enough power so that it can operate effectively without continually going to the EDPCC to get decisions or backing. Examples of the functions of this group are:

1. Provide systems and programming support for all departments without their own software staffs. Provide similar services for the exceptional needs of software groups of individual departments on an ad hoc basis.
2. Furnish information as required by the EDPCC, and ensure the implementation of its decisions.
3. Establish standards in cooperation with the EDPTC; promulgate such standards throughout the corporation and ensure adherence to these standards.
4. Through the use of bulletins or releases, disseminate technical information throughout the corporation.
5. Coordinate data processing educational efforts for both technical and managerial personnel throughout the corporation.

Smaller Companies. Whether the company is large or small, an EDPCC is helpful and its duties will be substantially the same. Instead of having individual systems and programming groups within each department, such groups can operate the same way but should be located within a centralized group. This tends to maximize responsiveness to the individual departments while minimizing the problems of personnel with little or no opportunities for intellectual or technical growth, and with lesser advancement opportunities inherent in small departments. The EDPTC would not be needed as a formal committee, since its functions would be handled internally by the central group.

The key to successful implementation of such a plan is the manager of the central group. In addition to other characteristics, he should be a salesman with a "can do" attitude. It normally is difficult to get a good computer technician who is also a good salesman. If a choice between the two becomes necessary, at least in the early stages, prefer the less technical person. Problems with people are paramount in the inceptive stages.

Command and Control

A new dimension called command and control has been added to the centralization versus decentralization issue within the government. Essentially, the reason for this is traced to the apparent divergent views or disillusionment over the centralized computer-systems approach and a need for standardization. There are few people in the computer industry who are not aware of what is termed the "World-Wide Military Command and Control System" (WWMCCS). In reality it is computer hardware and software, the organization, people, training, material and resources, designed to support commands at the highest levels in their decision-making capacity. It also includes the means of communications for the collection and transmission of information necessary for this purpose.

There will be no attempt here to delve into decision making as a topic. Its functional aspect, however, is a natural outcropping of any discussion on centralization of control. Within this context, the function is described in terms of command, control, and communications. The central purpose of this discussion will be to synthesize some of the conceptual issues and the more pragmatic approach. Thus, it provides a takeoff point for further study of EDP location within a company.

Some of the characteristics of command and control, as they exist in WWMCCS, might be described as follows:

1. Command prerogative and responsibility exist by level and by type of command authority needed.
2. Standardization is an imperative because it concerns data bases,

data management systems, nonfunctional and functional software, applications packages, and simulation models.

3. Top management exerts its guidance through a WWMCCS Council (Deputy Secretary of Defense level). Note the coincidental similarity between this council and the suggested departmental-level EDPCC approach suggested for corporations.

4. Policy making evolves through a policy group at the Joint Staff level, which reports to the Chairman, Joint Chiefs of Staff, and is made up of service representatives and other Department of Defense agencies.

5. Committee and working group relationships are established for coordination of WWMCCS implementation.

6. Certain organizations having specialized personnel are used to take advantage of available expertise for the WWMCCS as a whole.

One factor immediately apparent is that computer centers proliferate the defense structure. It would be hard, however, to say that central control exists or does not exist. Since installations of WWMCCS computers is taking place at the time of this writing, the level at which decision making will take place, and for what reasons, remains to be seen. The structure exists as a hierarchy of decision points, and it might be that centralized control will generally be exerted at the appropriate level for a particular type of decision.

Standardization throughout WWMCCS has been stated as a prime objective. Nevertheless, there are many critical problems having to do with standard data elements and codes, standard nonfunctional and functional software packages, operating systems, data-base standardization, standard data-management systems, applications, reporting systems, and display systems. The phasing of hardware installation is aggravating these problems, and again it is hard to predict an optimistic future for WWMCCS standardization as of this writing.

It would seem there is more chance of failure in terms of systems development, if only because there are so many points at which failure can occur. Further, some failure may affect other points in the structure. One mechanism that has been established to minimize or prevent chance of failure is a Joint Technical Support Agency (JTSA), which is responsible for software standardization, test, and evaluation. The JTSA, in turn, coordinates systems development throughout the WWMCCS community. For this purpose, JTSA is responsible to the Defense Communications Agency (DCA) and the Joint Staff, who are, in general, responsible for systems development. The DCA receives guidance from both the Joint Staff and the Assistant Secretary of Defense, Telecommunications, in terms of technical matters and system engineering.

ORGANIZATIONAL LOCATION

An opinion with great credibility is that the computer organization should be at the top for proper management, maintenance of objectives, and the decision-making process, and for a proper balance of authority and responsibility. On the other hand, if there is little or insignificant use made of a computer, it might be more properly placed in some subordinate organizational element. In either case, improperly located computer organizations are sources of trouble and become costly problems.

Soft-goods department stores can be used as an example of firms with homogeneous organizations. Assume that a data processing organization in a chain is placed at the top and properly used by management. In a competitive chain, the data processing organization is widely separated from the top and not properly used. It isn't difficult to predict which chain will be more successful.

One could argue that, with $20 billion invested in data processing, businesses surely know how to use it and where to place it within their organizations. On this point, some historical perspective will help.

In the context of staff placement it was stated that normally a staff function should be placed where the most responsible overall staff work had been previously assigned. EDP's being placed directly under the manager appeared to be the evolving pattern. If staff and machine operations are placed properly, they can alleviate the concerns of functional managers about responsiveness to needs. Analyst and programming groups should be segregated. With the two different elements reporting to different major organization elements, neither one could attempt an information coup with top management.[5] Of course, these cautions were expressed as dangers extant with the times. After a decade of computer use since these warnings, however, these cautions have not passed into oblivion. Implicit in the statement was concern over information control and evaluation and response to the needs of functional managers.

In a different manner these cautions are still expounded, although they are articulated in a more explicit way. A more recent article stated:

> The data processing department is the entity within the organization which: (1) must communicate with other units; and (2) must function as a communication device for other departments. But unless the functions of the computer groups are directed toward providing the connecting link in the form of an "information system" within the organizational setting of the company, these requirements cannot be met

5. L. R. Fiock, "Seven Deadly Dangers in EDP," *Harvard Business Review* May-June, 1962, p. 94.

by the data processing unit, and data processing will not have any significant impact on the way the business organization is managed. The business must be treated as a unified whole and business activities rather than organizational elements must be taken into consideration when the data processing department attempts to achieve its objectives.[6]

Examination of the foregoing statement reveals some issues important to placement of the data processing organization within the firm:

1. Information control and evaluation.
2. Response to the needs of functional managers.
3. Contributing to the objectives of the firm, as well as other organizational elements.
4. Interactive communications between all departments.
5. Proper managerial level.
6. Balance of authority and responsibility.

Functional Location

Decentralizing and embedding the data processing function present no really significant problems regarding organizational placement. However, if all data processing functions are centrally organized as a unit, then locating the resulting organization in a functional department is a possibility. If the functional department can justify and use the entire capacity of the computer, there are no really significant problems except as might arise in interaction between this department and others.

Placing the computer within a functional department because of exclusive need highlights the appeal for Dr. Hopper's minicomputer concept (see footnote). Although it was described earlier in the context of ultimately eliminating operating systems, it excites the imagination to think of the power of information flow throughout a firm with such a network of minicomputers. One can certainly eagerly await the fulfillment of her concept and the thesis of minicomputer use.

Figure 2.1 shows the assignment of a data processing organization to a functional department. For more than any other reason, this assignment is a traditional placement due to the nature and history of earlier data processing functions in the accounting and records area. The arrangement, however, might not be appropriate if subsequent work is done for other departments, for often it is sensitive to the requirements of the department it serves.

If more than one department has data processing requirements in an arrangement that places the computer in the functional department, there

6. Joseph A. Orlicky, "Payoff: A Management Challenge," *Data Management* (August 1971), pp. 24-27.

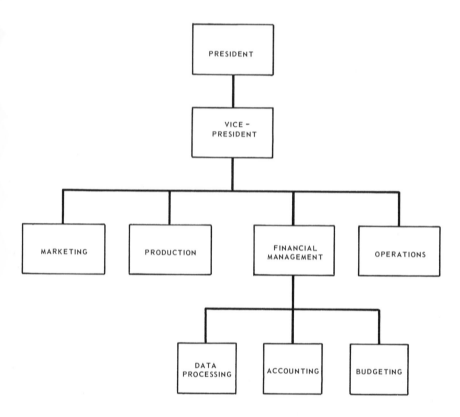

ASSIGNMENT OF DATA PROCESSING TO A FUNCTIONAL DEPARTMENT

Fig. 2.1.   Assignment of data processing to a functional department

are only two basic alternatives. Either one functional department does the work for the other departments, or each functional department is furnished with a computer. In the first alternative, managers often are reluctant to have another functional department perform some of their operations. Not only do they feel that they are losing functional responsibilities and personnel, but also that they have no control over when their data will be processed. If another functional department does the processing, that department's work might have the highest priority. In the second alternative, computers in each functional department tend to be smaller than if there were a single, central-ized computer. (Again Dr. Hopper's minicomputer concept gains more appeal.)

The problems introduced above would be classified more in terms of functional considerations and response to the needs of functional managers. Implicit to functional considerations is the need for interactive communications between all departments, although many managers do not want full knowledge of their activities to be gained by someone outside their organization. If, for instance, theirs is a profit center, they would feel that their ability to show profit to top management might be impaired or destroyed by other profit centers that could turn market knowledge to their own advantage. This is a serious problem and one for which there is no clear-cut answer, at least for the purpose of this discussion. Profit centers often become primary vehicles for contributing to the objectives of the firm. In this context, then, placement of the computer organization is important from the standpoint of departmental objectives and their interaction with the firm.

The use of computers for purposes of analysis and evaluation is becoming more and more prevalent in a great number of corporations of varying sizes. Effective techniques have been developed for this purpose, so that simulation of entire industries is possible within certain limits. Although not yet able to solve problems of the magnitude that businesses face, decision making based on forecasting techniques and use of problem-solving models enable managers to test objectives at all levels within a firm and between firms within an industry. Using constraint equations, for instance, permits optimization of systems, and accordingly supports the interests of the entire organization. In light of this, then, placement of data processing departments should be considered from the standpoint of contributing to the objectives of other organizational elements as well as to the firm.

Pertinent points related to organizational location are discussed below.

Special Assistant to Top Management

If the computer is located under a special assistant to top management, data processing will have the authority of top management to ensure that operating groups comply with its directives. The areas of responsibility will be clear-cut but limited. Through the special assistant's close association with top management, the operating groups will understand the needs of the individual top managers. There will be attendant difficulties, however, since the span of control of top management will be extended. Inasmuch as the special assistant normally does not have much connection with other management levels, he may not be expected to develop an integrated and interactive information control, analysis and evaluations system.

Departmental Administration

Another possibility is to have the processing centralized, with one person in each major department in charge of the program within his department. The advantages of such an arrangement are that the responsibility would be delegated closer to operations, those handling the data would understand the problems involved and the data quality, and it would be easier to improve procedures. The major disadvantages are the difficulty in securing agency-wide coordination, and the increased possibility that a full-time person would not be assigned the responsibility for the system in each department.

Director of Operations or Administrative Management

A practice that has gained considerable acceptance has been to place data processing under management that furnishes the traditional staff services. Since the manager is a neutral executive, the services tend to be impartial. Observation of several installations operating under this concept indicate that almost invariably the degree of integration of the system is quite low. Problems of establishing and maintaining meaningful priorities are difficult. Furthermore, since such a manager usually is not a dominant person in the organizational hierarchy, he is not in a position to design and install an integrated system, or to enforce priorities he establishes.

Vice-President for Information Systems

A department of information systems, headed by a vice-president, is a concept gaining limited acceptance. Under this arrangement, the chief executive delegates to the vice-president all responsibility for management information. He makes the assignment so that it is understood by all, giving his authority to cross organizational lines for resources that will provide high-quality personnel. To be effective, the assignment should be in writing, widely circulated, and possibly redefined at least annually.

The assignment of the computer to a vice-president for information systems appears to have considerable merit for a large corporation. Normally, without delegating this specific responsibility, one would hesitate adding another item to the things top management must control. However, the factors of balance of authority and responsibility, proper managerial level, and contribution to the objectives of the firm give weight to this approach for personal control by top management.

INTERNAL ORGANIZATION OF DATA PROCESSING

Up to this point, study has been made of centralization versus decentralization impact on different parts of the company. Organizational location within the firm has been examined. There has been no attempt to state any best solution(s). Indeed, this would be almost impossible because of the heterogeneous nature of organizations. It was pointed out that the manager of data processing, in order to be effective and contribute to the objectives of the firm, must understand the concepts and meaning of his organization as it relates to others within the firm, must know how the organization of the firm relates to the industry, and must be aware of the impact of changes taking place within and between each organizational element.

The size and budget of a firm will dictate to a large degree just what type of data processing organization can be established. The choice of personnel, both in number and competence, will further complicate the considerations. One common thread should exist for all organizations, regardless of size and structure—that is, how to process information for management purposes. This factor will bear heavily on the internal organization for data processing. Informational activity creates organization. The handling of information permits direction to be given through a variety of feedback arrangements. Again there are problems connected with the internal makeup of a data processing organization. An examination of a variety of organizations in terms of purpose, size, composition, and related problems follows.

Open Shop versus Closed Shop

When first studied, the problem of open shop versus closed shop was not an overriding factor or issue to be considered in depth. As new techniques for information analysis and evaluation have been developed, however, this division has taken on new meaning, and is a worthy subject for detailed study.

An open shop is defined as one in which the computer is located centrally. The departments making use of the computer provide their own system analysts, programmers, and possibly console operators for the computer. Programmers are still required in the computer center for the operating system and its modifications, to prepare other nonfunctional software packages (such as service routines), to give advice and assistance to users, and to establish programming procedures and routines for optimum use of the computer.

A closed shop is defined as one in which the system analysts, programmers, and operators are located within the central organization. In either classification, system analysts could be assigned to operating departments.

Open Shop

As more extensive use has been made of the computer and new uses found, there has been increased emphasis and meaning placed on the open shop or some modification thereof. For example, on university campuses the use of computers for student instruction could be classified as open shop. The students are, in essence, the system analyst, programmer, and/or operator, either singly or collectively. A natural outcome is that by the time the student graduates, he will have gained some expertise in all three areas, and will probably expect to put his talent to use in a computerized organization or in disciplines such as medicine, research, and engineering, where, for various reasons, individuals require a computer for their particular use. The list of those fitting into the open-shop concept is virtually endless.

While the open shop may add to privacy and fewer persons may result in economy of effect (because of combined talent and competence), there are, nevertheless, some serious drawbacks to the open shop. In many instances poor utilization results in higher costs of operation. Many users will waste time, cause reruns, bring about operator-induced hardware problems, and increase the need for maintenance. Further, the output of open shops normally receives only a limited use. With financial applications, when an audit trail is necessary, closed shop operations usually are more successful. There are other factors involving open shops, including security. This is discussed in Chapter 5, and has been a subject causing great anguish—in fact, businesses have failed because insufficient attention was given to security. This one factor alone would militate against any open-shop organization where its continued existence is vital to the continuation of the firm.

If the philosophy of operation is open shop, the expected basic functions of data processing are computer operation and scheduling, computer maintenance, operating systems programming, establishment of programming standards and procedures, and training of personnel in other divisions. Figure 2.2 is an example of the organization of a typical open shop.

Scheduling, if it is a major problem, might be the function of the direc-

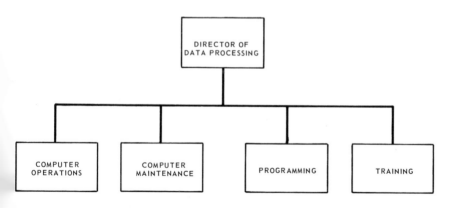

OPEN-SHOP ORGANIZATION

Fig. 2.2. Open-shop organization

tor. Otherwise, it can be done in computer operations, with decisions in exceptional cases from the office of the director. The size of the staff is variable, depending on the extent of user involvement. Maintenance, in all probability, will take place through contractor service. The functions of maintenance might be those of ordering the service when needed, maintaining non-computer equipment, and operator maintenance.

Establishing an open-shop organization can be difficult and complex. One must assure that certain standards of operation are met by users, who are not responsible for the functioning of data processing. Interface between users generally would be minimal, if not nonexistent. Accordingly, there would be no attempt to understand or solve problems that may arise. The converse may be true, since user dissatisfaction would probably be greater and of a more continuous nature.

Those who embark upon establishing open-shop operations should be as meticulous as possible in structuring the organization. They should foresee as closely as possible the necessary delineation of user responsibilites to prevent as many problems of user interface as can be avoided. The open shop looks simple at first glance, but in fact may be very complex in the execution of its operations.

Closed Shop

There is no exact standard (nor should there be) for organizations that have to meet a wide variety of needs and of firms. Accordingly, the closed-shop or organization developed here will contain the subsets and ingredients of organizational structures that contribute to the objectives of the firm.

The closed shop is a self-contained unit concerned with lines of communication, information flow, and the decision-making process. It collects data, analyzes and evaluates information, displays the results as appropriate, disseminates information, and provides other support functions as required. As a result, the range in types of applications, number of users, amount of equipment, and number of personnel may be great. Figure 2.3 is an example of an organizational element that might accomplish these functions. It is recognized, of course, that the organization formed will not fit all companies. It has been designed for a large corporation, and modifications should be made to fit the peculiar requirements of any company organizing for data processing,

System Analysis and Design, and Programming

One question that arises is whether data processing should do system analysis and design. When systems analysts are in another department than that of the programmers, their work may become too theoretical. The analysts may not have a practical appreciation of programming techniques and

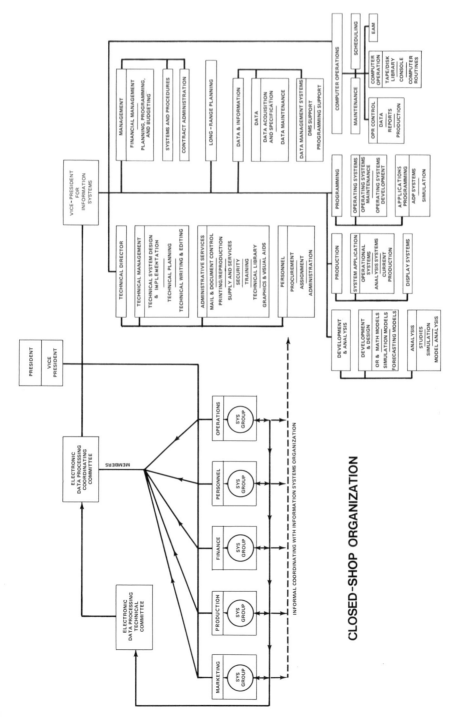

Fig. 2.3. Closed-shop organization

47

machine capabilities and limitations. Programmers, on the other hand, could lose time because of the difficulty of communication through formal organizational channels.

In one very large government computer center, this argument has continued for years. Within the computer facility, programmers are not allowed to be assigned to analytical organizations. The programming element does very little application programming except for one system that has the highest priority. As a result, the greater proportion of program development, maintenance, modification, and documentation is done by expensive personnel on a contractual basis, This situation causes lags in analyst support to users. In some cases very serious problems arise when certain programs are too highly secret for the details to be given to contractual people. The analytic organization has skillfully masked its efforts to attain programming expertise within that unit. One almost believes that top management pretends not to recognize the situation. Many of the users have skilled analysts and programmers and, as a result, will not agree to separate the skills. Thus, through an evolutionary process, the users are building their skills while the computer facility suffers an ever-widening gap in capability to satisfy the users.

The last point gives rise to another issue in differentiating between the functions of systems analysts and those of programmers. Where one leaves off and the other begins depends in most part upon the philosophy of each installation. As a general rule, a systems analyst should know where his work ends and the programmer's begins. The programmer's understanding of this should coincide with that of the systems analyst. As a practical matter, a physical delineation of work load would enhance ease of communications, better mutual understanding, and sharing of technical knowledge.

It is suggested that the systems analyst talk with the user and prepare the specifications of exactly what will reach data processing, He should also specify the details of the output desired, and establish the system to be followed until the results reach the users. The programmer should handle all operations from the time data reach data processing until the report is finished. This flow of work is shown in Figure 2.4. The advantages of such a division of work are:

1. The assignment of work is specific.
2. The systems analyst will not work in a vacuum. He will have a specific knowledge of the equipment and techniques of data processing.
3. The programmer will understand his environment and will have knowledge of equipment, procedures, programming, and other data processing techniques.
4. It provides a natural progression of advancement, beginning with the operator and ending with the systems analyst.

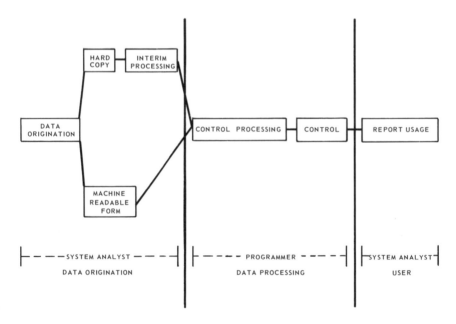

FUNCTIONS OF SYSTEMS ANALYSTS AND PROGRAMMERS

Fig. 2.4. Functions of systems analysts and programmers

The disadvantages are:

1. Both the systems analysts and the programmers must have both broad and specific knowledge.
2. The programmer communicates with the user only through the systems analyst. If contractor personnel are used, this disadvantage is greatly magnified.
3. The systems analyst must be fluent in the language of the user and that of the programmer.

Long-Range Planning

The growth rate of the computer industry has been phenomenal, but its future is not clear. One has only to look back at the frantic rush toward each new generation of computers to realize that planning—especially long-range planning—has been deficient. New equipment, new techniques, new services, and new firms spring up so quickly that one cannot keep up with the state-of-the-art. The picture, then, is more of a vignette—that is, it shades off at the edges. Indeed, what is the current generation of computers? This plaintive query is of little importance compared to the problem of long-range planning and how it is to be accomplished. Installation expenses, equipment obsolescence, organizational needs, system changes and flexibility, new user requirements, and long-range objectives dictate a need for proper planning. This was discussed at length in Chapter 1, but is mentioned here because of the necessity for long-range planning and its effects on the organizational structure of the company.

Functional Project and Matrix Management

The subject of organization would not be complete if project or matrix management were not examined. Project and matrix management received widespread attention in many industries, as well as government, over the past few years. It would be difficult to estimate the full impact these forms of management have had on organizations. To quote Gerald DeMaagd[7]: "Considering the dynamic nature of data processing and its continuing requirements for change, the matrix concept of organizational structure has the features of flexibility and adaptability that make it a natural for the field."[7]

In the WWMCCS, a project manager has been assigned the responsibility for implementing the operations. The Department of Defense is firmly oriented toward project management. There has been sufficient discussion relating to functional organization, so that further amplification is not needed. Some explanation of project and matrix management will be given, followed by some advantages and disadvantages of each. The individual company must select the form most beneficial for its purposes.

Project Management

Project management has been defined by Cleland and King[8] as follows: Project management is carried out by a set of managers acting as unifying agents for particular projects in respect to the current resources of time, funds, materials, people and technology. The project managers act as focal points for their project activities through a unique organization superimposed on the traditional functional organization structure. The project managers are, in effect, the general managers of the company for their particular projects. They actively participate in planning, organizing, and controlling those major organizational and extraorganizational activities involved."[8]

The structure of a project organization is somewhat basic and standard. It is portrayed in Figure 2.5.

7. Gerald R. DeMaagd, "Matrix Management," *Datamation* (Oct. 15, 1970), pp. 46-49.

8. David I. Cleland and William R. King, *Systems Analysis and Project Management*. New York: McGraw-Hill Book Company, Inc., 1968.

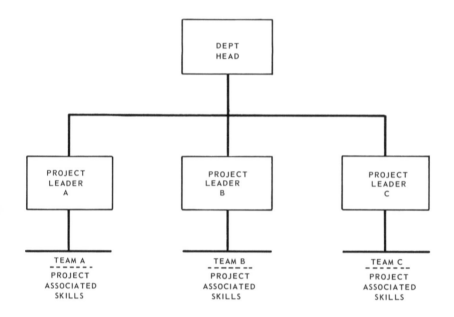

PROJECT ORGANIZATION

Fig. 2.5. Project organization

The main advantages of project management lie in (1) the concentration of varied skills to accomplish some project and (2) the focusing of management control. The combination will reduce the risk of failure and enhance the capabilities for rapid response and corrective action when needed. A project team usually plans the project to show critical points that will require special attention before success of the project can be assured. Thus, performance is emphasized.

Cost may be a prohibitive factor and disadvantage if efforts and facilities must be duplicated because of the number of projects. Another disadvantage is that personnel may have more than one supervisor, thereby causing conflicting authority. This problem may require some sensitive handling to establish and maintain a favorable environment.

Matrix Management

Matrix management is essentially a relationship between project managers and functional and resource managers. It is shown in Figure 2.6. Apparently there is some mix between project, functional elements, and resources.

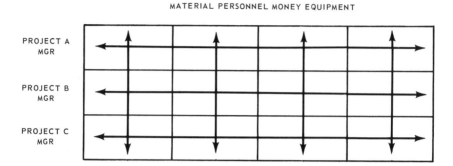

Fig. 2.6. Matrix management

The criteria for such an organization involve project deadlines, cost factors, and some emphasis on performance. Conflicts will or can arise because of an obscure chain of command, since both a horizontal and vertical organizational structure can exist simultaneously. The advantages of matrix management can be summarized as follows:

1. There is a single manager for all matters relating to the project.
2. There is a faster response to project needs.
3. Concentration of skills and movement between projects is possible.
4. Personnel remain functionally situated.
5. There are integration and balance between elements.

Disadvantages are mainly centered in the conflicts that may arise between project and functional organizations over resources and authority. One other disadvantage is the need to assure that performance overrides, or at least is not subsumed by time or cost facors.[9]

SUMMARY

Objectives and organization are inextricable. A manager of a data processing organization must be aware of and understand the concepts and meaning of his organization, the relationships among his division and others

9. *Ibid.*

within the firm, how the organization of the firm relates industry-wide, and the impacts of changes taking place within and between elements, in order to be effective. He should be capable of determining and analyzing information from external and internal sources so that the company can either meet its objectives or recognize potential failure to meet these objectives as early as possible. Advantages and disadvantages are attributed to both centralization and decentralization, none of which are overriding in magnitude. For the ADP manager, two areas of concern are involved—centralization of hardware and centralization of software.

The degree of centralization of system and programming efforts depends upon the desires of top management. Complete centralization or complete decentralization may not be desirable. Each company should examine its organizational structure with regard to guidelines and, if it is too centralized, movement should be made toward decentralization. If it is too decentralized, some centralization efforts should take place.

As regards installation of computers in centralized or decentralized locations, if the relative volume of computing as contrasted with that of data processing is high, the answer almost has to be *centralize*. If the volume of data processing is high, there is a much better possibility of decentralization. Even here, however, one is led by economic and personnel reasons toward a centralized computer installation. From either standpoint, computer power should be centralized.

If data processing is decentralized to functional departments, there will be a tendency to restrict usage to that department, and costs will be higher. If it is centralized, data processing should report to officials as high as the highest users, and responsibility for information systems should be assigned to a vice-president. This should help development of an integrated data processing system. It should also result in a system that will be advantageous for the company as an entity. In the advent of an integrated system, changes in functions, organizational relationships, and structure may be needed.

Depending upon whether there is an open-shop or a closed-shop operation, there is considerable variation in the organization of data processing. No single organizational chart can be recommended for all data processing organizations, but certain functions must be provided in all charts. The means by which these functions are accomplished depend upon the management's philosophy of organization. The major purpose of an organizational alignment is to achieve a desired policy or purpose at a minimum cost, in the shortest length of time, and with the least amount of disorder and confusion. The organization that accomplishes this purpose is a beneficial organization. Project and matrix managements have been helpful in many cases. These types of managements should be considered, especially in large system and/or programming projects.

EXERCISES

1. Discuss the organizational implications of feasibility and applications studies, including, at a minimum: trends, organizational location, attributes of members, steering committees and their charters, and the use of consultants.

2. What is the interrelationship between the objectives of a company and its organizational structure?

3. You have been assigned by the president of your company to prepare a first draft of a charter for a feasibility and applications study. This draft is to include a proposed organizational assignment for the study. The company has two similar organizational locations in cities 100 miles apart. Its primary business is the wholesaling and retailing of electric and electronic components and equipment. Prepare such a draft.

4. Discuss the centralization versus decentralization problem and its impact on data processing. What factors should be considered in the decision to centralize or to decentralize?

5. Discuss the problem as to where analysts and programmers should be located. Consider in this answer: open shop versus closed shop and organizational location of data processing.

6. What are the functions of open-shop data processing? In what circumstances would you recommend open shop?

7. Sketch an organizational chart of a data processing division in a large company. The division reports directly to a vice-president for information systems. Show how this chart would change, depending upon such factors as size of company, organizational preferences of management, and the homogeneity of the firm.

8. Why are project and matrix management particularly helpful in large systems and programming applications? Discuss their advantages and disadvantages. Under what circumstances would you recommend their use?

3 ◀ SELECTION OF PERSONNEL

> Every organization, large or small, in the last analysis is dependent for its success on the quality of effort of the people who have been chosen to operate the concern. The concept of personnel administration—of getting qualified people to work together effectively in an organization—is indeed the capstone of successful management.[1]

Probably the dominant factor in the success or failure of any organization is the people with authority and responsibility for operation. These people must be carefully selected, thoroughly trained, adequately supervised, well motivated, and in the right jobs. The key elements that this chapter examines are those involved in the careful selection of competent personnel for the right jobs. The magnitude of the personnel problem in the data processing field will be considered, as well as sources of people, selection methods, and the relationship of position descriptions to the selection process. Problems and trends in the selection of five primary professional positions in data processing—director, systems analyst, systems programmer, business programmer, and scientific programmer—will be discussed in detail. The scope of each position will be delimited, and the desired characteristics of the individual to fill each position and the method of selecting him will be discussed.

GENERAL

Personnel Situation

In 1966 the shortage of systems analysts was estimated at about 40,000 and of programmers at 100,000. Anticipated growth in the number of computers used for business data processing from 1966 to 1970, effects of changes in programming languages on types and numbers of personnel needed, and sources of such personnel were considered. The 1970 shortages were esti-

---

1. Cathryn Seckler-Hudson, *Organization and Management: Theory and Practice.* Washington, D. C.: The American University Press, 1955, pp. 157-158.

mated at 120,000 systems analysts and 100,000 programmers. In analyzing the personnel situation in the data processing field, others have made estimates that varied from these figures. However, all estimates in the late 1960s showed a shortage of computer personnel and a growing shortage in the 1970s.

The recession starting in 1970, however, resulted in a new phenomenon—unemployment in the computer industry. Although computer professionals were reported as better off than those in some other fields, there was unemployment in this area. A survey showed 1.3 percent for data processing personnel, as compared with 3.6 percent for all white-collar workers. These figures were prior to RCA's decision to leave the computer field.[2] This should cause the 1.3 percent figure to rise, although it will not approach the 3.6 percent. A *Computerworld* article showed a year of layoffs and a half-year of no activity, followed by increasing demands for computer professionals in 1971.

This recession, however, has not had any substantial effect on long-range projections of the needs for computer professionals. The Department of Labor estimated that the 175,000 programmers employed in 1968 would rise to 400,000 in 1980. During the same period of time, requirements for systems analysts would increase from 150,000 to 425,000.[3]

Even with unemployment in the millions, the number of people required for ADP has outstripped the supply of qualified candidates. The key word in this conclusion is "qualified." The word implies a blend of personal characteristics, education, training, and experience. Data processing case histories have showed that many people who were sincerely desirous of succeeding in data processing have in fact failed. These failures may be recognized at varying times in the long process of selection, formal training, on-the-job training, and production. Their effects on the installation that made the poor selection can be disastrous. The entire process probably lasted for more than a year. Not only had that year been lost because no usable production occurred during that period of time, but also the next year, required to train a new selectee and make him productive. If it is accepted that one of the prime ingredients of a successful installation is high-quality personnel, it follows that the selection process merits high priority.

Sources of Personnel

Methods of finding sources of personnel, of course, apply to two areas—hiring from outside the company and selecting from within. At different times,

2. E. Drake Lundell, Jr., "Employment Takes a Better Turn," *Computerworld* (Oct. 13, 1971), p. 4.
3. Alan Drattel, "Study Shows Sharp DP Job Rise by 1980," *Computerworld* (Sept. 8, 1971), p. 1.

and from company to company, the pendulum has swung from one to the other. Is it better to select people who know the business but not the computer? Is it preferable to choose those who know the computer but do not know the business? At what point does the answer change, when absolutes of knowledge in these two areas become gradations of each? Is management in a position to make the better choice? In many firms there is evidence of untapped potential among its employees, but management's problem is to make the proper selection. Similarly there are many competent computer professionals outside the firm, but how does one select an applicant who will be valuable to the company?

Selection from Within

Despite the glamor of data processing, other operating departments still have their functions to perform. Thus, they do not relish losing good employees. If top management does not give overt support to the principle of transferring the best personnel from individual departments, the managers of these departments will not offer their best people. Failure to pay heed to this can result in data processing's being staffed with incompetents, and a much greater chance that the installation will not succeed.

Although most companies use their current personnel to form the nucleus of the new data processing organization, it should be pointed out that this source of personnel is not a "bottomless well." Assuming that the selection procedure is optimal, the initial establishment of data processing will select those best qualified. Because of the relatively high turnover in data processing, it will be necessary to acquire more personnel at a later time. Unless positive steps are taken to replenish the remainder of the personnel pool with people who are at least on a par with those who were first selected, each successive selection will be made from less-qualified personnel.

In the 1950s there was a strong preference for selection from within. In the 1960s, however, there had been a diminution of this method of selection. By the early 1970s, selection from within had lessened even further. A company reported being forced to lower its acceptance standards if it were to continue recruiting from within, having exhausted the talent able to meet earlier high standards. A federal bureau had a similar experience in a second recruiting for systems analysts and programmers.

Some administrators questioned the policy of continued selection from within, particularly when second recruiting efforts showed that none who took the tests received ratings above the minimal selections of the first recruiting.

> This [selection from within] is believed to be a dangerous doctrine representing a considerable overemphasis on knowledge of local paper work. In the present era of greater equipment and software subtlety,

and because of the desire to implement a true service almost universally, ability to develop new conceptual schemes for doing work seems more important than knowledge of local procedures. Too much of the latter might even be a deterrent to imaginative innovation. However, it must be confessed that the majority of organizations polled in a recent recheck said they were making no changes in their practices on this score and, further, that they did not think changes in the state of the art would make changes in such practices necessary.[4]

If only a particular application is to be automated, personnel from that application area should be given particular consideration. Generally, they will be best informed about the system. Furthermore, although this may not be important, there is a possibility that their former positions will not exist after the new system is installed. If, on the other hand, the installation is to service the company as an entity, selection from an operating area might tend to prejudice both the way data processing will be oriented and the consideration that will be given by other areas of the company.

Selection from Outside

Selectees from outside the company may be segregated into two types: experienced and inexperienced. The advantage of selecting personnel who know the computer is that they will be productive earlier than inexperienced people, who will need a period of training before becoming productive. If the experienced person comes from the same industry, i.e., from bank to bank or from grocery chain to grocery chain, other beneficial by-products that might be realized are the techniques and practices at his previous place of employment. Furthermore, since he has worked in data processing previously, it is possible to get more substantial information concerning his potential in the new data processing organization. His employer, fellow employees, and those in professional associations constitute excellent sources of such information. The disadvantages include the higher pay required to entice an employee to leave his current company, the tendency of this type of pirating to raise general pay rates in data processing, and the probability that a person who has left one employer for a higher salary will do so again.

Selection Methods

The fact that some of those selected become very successful in data processing, whereas many of those who appear to be the best qualified fail miserably, suggests the need for better or more extensive testing and/or

4. Harry H. Fite, "Selection of Data Processing Personnel." Unpublished paper written for the Center of Technology and Administration of The American University, Washington, D.C., pp. 9-10.

selecting methods. More tools are available to the person selecting from within than from without. One can observe the applicant while he is working. In selecting from within, one can interview, test, and observe. Although the tests should differentiate between scientific and business types of personnel, they do not supplant personal interviews and observation. Furthermore, compatibility of the person with the company, his attitude toward the work, and his personal characteristics are also important factors. Tests should be used to eliminate those who are definitely not qualified, but personal observation may constitute the best basis for final selection.

The U.S. Civil Service Commission has devised written tests for inexperienced personnel entering federal employment. For programmer and systems analyst trainees, the test usually is the Federal Service Entrance Examination (FSEE), a written test, primarily a test of intelligence, knowledge, abstract reasoning, and arithmetic reasoning. This examination is administered to college seniors and graduates interested in entering the federal civil service. The examination, of course, is designed to eliminate those who are not eligible, and to structure those who pass in the order of the grades achieved. The person desiring to make selections has at his disposal not only the grade scored on the test, but also the scores on the individual segments of the test. The employee's application furnishes pertinent background information about himself. Individual agencies use the FSEE as a basis for eliminating nonqualified employees in selection from within. They may use only part of the FSEE, or they may devise their own tests. Many, however, use parts of the FSEE, such as arithmetic reasoning, abstract reasoning, and intelligence. The passing grades are established, based upon previous experience in the agency, but at times they must be lowered in order to get enough eligible candidates.

Interviewing of the candidate does not play a major role for people first entering civil service. In practice, it is usually not policy to pay the expenses of a person who comes to the installation to be interviewed. Therefore, only local people or those willing to come without expense reimbursement are interviewed at the installation. Recruiting teams, however, are permitted to travel around the country to interview prospective employees.

On the basis of background and experience, applicants for higher positions can get on the Federal Administrative and Management Examination (FAME) register. This is an "unassembled examination" in which the applicant does not take a written test. The principal means of hiring from this register include examination of background and experience, correspondence with previous employers and references, and occasional interviews.

Many state and local governments follow procedures similar to those of the federal government. In private industry the interview and an examination of background play a more major role. Written examinations, such as the IBM Programmer Aptitude Test (PAT), are used primarily as screening devices. A fairly substantial reliance is placed on employment agencies to get candidates for positions, especially when seeking experienced people. Local chapter meetings and annual conferences of professional associations have also been used as areas for recruiting. Psychological tests and consultants have helped in the selection of data processing personnel.

Job Definition

All else being equal, it appears that a more effective selection procedure is possible in those areas in which the positions are clearly defined. In such instances it is possible to delineate the individual operations and the personal characteristics that should contribute to success. In companies where there is no specific line of demarcation between positions, and where the duties are not clearly defined, the possibility of selecting qualified and competent personnel scientifically is lessened.

Positions

The variation in job definitions in data processing can be shown by comparing two lists of data processing positions published within a year of each other. The U.S. Department of Labor lists 13 occupations in electronic data processing systems.[5] The *Data Processing Manning Survey* has 23 different job descriptions, 7 of which are associated directly with electric accounting machines (EAM) and not with the electronic computer positions in the Department of Labor list.[6] In no case does a position in both lists have identical functions. Of the 13 positions listed by the Department of Labor, 7 are not included in the other list, whereas 10 of the 16 computer positions in the Manning Survey list do not appear in the former.

In the area of programming, for example, the federal list has assistant head under whom are programming, senior programmer, computer programmer, programming technician, and programming clerk. The survey includes only chief programmer and programmer. Conversely, the federal list does not include any systems analyst positions, whereas the survey has project planner, systems analyst, and computing analyst. Although the references cited are based on 1950 information, the situation has not improved materially since then. Differences in titles (and definitions) make it difficult, if not impossible, to assess an applicant's experience from the titles of the jobs he has held.

5. *Occupations in Electronic Data-processing Systems.* Washington, D.C.: U.S. Department of Labor, January 1959, pp. 9-26.

6. "Data Processing Manning Survey," *Research and Engineering* (March/April 1958), pp. 31-33.

Influencing Factors

Analysis of data processing positions in various installations reveals many differences in the distribution of positions. Some of the factors that appear to influence the decision as to where to establish the limits of individual position descriptions are discussed below.

Size of Organization. In a data processing installation with only a few computer personnel, each person normally is responsible for a wider range of activity than in an organization with a large number of computer personnel. In the small installation the programmer, in addition to his programming duties, often does systems analysis and runs the computer in production operations. It is not uncommon in installations of that size for the head of data processing, despite advice to the contrary, to spend a large proportion of his time writing programs and even running the computer.

Philosophy of Operation. Chapter 2 showed that the functions of the data processing division differ significantly, depending upon whether the operations are open shop or closed shop. With the major organizational differences, it is expected that individual position descriptions also will differ considerably.

Wage Level. The labor situation is another factor that can influence position descriptions. If computing personnel are plentiful, installations with more than a few employees can subdivide positions into smaller areas. With limited individual responsibilities, the rate of pay normally is less. If, on the other hand, computer personnel are scarce, the range of their duties can be expanded, permitting payment of higher salaries. This is particularly evident when one of the better employees is offered more money at another installation, and the job description does not permit his pay to be raised. By redefining the position, expanding its responsibilities, and minimizing the degree of supervision, it is often possible to raise the salary rate.

Personal Attributes. To paraphrase Parkinson's law, work tends to expand to fill the space available to do the work. Similarly, although the written description may not change, duties actually performed tend to reflect a person's particular talents and interests. Numerous audits have uncovered job descriptions that, although accurate when written, have not kept up with actual changes in duties.

Communication Problems. The decision to expand or contract the duties of individual positions should consider communication problems that may arise as side effects of the expansion or contraction. If the programmer talks to the customer, designs the system, writes and debugs the programs, and then makes the production runs, there is a minimal problem of communication. If, on the other hand, more than one person is involved in the process, the problem of communication increases geometrically as the number of people increases arithmetically.

DIRECTOR OF DATA PROCESSING

In establishing a data processing installation, the first person to engage is the director. As used here, the director of data processing reports to general management—the vice-president or director of management information. He is completely responsible for the systems analysis and design, programming, EAM, and computer operations and related training. Possibly he also has operations research personnel, character recognition, and communication equipment.

Characteristics

In the early 1950s when computers first were used for business applications, knowledge of the computer or of data processing was considered the most necessary characteristic of the director of a computer installation. As a result, the early directors were primarily either mathematicians or those who had headed up EAM installations. The failures of the mathematicians often were attributed to lack of administrative ability and a need for more practicality. In one case it took years to automate the payroll of a large industrial concern because of a desire to incorporate into the system every idiosyncrasy of the manual and EAM system. The usual EAM manager was a technician who knew the equipment and the applications on it. He was not well educated and did not have the overall view of data flow through the company. He was not considered to be in the upper management areas in company operations. With this type of management, it was not surprising to hear the challenge, "name one successful installation."

By the late 1950s opinions of the necessary characteristics for the manager of data processing had changed. It was suggested that the most important selection, that of the manager of data processing, should be done with considerable care, since he should be alert, inquisitive, and should get along with people. He also should be able to apply logic to a statement of the problem, he should be able to hypothesize possible solutions, and he should have an aptitude and desire for systems work. Some knowledge of data processing equipment and its capabilities is desirable, but not essential.

There were many technicians in charge of data processing during the 1960s, but there was a shortage of good managers. This was not an effective arrangement, since the head of a computer installation should have the administrative ability to coordinate the skills of his technicians, making them productive. In the early 1960s the Data Processing Management Association first offered nationwide examinations for a certificate in data processing. This examination, given annually since then, tests candidates in attributes considered desirable for managers of data processing. By the 1970s there was substantial agreement that the director of processing should be a good administrator with a knowledge of the functions of the company. More and more people with this background, plus a substantial understanding of data processing equipment and its potential benefits, are becoming available. The current manager of data processing is emerging as a fairly young, well-educated man with relatively high intelligence and a good knowledge of computers and systems. He knows how the company operates and how information flows through it.

Changes in professional organizations mirror those developments. In the early 1950s the National Machine Accountants Association was composed primarily of managers of EAM installations. The publications and meetings for the most part were devoted to equipment and machine techniques. Only a low percentage of these managers had college degrees. About 1961 the name was changed to the Data Processing Management Association (DPMA). At first the change was in name, not in the method of operation or in membership. For example, in the Washington, D. C., chapter in 1961, six of the ten meetings were devoted to individual computer manufacturers displaying their new equipment and explaining what it could do. Two of the remaining meetings featured sports (the best attended) and a social gathering. By 1971 the chapter membership more than doubled. If one were to use the mode as a measure of a typical member, he would be in his late thirties, have a college degree, be a company official (such as assistant vice-president), know both computers and systems, and have a strong desire to improve himself. In 1971, eight of the ten meetings were devoted to such subjects as systems design, people problem in systems implementation, education and training, optical character recognition, and data-base design. The metamorphosis is also evident in the international organization, which has more than doubled in size from 1961 to 1971 and has experienced a similar upgrading in type of membership. A survey in 1969 showed that 72 percent of the reporting companies required college background for the manager of data processing. More than 45 percent required college degrees.[7]

7. "EDP Salary Study—1969," *Business Automation* (June 1969), p. 58.

Selection

Since, as indicated previously, the director of data processing, in addition to other personal characteristics, must be a good administrator with a knowldege of the functions and operations of the company, he should normally be selected from within. In fact, if the company has no one who is capable of assuming the position, it is possible that automation is premature. Although there are no universally accepted criteria, it is suggested that the field of applicants be narrowed to those who are mature, know the company's operations, have demonstrated the ability to operate effectively with the department heads and induce constructive action, have the confidence and support of top management, and have a considerable knowledge of computers and systems.

This does not, of course, preclude the hiring of data processing managers from outside the company. Advertisements for data processing managers and employment agency listings indicate that data processing managers often are recruited from outside. In banks in the Washington, D. C., area, for example, two directors of data processing moved to better positions in other banks, one becoming an assistant vice-president in a suburban bank and the other becoming a vice-president of a bank in another state. In each case, however, the function essentially was that of developing and implementing a computer-based system for a multibranch bank.

In the preceding examples the managers moved from company to company, but essentially stayed in the same job in the same industry. The director of data processing of the Federal Reserve Board left to become the director of data processing of one of the largest banks in the world. He is now the manager of Telecommunications and Information Systems for a federal agency. In other cases the directors of data processing of the Federal Communications Commission, the State Department, and the Labor Department came from the Department of the Navy. The director of data processing of a Navy bureau came from the Army Map Service. These are only a few examples of many similar moves.

Nothing about managing a data processing installation indicates that only men should be considered in this particular area. Nevertheless, a 1960 survey showed that only two of 489 firms had a woman manager of data processing. To name a few of the many excellent women in managerial positions: Mrs. Eleanor Irvine has her own corporation in computer personnel consulting. Commander Grace Hopper heads the Programming Languages Section of the Department of the Navy. Dr. Ruth Davis is the Director of the Center for Computer Sciences and Technology of the National Bureau of Standards. Geraldine Oxley is the director of electronic research for the New York Life Insurance Company. By 1971 the percentage of data processing managers who were women had increased considerably but was still distressingly low.[8]

SYSTEMS ANALYSTS

In planning for a data processing installation, several systems analysts are needed early. It is not a simple task to get them. Competent analysts are scarce, and it takes several years of good, practical experience and on-the-job training to produce a systems analyst of any real value. Within this context, the systems analyst plans the system from data preparation until such data reach data processing. He describes the input to data processing and the desired output. Also he plans the system from the time the output data are released by data processing until they are used.

Characteristics

Seven different sources indicate 25 desirable characteristics for systems analysts.

As Table 3-1 indicates, although 25 characteristics are cited by seven different references, four or more of the references concur in only six of them. The prime factors, logical ability and thoroughness, are mentioned by six of the seven, followed by the five recommending ability to work with others and resourcefulness. Of the seven, only four list imagination and oral ability. The ideal person for systems analysis work, therefore, is one who is logical, thorough, resourceful, imaginative, expresses himself clearly, and works well with others.

Selection from Within

The prime source of systems analysts is personnel already working in the organization. The background amassed in the standard operating procedures permits them to develop systems without indecision and confusion. Since they have knowledge of the current relationships, they should be able to foresee the side effects of system changes that might result in repercussions elsewhere. Furthermore, time need not be spent in orienting them to company procedures and relationships.

Some consider the qualifications for systems analysis to be knowledge of the policies, procedures, and practices in the areas to be studied. The implications of this, of course, are that recruitment must be either from the area affected or from the audit and/or systems personnel concerned with

8. Helen M. Milecki, "Women in ADP Management," *Data Management* (February 1971), pp. 18-23.

TABLE 3.1

DESIRABLE CHARACTERISTICS FOR SYSTEMS ANALYSTS

Characteristic	Source						
	1	2	3	4	5	6	7
Logical ability	x	x	x	x	x	x	
Thoroughness	x	x	x	x	x	x	
Ability to work with others	x	x		x	x		x
Resourcefulness	x	x		x		x	x
Imagination	x	x		x		x	
Oral ability	x	x		x			x
Abstract reasoning		x	x				x
Emotional balance	x			x			x
Interest in analysis	x			x		x	
Writing ability	x	x		x			
Curiosity	x	x				x	
Decisiveness	x						x
Empathy		x		x			
Mature judgment	x					x	
Practicability	x	x					
Ability to observe		x					
Dislike for inefficiency		x					
Initiative			x				
Integrity	x						
Intelligence		x					
Interest in science and technology							x
Interest in staff work	x						
Numerical ability							x
Open-mindedness	x						
Selling ability	x						

SOURCES: (1) Department of the Army; (2) Sperry Rand Corporation; (3) Ned Chapin; (4) Univac Division of Remington Rand; (5) Diebold, Inc.; (6) Gordon L. Murray; (7) Department of Labor.

that department. Since personnel will not have to be familiarized with operations and procedures, time saving results.

Experience does not result in a clear-cut verdict that systems analysts should be recruited only from within. If the in-house talent is equal in caliber to that of those applying from outside, then the knowledge of local people and procedures can be quite valuable. If higher-caliber people are selected from outside, however, the time lost in the familiarization process can be regained over a period of time. Both in private industry and in government, there is quite a traffic in systems analysts from one computer installation to another. In times of business contraction, however, for all practical purposes this migration of systems analysts stops. Before the 1970 recession, advertisements for systems analysts were exceeded only by those for programmers. Analysts who held jobs in 1970 and 1971 were only too glad to stay in them. Previously, a manager did not discharge the marginal analyst—at least he produced something. If a manager did discharge the marginal analyst, he might not be able to get a replacement who would produce as much. But with large governmental contracts terminated or renegotiated, and computer software firms unable to get business, analysts suddenly became available. For the first time, the manager has been able to weed out the marginal systems analyst and replace him with one who will be more productive. It appears that the availability of systems analysts will be cyclic. In good times they will be scarce; in recessions, plentiful.

Backgrounds

According to Sperry Rand, a knowledge of the capabilities and limitations of computers is "essential" for systems analysts. Previous experience in a computer system is "extremely valuable"; experience in coordinating manual operations with computer procedures in planning a conversion, "desirable"; and conference-type experience, "useful." Those who already are making analyses for more efficient systems have the ability to cross departmental lines and can view broad relationships between operational areas.

A survey of more than a hundred governmental installations showed a strong consideration of previous systems experience as "very important." About half as many rated pervious computer experience in the same category of importance. Only 11 percent of the installations rated tabulating experience as "very important." There was little difference between scientific and business-type data processing installations in this regard. The results of this survey are listed in Table 3.2. From the standpoint of educational requirements the same study produced the results shown in Table 3.3.

TABLE 3.2

EXPERIENCE REQUIREMENTS FOR SYSTEMS ANALYSTS

		Percentage Considering Factor "Very Important"	
Factor	*Number of Installations*	*Scientific*	*Data Processing*
Systems work	113	86	93
ADP operations	107	54	47
Tabulating work	108	13	11

SOURCE: Harry H. Fite, "Selection of Data Processing Personnel." Unpublished paper, Center of Technology and Administration, American University, Washington, D.C.

TABLE 3.3

EDUCATIONAL REQUIREMENTS FOR SYSTEMS ANALYSTS[11]

	Number of Installations	Percentage Considering Factor "Very Important"	
		Scientific	Data Processing
High school	105	93	92
Manufacturer or technical training	97	58	56
Mathematics major	98	25	8
College science major	91	9	5

SOURCE: Harry H. Fite, "Selection of Data Processing Personnel." Unpublished paper, Center of Technology and Administration, American University, Washington, D.C.

Although men outnumber women by a ratio of eight to one in data processing, women have proved to be good at systems analysis. There is no valid reason to discriminate against them. The use of older, experienced people in systems design is recommended. In order to counteract any tendencies toward conservatism, however, some younger analysts should be included.

Methods

As early as 1959 the Department of the Army followed the methods listed below as methods of measuring the characteristics of potential systems analysts.[9]

1. General interview: To clarify and verify the information submitted in the application and to size up the applicant's characteristics and interests.
2. Case-problem interview: Candidate is given a problem or problems. He is asked to state orally his approach to the problem(s), his reactions, and his interests.
3. Group oral interview: Candidates, under observation, work as a group to solve a problem.
4. Discussion of work product: Written product of candidate is discussed to see if the characteristics of good performance are present.

9. *Army Civilian Career Program for Comptroller Functional Area.* Washington, D.C.: Department of the Army, Sept. 30, 1959, p. 60.

5. Examination of work product: Examination of a candidate's writing to see how conclusions were reached and presented.
6. Reference inquiries: To see how applicant has faced problems in the past. Questions should be on specific job elements instead of on total performance.
7. Written case problem: Like case-problem interview, except that it is in writing.
8. Verbal abilities test: Measures vocabulary, reading comprehension, and judgment.
9. Abstract reasoning test: Measures ability to reason from various symbols, but knowledge is not a factor.
10. Administrative judgment test: Measures ability to use judgment in administrative situations. Knowledge of administrative processes is a factor.

Although the Army methods were published in 1959, many of them continue in the 1970s as the major methods of selection of systems analysts. General interview and reference inquiries head the list, followed by tests of verbal abilities and abstract reasoning. Case-problem interviews and group oral interviews are used occasionally, the latter especially when several analysts are needed.

The usual method of selection for systems analysts is a combination of interviews and tests. Interviews are quite unreliable. Although tests are not valid, nor are they reliable enough, they are helpful. At least they screen out those who have little or no chance of succeeding. Most systems analysts selected from within are chosen by a combination of tests and interviews. The tests most often used in the federal government are the verbal abilities test, the abstract reasoning test, and the administrative judgment test. For selection of systems analyst trainees from outside the government, the Federal Service Entrance Examination is used normally.

PROGRAMMERS

The key to success of any computer installation is its programming. Since one good programmer often is worth four mediocre programmers, the director of data processing tries to select those best qualified. The principal staffing problem of the computer field is getting programmers. In order to get them, it is necessary to develop new and improved sources. Programming problems are aggravated by turnover, which in turn results from the demand for programmers being greater than the supply. Increases in trainee starting salaries motivate programmers with a few years' experience to change jobs to keep ahead of the trainees. Few programmers are released because of poor-quality work, except during periods of recession. What will be needed, if the estimates of the Department of Labor are correct, will be better schools and training facilities for computer programmers, more precise selection methods, and positive programs of salary and work assignments.

A programmer is defined as a person who prepares plans and procedures for converting data into their processed state when they reach data processing. He prepares block diagrams, flow charts, instructions (machine, mnemonic, or higher-level); and tests and debugs the programs. A systems programmer is one whose prime area of application is the operating system. He makes changes and amendments to the operating system to make the computer more useful for the operations of the company. He also assists other programmers in interacting effectively with the computer. Business programmers write and debug programs for business applications. Their normal language is COBOL or PL/1. Scientific programmers usually write and debug programs for engineering, mathematical, or similar applications. Their normal language is FORTRAN, ALGOL, or BASIC. The discussion of the selection of programmers will be segregated into the categories mentioned.

Systems Programmers

Characteristics

Since literature on the desirable characteristics of systems programmers is comparatively scarce, these traits were compiled from experience and discussions with directors of data processing who had hired systems programmers.

First, from an experience standpoint, a programmer should have programmed in several computer languages, including FORTRAN, COBOL, and at least one assembly or machine language. The machine-language experience is necessary, as practically all operating systems are written in the language of the computer. The knowledge of other languages will help him understand what other programmers are trying to do, so that he can assist all in interacting with the computer. Second, his paramount interest should be programming, as distinguished from applications. Since his work will be absorbing, he will have no desire to leave for other work. Third, he should be stable and able to work under pressure. Quite often those he works with will be programmers whose efforts have been thwarted (or they so believe) by the operating system and/or the computer. As such, these co-workers are often upset before seeing him, and are under pressure to get their work done. Fourth, an ability to understand people under emotional pressure and work with them effectively will certainly help him in dealing with others. Fifth, he must not feel superior to the programmers with whom he must interact. At least, if he thinks that he is superior, he shouldn't show it. Finally, ability to teach will help him train other programmers so that they may interact more effectively with the computer. This, in turn, will lessen the many crises that beset the systems programmer in his daily work.

Selection

It does not matter very much whether systems programmers are selected from within or from outside the company. The problem is to find them. Even during depressions there is a severe shortage of systems programmers. Usually those interviewed will not have all of the characteristics and background listed above. The best ways to determine whom to select are by talking with their references and people with whom they have worked, and by personal interview.

Business Programmers

Characteristics

Twenty references list 23 different characteristics for a computer programmer. Only seven of these characteristics, however, are named by more than three of the references. According to these, a programmer should be intelligent, have both logical and verbal abilities, have a systems approach to problems, and be accurate, ingenious, and interested in programming. If a person is intelligent and is interested in programming—not just for the pay, but in programming as an activity—he stands an excellent chance of succeeding as a programmer of business applications.

Selection from Within

When computers were first used for business purposes, they were often put under the control of engineers and mathematicians. Those in charge decided that it was easier to teach the machine to someone who understood the business than it was to teach the business to someone who knew how to program but didn't know the business. The problem was to find people who could use the computer to best advantage. Most companies had formal recruiting programs of promotion from within, since that assured knowledge of company operations and organizations.

There was a strong preference to train existing employees rather than hire new ones. This policy was more successful in business data processing than in scientific computations, where most companies had to bring in some programmers from outside. Although there are advantages to hiring business programmers from within, it is not essential that this practice be followed.

Some experienced "outsiders" should be added if most of the programmers are comparatively inexperienced, selected from within, and trained to program.

Some of the advantages of recruiting from within are:

1. The employee has more knowledge of how the company operates.
2. Employee morale is improved.
3. More is known about the ability of the employee.
4. The selection procedure is less expensive.

Among the disadvantages are:

1. It may be necessary to lower acceptance criteria in order to make successive selections from within.
2. Fresh viewpoints will not be brought into the company.
3. If the selected employee fails as a computer programmer, problems will arise in placing him in another position.

Selection from Outside

Despite the advantages of hiring from within, it often becomes necessary for a company to recruit programming trainees from outside. The System Development Corporation in a large-scale recruiting drive covered most major and medium-sized cities in the country. Newspaper advertisements were used as a prescreening device, indicating minimum knowledge requirements and a willingness to relocate. Personal interviews were combined with psychological-test batteries. Instead of a high-pressure approach, the applicant generally was encouraged to find out about the field for himself and then decide if he wanted to become a programmer. Offers were made to one of nine persons interviewed.

Largely, the sources for outside programmers are private employment agencies, recommendations from the current staff, advertising in trade publications and newspapers, and college recruiting. The more effective companies hire mostly from outside or not at all. Probably, because of their higher standards and rigid pay scales, the more effective companies find it quite difficult to hire and keep programmers.

Background

Programmers in business data processing find a good, basic background in college mathematics and business administration, including accounting and statistics, to be helpful. The minimum requirement normally is a high school education with algebra and geometry. The majority of business firms require at least a college background as a minimum requirement for programming. Evidently, governmental installations do not put so high a premium on education as private industry does. Only 10 percent of the data processing installations in government require a college education. Table 3.4 shows the educational background of programmers found by a University of Southern California study.

TABLE 3.4

EDUCATIONAL BACKGROUND OF BUSINESS COMPUTER PROGRAMMERS

Factor	*Percentage*
High school diploma	98
College diploma	48
Some graduate training	7
Academic major (expressed as a percentage of those indicating·a major)	
Accounting	5
Business administration	13
Engineering	23
Physics	5
Mathematics	16
Others	38

SOURCE: *The Role of Humans in Complex Computer Systems.* Department of Psychology, University of Southern California, January 1959, p. 36. Sponsored by the Office of Naval Research.

Age

In the selection of computer personnel, arbitrary restrictions are established with regard to age, sex, and race. There is a common belief that programmers must be young, to be flexible in thinking and to attempt new ways of doing things. No significant age differentials can be found between computer programmers of installations considered effective and those found to be less so. Most officials want programmers in the 25-45 age group. Further analysis, however, indicates that learning ability depends primarily upon the individual, not his age. A program combining older, experienced programmers with younger ones may prove most satisfactory. It is felt that the enthusiasm for new and untried methods of the younger programmers stimulates the older ones. The conservatism of the senior programmers, on the other hand, tends to stabilize the younger ones.

Sex

About one-fifth of the programmers are women. They often are extremely successful, possibly because they are happier with detail work. Deterrents to the use of women in programming positions are the high turn over and late shifts. The experience of this author has not validated that claim. Due to the ability of male programmers to transfer to higher paying positions in other installations, turnover was higher among them. As expected, absences due to pregnancies were higher with young female programmers than with older ones. The tendency of married female programmers to take leave to nurse a sick child was counterbalanced by the time male programmers took off for sporting events. Assignments were made without reference to the sex of the programmer, despite the fact that, for months at a time, all machine debugging was done on the "graveyard shift."

Race

Few references, if any, are available concerning the degree of success of business programmers according to race. Based on his experience with government and private industry, this author is unable to distinguish any correlation between success of a programmer and race. One of the most successful computer installations in his experience is a medley of black, brown, white, and yellow programmers and analysts. In professional societies, such as the Association for Computing Machinery (ACM) and the DPMA, there exists a scarcity of nonwhite members. Although the population of Washington, D. C., is far more than 50 percent nonwhite, generally few nonwhites attend chapter meetings.

Testing

The IBM Programmer Aptitude Test (PAT) is without doubt the most usual test administered to potential computer programmers. This author has found it useful as a screening device to eliminate those with little chance of success in programming. There is, however, no significantly higher success rate between those getting "A" on the test and those getting "B." In a class in which programming was taught, 19 received scores of "A" in the Sperry Rand programmer aptitude test (similar to the PAT). One person with a score of "B" was included in the course. He was the second-best programmer in the class and has been outstanding in on-the-job programming. In either test a score of "A" or "B," and an above-average IQ together with a strong desire to be a programmer, appear to be the prime ingredients of success.

A survey of 262 companies showed that 96 of them used tests for selecting programmers. Usually, these tests were arithmetic reasoning, verbal abilities, and abstract reasoning. Four of the tests used were found to help in selecting programmers. Nevertheless, there was no significant correlation with the supervisors' ratings of programmer proficiency. Another survey tested programmers as compared to nonprogrammers. The former were superior in numerical ability, symbolic reasoning, numerical reasoning, and tables. The tests, however, were not considered to be a significant measurement of ability, initiative, or potential.

In measuring the qualities for which interviews do not provide specifics, psychological tests are helpful. These tests, however, should be selected carefully and used cautiously. Furthermore, the result should be used in conjunction with other selection means and not as the only criterion. It is suggested that potential programmers be given a well-rounded battery of tests that measure mental ability, mechanical aptitude, abstract reasoning, and personality.

The DPMA started a nationwide annual test of computer programmers in 1970. It is still too early to evaluate this test. It offers the possibility of being relatively sure that any candidate who has passed the test has a certain basic knowledge of programming. Less than 40 percent of the 1100 taking the initial examination passed.

Scientific Programmers

Characteristics

It is probable that the desirable characteristics of a scientific programmer are similar to those of a business programmer. However, the systems approach to problems is possibly less important in scientific than in business programming.

Selection

The policy of training current employees instead of hiring new ones is more successful in business data processing than in scientific and engineering companies. Knowledge of how the company operates, which is the major advantage of hiring from within in business data processing, is of little importance to scientific programmers. The business programmer hired from outside must spend quite some time learning about the company and its methods of operation. The scientific programmer, on the other hand, can produce almost immediately. A much higher proportion of scientific programmers, therefore, is hired from outside the company.

The University of Southern California survey[9] found that programmers in scientific work generally are better educated than those in business data processing. As indicated in Table 3.5, 87 percent of the scientific programmers have college degrees, as compared with 55 percent of business

9. *The Role of Humans in Complex Computer Systems.* Dept. of Psychology, University of Southern California, January 1959. Sponsored by the Office of Naval Research.

TABLE 3.5

EDUCATIONAL BACKGROUND OF SCIENTIFIC
COMPUTER PROGRAMMERS

Factor	Percentage
High school diploma	100
College diploma	58
Some graduate training	29
Academic major (expressed as a percentage of those indicating a major)	
Accounting	2
Business administration	1
Engineering	6
Physics	10
Mathematics	66
Others	15

programmers (Table 3.4). Almost two-thirds of the scientific programmers majored in mathematics.

Testing

Rowan[10] reported that the Thurston Primary Abilities Test and the Thurston Temperament Schedule were used to predict success on the job. The subtests involved were verbal meaning, reasoning, space, and emotional stability. A multiple coefficient of correlation of 0.52 was found between the supervisor's ratings and the results of these tests. It was recommended that special-ability tests be used only to eliminate personnel lacking the minimum necessary aptitudes. The Thurston Primary Abilities Test, supplemented by the Michigan Vocabulary Test or Miller Analogy Test, gave additional information with respect to verbal skills. Furthermore, the two Thurston tests used in conjunction with each other were considered valid for selecting scientific programmers.

SUMMARY

General

Until the recession of the early 1970s there was a shortage of qualified

10. T. C. Rowan, "The Recruiting, Selecting, and Training of Programmers," *The Magazine of Datamation* (May-June 1958), p. 17.

data processing managers, systems analysts, and systems, business, and scientific programmers. Based upon the increase in computer installations expected by 1980, unless steps are taken to educate and train competent people, the current surplus will become a deficit. In selecting people both from within the company and from without, problems will have to be faced. Judging from the number of poor selections in data processing, selection methods have also been poor. In order to make a selection, it is necessary to have a definition of the job to be filled. The primary factor in job definition is to describe it clearly and specifically. Depending upon several factors, the positions vary from installation to installation. No general criteria to cover the great majority of all situations can be established. On the contrary, it appears to be necessary to consider the problems of each data processing installation and to devise the job definitions for each position specifically and individually.

Director of Data Processing

Managerial skill is the primary factor in the selection of the director of data processing, with technical competence as a secondary factor. The director should know the problems and objectives of the organization and of each segment thereof, and should be able to deal effectively with people at all levels. He should be selected from within the company and have imagination and adaptability. Future developments in hardware and software will necessitate a flexible, knowledgeable manager with skill in both large systems and in man/machine interface.

Systems Analysts

The ideal systems analyst should be logical, thorough, resourceful, and able to work with others. He should speak well and show imagination. It is preferable to select systems analysts from within the company. If the "local talent" is inferior, however, analysts may then be selected from outside. A combination of interviews and tests ought to be used in making the selection. Knowledge of systems work and of computer operations are a requirement and a definite plus factor, respectively. Education beyond high school is not required extensively. A mathematics or science major, however, is generally considered helpful in scientific installations. With the growth of large integrated systems, new skills, such as communications and psychology, must be added to the repertoire of systems analysis and design teams.

Programmers

Systems Programmers

The good systems programmer is the dedicated programmer with a background in FORTRAN, COBOL, and an assembly or machine language,

He must be able to work under pressure and deal effectively with people who, in turn, are working under pressure. The shortage of qualified systems programmers is so severe that the problem is finding them and assuring their competence for the job.

Business Programmers

Intelligence and interest in programming as an occupation are prime requisites for good business programmers. The best source for such programmers has been from within the company. Regardless of previous experience, the recruitment of some experienced outside help from any source (including college graduates) has been successful. A background of high school education suffices for most business programmers. Many companies depend on a combination of interviews and tests to select potential programmers. In the federal government the civil service tests of abstract reasoning and arithmetic reasoning yielded the best results. Outside the government, however, IBM's PAT is widely used. The DPMA's programmer test possibly will be a valid means of selection.

Scientific Programmers

The characteristics of scientific programmers are similar to those of business programmers. Their desirable background, however, differs. As stated previously, scientific programmers are generally better educated than their business counterparts. Degrees in mathematics are held by the majority of scientific programmers. Since knowledge of the company and its operations is not especially important to scientific programmers, a large proportion of them are selected from outside. Certain tests have proved valid for selecting potential scientific programmers.

General

Rather than try to devise better tests and make optimal selections, the primary effort should be on taking constructive steps to build a "pipeline" of potential programmers. Recruiting, training, and working conditions are the keys to such action.

EXERCISES

1. What are the advantages and disadvantages of selecting computer professionals from within the company? Do these vary for different types of professionals? Discuss.
2. What are the advantages and disadvantages of selecting computer

professionals from outside the company? Do these vary for different types of professionals? Discuss.

3. Discuss the role of job definitions in selecting computer professionals.

4. What factors influence job titles and job descriptions?

5. What characteristics should one look for in selecting a director of data processing? Would your answer differ if your company were getting a computer for the first time, as contrasted with getting a new director for an ongoing computer installation?

6. Discuss the mobility of different types of computer professionals —their ability to move from company to company.

7. What characteristics would you look for in selecting systems analysts? Would these vary in business data processing, as contrasted with scientific or engineering work?

8. What methods are available for assessing the capabilities and characteristics of various candidates for the position of systems analyst?

9. Differentiate between systems programmers, business programmers, and scientific programmers with regard to duties, desirable characteristics, and desirable backgrounds.

10. What tests would you use for selecting scientific programmers? Are they valid? What changes would you make in your answer if the selection were for business programmers.

11. You have been selected as the director of data processing for a large department store that is converting from electric accounting machines to a medium-sized computer. Develop a plan for acquiring your professional computer personnel.

3 ◀ SYSTEM DESIGN

Since 1950 the internal speed of computers has progressed from milliseconds through microseconds to nanoseconds. Input/output devices have increased from 150 to 200 cards per minute input and 200 lines of print per minute to speeds in excess of 2000 cards and 3000 lines. Installation costs have been reduced greatly while the reliability of the computer has increased markedly. In contrast to these magnificent gains in the development of computer hardware, ability to make use of these improvements has moved at a snail's pace. True, there have been some significant developments, such as time sharing, multiprogramming, and multiprocessing, but these are only a beginning. The basic need of the data processing field is to make use of the equipment now on the market, rather than to buy newer and faster computers. If the developers of equipment were to rest on their laurels and not develop another item, it would be years before the current equipment could be used to any degree approaching its true potential capability. Since the hardware developers show no sign of decreasing their efforts, it is likely that the relative efficiency with which computers and related equipment are used will decrease rather than increase in the 1970s. From the standpoint of business data processing, the areas of systems design and computer programming are the locations of most potential benefits, and therefore efforts should be concentrated in those areas.

A survey of more than 100 computer installations showed that the most common job on third-generation equipment was the simulating or emulating of second-generation computers. The most common job on second-generation equipment was simulating first-generation computers or doing work almost exactly as it was done on EAM. Computer users were asked to compare their system to the system in use in the early 1950s. If they had the same system but merely had put it on a bigger and/or faster computer, it was defined as no improvement in the system. The majority admitted that they were still using the same system. Various users estimated increased efficiency between 25 percent and 100 percent. The highest figure given was that the current system was three times as good as the system used 20 years ago.

From the figures in the preceding paragraphs, it is clear that computers are at least 20 times as good as they were in the early 1950s. In contrast, systems are at the most only three times as good. The difference between these two areas represents unused computer potential, which is increasing rapidly. If there are any indications that the trend will be reversed, this author is not aware of them. Picasecond speed is expected soon. When the distance that electricity can travel limits the speed of computers, a possible change will be systems of computers instead of computer systems. The inference is that systems composed of minicomputers, by their parallel operation, will overcome limitations imposed by the distance electricity can travel in a unit of time. In contrast, aside from the minicomputer concept, no marked improvement in systems design is anticipated in the near future. Apparently few potential systems designers receive adequate education and training for developing their ability to design complex systems that work. Universities and colleges do not have curriculums that fill the void. There is no national program to develop good systems designers. There are many systems designers, but few with real ability. If computers are to be used anywhere near their potential productive capacity, effort should be concentrated in developing a new breed of better educated and more able systems designers.

To a large proportion of those in the data processing field, the term "systems analysis" includes the gathering of facts, their analysis, and the design of a new or improved system. Systems analysis has been defined as a function in which the relationship of the application to the total information system is analyzed. Systems design, on the other hand, specifies the system to be used, and devises combinations of services by which the data is converted to meet the requirements of the system analysis. In any event, the gradations between systems analysis and systems design are subtle.

For the purposes of this chapter, system investigation is defined as the gathering of information concerning the objectives of an organization and the manner in which these objectives are achieved. Systems analysis is the examination of the results of the investigation and their realignment and combination to provide the basis for the design of a new system. Systems design is the use of the information from the system analysis phase to devise optimal methods of achieving objectives. This approach largely eliminates the problem of gray areas where system analysis and system design merge. It enables the concentration of effort on the area of greatest need—that of the system design.

Much has been written and many guides are available on how to collect data concerning input, files, output, and the way in which the system operates. The methodology is fairly straightforward. Further elaboration here will not result in any significant contribution. Most of the emphasis of this chapter, therefore, will be devoted to systems design, about which comparatively little has been written. Furthermore, many current data processing systems are deficient in this area of imaginative and effective system design. This chapter is divided into four areas: systems concepts, systems elements, systems development cycle, and information system design.

SYSTEM CONCEPTS

System

A system has been defined as an assembly of procedures, processes, methods, routines, or techniques united by some form of regulated interaction to form an organized whole. Another definition is a particular combination of human service, material service, and equipment service for handling information for a purpose. In either definition it is a combination of people, equipment, material, documents, and procedures working as an entity to accomplish specified purposes.

Information System

The military services found that many advantages resulted from centralizing selection of equipment for proposed systems rather than from decentralizing such selection to individual activities or commands from which the systems were proposed. The Air Force uses the term "data system" to describe the input to a data processing system, the files to be maintained, the output of the system, and the general procedures to be followed in converting the input to the desired output. Various agencies design the data systems they desire, but the equipment for Air Force installations is selected centrally at Hanscom Field, Massachusetts. The addition of detailed procedures and personnel and the implementation of such procedures result in a system in operation. Both the Army and the Navy use substantially the same practices. Their selection offices are in northern Virginia, fairly close to the Pentagon. The Army uses the term "information system" instead of the Air Force term "data system." Since the basic purpose of any data processing system is the information that can be derived from it, rather than its inherent data, the term "information system" is a more complete description.

Integrated and Fragmented Systems

Definitions

Integrated System. An integrated system is one that transcends organizational lines. It considers the objectives of the firm as an entity, and aims at the accomplishment of these objectives. The basic rules for integrated data processing are:

1. Capture the data as close to the source as possible.
2. Process both original data and additional data on machines that read and produce punched cards and/or punched paper tape and/or magnetic tape and/or disks.
3. Treat as an entity the data processing requirements of the company.
4. Cut across departmental lines to consolidate data processing.
5. Embody the principle of "once in, many times out."

Fragmented System. The opposite of an integrated system is a fragmented system. Under the fragmented system each application or subsystem exists as a separate entity. Files may be maintained separately for each application, and data from one file may be maintained in part or whole in another file. Although a fragmented system may capture data as close to the source as possible and further processing is completely mechanical, normally it is restricted to a particular department. The same data may enter the system more than once.

Degree of Integration

In actual practice, there are very few completely integrated systems and very few completely fragmented ones. Instead, they generally range from those that verge on being completely fragmented to those that approach being wholly integrated. Rather than characterize a system as being fragmented or integrated, it is more accurate to specify the degree of integration.

Advantages and Disadvantages of Integrated Systems

There is no intention here to infer that an integrated system always is superior to a fragmented one. Each has its advantages and disadvantages. Analysis of these advantages and disadvantages, however, indicates that an integrated system has far greater potential advantages. Before making the decision to install a comparatively fragmented system (often actuated by the desire to "crawl before you walk"), one should analyze carefully these advantages and disadvantages.

Advantages. The major advantages of an integrated system are:
1. It will meet the information needs of the organization more precisely, since the emphasis of the design is on needs, not on current practices.
2. Data should be more accurate, complete, and timely.
3. The potential information, savings, and/or profit are greater.
4. The resulting system will be more creative and objective. These will enable the better use of advanced management techniques.
5. Control techniques not directly connected with computer operations may be installed.

6. Duplicate records, duplicate effort, and random uneconomical practices are eliminated, resulting in lower clerical costs.
7. Materials, facilities, capital, and effort are controlled more effectively.
8. The need for interfunction controls is reduced.
9. If the original design is done well, the need for changes due to inadequate system design is reduced.
10. It is possible to install each subsystem individually, without the need for costly reprogramming. Similarly, current applications often can be made a part of the integrated system if this is done early enough in the implementation.
11. The full capabilities of the computer can be realized to a greater extent.

Disadvantages. The disadvantages of an integrated system are:
1. It is more difficult and costly to design and install.
2. It takes more time to design and install. Management often will not wait indefinitely for results; it wants to see some results relatively quickly.
3. More planning and personnel training are required.
4. Organizational changes may be needed.
5. Ultimate savings and profits tend to be deferred.
6. It is difficult to visualize the complete system in detail.
7. Few people have the ability to design and install a successful integrated system.

Integrated and Total Systems

Some writers use the terms "integrated system" and "total system" interchangeably. Others consider the latter to be more integrated than an integrated system. Some suggest that files in an integrated system are organized on a functional basis. In a total system they are organized around assets. In this discussion a total system is considered to be synonymous with a completely integrated system.

Real-Time Systems

A real-time system is one in which transactions are processed as they occur, and the response time of the system is sufficiently rapid to meet the needs of the system. In this definition a computer is not an essential element of a real-time system. If the required response time, for example, is 2 or 3 minutes, a clerk having access to current information on cards in a tub file

Definition

can answer telephone calls on stock availability. At the other extreme, however, a real-time system to locate enemy planes and to assign missiles or planes as interceptors requires a more rapid response time. Considering the speed at which planes and missiles move, the number of possible interceptor units, and the number of possible targets, a computer is the only feasible means of operating such a system anywhere near the needed speed.

Elements

Real-Time Transactions from Remote Locations. In a slow-response system, remote transmittal might involve such devices as telephone, Teletype, and/or air-pressure tubes. In a rapid-response system, it might involve analog devices to record data (such as aircraft positions), direct transmission to computers, translation to digital data, and direct entry into a current "file" of enemy aircraft positions.

Querying the System from Remote Locations. In the slow-response system, the types of devices used to enter transactions into the system can be also used for querying. In the rapid-response system, the device often will be a remote console connected directly with the computer. The system may include a cathode-ray tube or tubes. Thus, one can ensure that the proper question was sent so that the reply can be accelerated.

Real-Time Entry of Transactions into the System. This is contrasted with batching transactions and their entry periodically.

Data Availability on a Type of Random Access Device. Magnetic tape might be suitable if the required response time is under 5 minutes. The unstructured order of transactions, however, would cause this to be a relatively cumbersome means of maintaining the file. Current mass-storage devices, however, permit random-access storage relatively economically. Such devices normally would be used in a real-time system. Magnetic tapes, however, do have uses in such systems. An example would be the maintenance of a log of all transactions of the system.

A Program-Interrupt Feature. In the slow-response system, the interrupt devise might be the ring of a telephone bell, the clattering of the teletype, or the arrival of a tube message-conveyor. On a computer it might be a combination of an operating system and peripheral signaling devices. When the interrupt signal is keyed, the operating system finds a convenient place to halt operations being processed, keeps a record of the status of such operations when they are halted, determines the cause of the halt, takes the proper action, and restarts operations after such action has been taken.

Furnishing the Desired Information. In many business systems, output of desired information is done by the same means by which the transaction or question was entered into the system.

Airline Reservation System

One of the most publicized examples of a real-time system in the business world is an airline reservation system. All elements of real-time operations are included in such a system. The clerk selling tickets has a device for querying the computer and for either making or releasing reservations. The computer program has an operating system so that transactions can be handled as they occur. Depending upon the particular version, data are maintained on disks or on drums and replies are furnished the clerk by means of the querying device.

Apollo

An Apollo moon flight is an excellent example of a real-time system. Many computers are involved both on- and off-line. A computer in the flight capsule sends and receives digital data. Radio is used to transmit and receive data between the capsule and various ground stations. Radar tracks the capsule. The analog data from the radar is converted to digital data and transmitted to a computer. The system has multiple means of communication and control, since safety of the astronauts and success of the flight dominate. Cost in this system is secondary.

Command and Control

This has been defined by the Department of Defense as an arrangement of personnel, facilities, and the means for information acquisition, processing, and dissemination employed by a commander in planning, directing, and controlling operations. An example of a tactical command and control system is the aircraft defense system described previously. A strategic command and control system would be, for example, one in which a record of all assets, such as men, vehicles, and materials is maintained on a computer. Pertinent factors concerning the environment in which the system operates and factors internal to that system are also kept. A command and control system is programmed to furnish information to decision makers. They, in turn, use all available information and management-science techniques in arriving at optimal decisions. Although command and control systems so far have been used almost exclusively by the military forces, the principles are equally applicable to business systems. A gradual spread of this type of system can be expected in that direction.

SYSTEM ELEMENTS

The chart in Figure 4-1 shows the elements of a system.

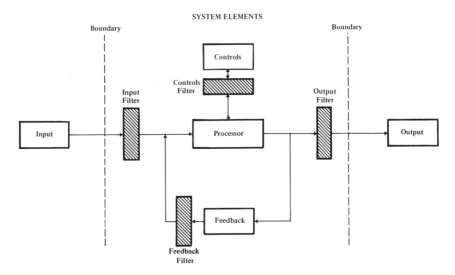

Fig. 4.1. System elements

Boundaries

The establishment of boundaries is a key element to be set at a place where the system to some degree is self-policing. Boundaries specify the limits of a system and must be within the ability of the designer to define. They delimit operations and concentrate system studies into specific areas. If boundaries are changed after the design and implementation have started, it is very possible that the entire effort will have to be restarted. If an integrated system is to be designed, it is necessary to define the limits of the system so that the analyst can look at the system as an entity. Once he understands what is included in the system, what is excluded, and how the system is intended to operate, he can establish the subsystems to be designed, and will know how the external environment affects the system. The concept of boundaries enables the analyst to segregate systems into subsystems of manageable size. In defining the elements of a system, boundaries constitute the best means of distinguishing between interfaces and feedback.

Processor

Since this chapter is limited to the development of an information system and not to the selection of equipment or the development of detailed procedures, the processor can be viewed as a "black box." One is not constrained by the limitations of specific computers or pieces of equipment. The effects of dominant personalities in actual systems are excluded so that a more perfect system can be developed. The processor may be defined as people and facilities working together to accomplish specified ends that are synonomous with the purposes of the system under consideration. In this sense, then, the processor may be referred to under its generic name—company.

Controls

Controls are that part of a system designed to ensure that the system operates according to plan. The controls may be external or internal. When they are internal, they are intended to monitor internal operations. Some controls, however, are external and can be imposed by law, regulation, or higher authority. For example, in public utilities, commissions may regulate prices to be charted. The Securities and Exchange Commission regulates the operations of stockbrokers and similar financial operators. Congress and various states pass legislation establishing minimum wages and fair employment regulations. The Defense Supply Agency may specify certain reports to be submitted by supply stock points of the Army, Navy, Air Force, and Marine Corps. All of these are examples of external controls imposed upon a system. Every system must operate within the limits imposed by such external controls.

Input/Output

Input is any information entering a system from external sources. If it crosses a boundary and enters the system, it is an input. Once the desired output of a system is determined, the input needed to produce the output may be specified. Although external controls, according to this definition, are an input to an ongoing system. They are a special input that must be considered in the design of the system. They impose restrictions upon system components, actions, and/or output. Other input is used to produce feedback and/or output.

Like input, output crosses a boundary. In this case, however, it originates within the system and goes to an external location. System output requirements, in general, are determined by system objectives.

Feedback

Feedback is data generated within a system and used by the processor to modify the operations of the system. The major difference between feedback and the interfaces (input and output) is that feedback does not cross a boundary, whereas interfaces do. Depending upon the system under consideration, a feedback may become a interface, or vice versa. Assume that a company, for example, has four subsystems. From the standpoint of the company as a system, however, these interfaces between subsystems are considered to be feedback.

Filters

A filter is a device that permits only certain things to pass through it, and stops all others. Filters may be imposed on input, controls, feedback, and output.

Input Filters

An example of an input filter would be the guard in a restricted building. If a person has his badge, the guard permits him to enter. If he does not have his badge, he is not allowed in the building.

Controls Filters

Operating regulations that differ between regular working hours and nonregular hours are examples of filters of controls. The rule might be that employees can keep their badges in their pockets during regular working hours but that after such hours, the badge must always be worn in plain view.

Feedback Filters

For an example of a filter of feedback, one might consider a warehouse system. After each issue of material, the material on hand (according to the record) plus the material on order might be compared with the reorder point. If the amount on hand plus the amount on order equals or is greater than the allowable low limit, no reorder action is necessary. If, however, this total is less than the reorder level, the feedback initiates the reorder action.

Output Filters

Exception reports are examples of filtered output. Only when the data are outside certain specified limits would exception reports be issued. This is an excellent means of eliminating "paper pollution" for the executive. Instead of having to look through many pages to determine if any action is necessary, he will receive only reports of items that should come to his attention. If he desires more reports, he can expand the parameters determining an exception. By contracting the parameters, of course, he can reduce the number of such reports.

Hierarchy of Systems

Earlier in this chapter the terms "system" and "subsystem" are used. This implies that a system can be subdivided into an unspecified number of subsystems. If there are two subsystems, say "A" and "B," subsystem A can get input from subsystem B and from sources external to the system. Similarly, it can send output to both subsystem B and to areas external to the system. Although subsystem B has similar sources of input and output, its input from subsystem A is identical with the output of subsystem A to subsystem B. Its output to subsystem A is the same as the aforementioned input to subsystem A from subsystem B. Figure 4.2 show the areas of input and output for two-subsystem and three-subsystem systems.

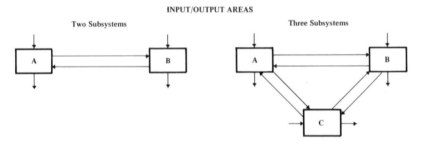

INPUT/OUTPUT AREAS

Fig. 4.2. Input/output areas

In a system with two subsystems, there are six different areas of input and output. In a system with three subsystems, there are 12 different areas of input and output. The formula for the number of such areas is

$$N = n(n + 1)$$

Table 4.1 lists the number of areas of input and output for different numbers of subsystems.

TABLE 4.1

SUBSYSTEM AREAS OF INPUT AND OUTPUT

Number of Subsystems	Number of Areas of Input and Output
2	6
3	12
4	20
5	30
6	42
7	56
8	72
9	90
10	110

It is evident that the number of areas of input and output increases much more rapidly than the number of subsystems. With each such increase in the number of areas of input and output, the difficulty of coordinating them increases correspondingly. The span-of-control concept evidently applies to subsystems to be coordinated as well as to the number of people to be supervised. It is suggested that the number of subsystems of a system normally be limited to five or possibly six. If such segregation results in unwieldy subsystems, they may be divided further into sub-subsystems as desired.

SYSTEM-DEVELOPMENT CYCLE

In developing and implementing a system, a cycle of events or phases is involved. The word "cycle" implies two things: There is an order in which the events occur, and the cycle is repetitive. This part of the chapter will describe each phase, stating what should be accomplished, the responsibilities of the different levels of employees involved, and approximations of the length of time to complete each phase. The phases in the system-development cycle are feasibility study, applications study, equipment selection and acquisition, preparation for installation, conversion, operation, and review and evaluation.

Feasibility Study

As used here, the feasibility study is a preliminary evaluation to determine if it is worthwhile to go through the rest of the system-development cycle. Summarizing from Chapter 2, typically, the study committee is composed of managers from each of the operating departments. It is established by, and has the overt backing of, top management. Appendix A is an example of a notice that top management should issue to implement a feasibility study. This notice gives the purpose for which the committee is established, to whom it reports, the full-time members of the committee, the members of the steering committee (if one is involved), technical and/or consultative services to be furnished to the committee, what the committee is to do, and a target date for the completion of the study.

The committee takes a broad look at the effectiveness of the system now operating. Is the system meeting the needs of the company? What is it costing? Is it possible (preferably probable) that a new system will better meet current or future needs? What might be the costs of the new system as compared with those of the old system? If the costs are lower, is the difference significant enough to make it worthwhile to go through the rest of the cycle? Will the costs saved, plus the added effectiveness of the system, make it worthwhile? If the new system will cost more, will the added effectiveness lead to a decision to continue the study? The recommendations of the committee are submitted to the steering committee, if there is one. The latter appends its recommendations, and both recommendations are sent to top management for the decision whether to continue through the cycle.

Depending on a number of things, if the current system is clearly inadequate and costly, the facts can be determined within a few days. Preparation of a report and forwarding it to top management will make the minimum time about a week. Processing through a steering committee might add another two or three weeks. In a more complex situation it might take two months to gather the facts, prepare the report, and staff it to top management. About a month, on the average, is sufficient for a feasibility study.

Applications Study

If top management approves a feasibility-study recommendation to continue further in the cycle, the next phase is the applications study. During this phase the system is designed and the organizational structure to implement it is recommended. The output from the applications study is a report to management whether to continue through the cycle. This report, in addition to organizational recommendations, lists the inputs, outputs, files to be maintained, computational requirements, and constraints for each application. It will be the basis for selecting the needed hardware and software. The design of the system will be treated later in this chapter.

Top management has the responsibility for establishing the committee to do the applications study. To increase the probability that this effort will succeed, management should give its clear support. This support is needed to ensure the cooperation of various echelons in the company. Appendix B is an example of an internal notice establishing the applications committee. Those who participate in the working group of the feasibility study usually continue in the applications study. The establishment of a new committee, however, facilitates dropping those who were not effective in the feasibility study, and thus their failure will not be advertised throughout the company. It also permits the addition of more technical people to assist in the design.

Milestones should be established for the applications study, and the study committee should report regularly to management (the steering committee or top management) on its progress. These reports should be reviewed and acted upon as soon as is feasible. This will help keep the study on schedule.

The system-design phase, basic to the applications study, is probably underestimated as to the length of time it will take. One year is the average length of time required. Experience has shown that six months or more will be needed to design even a comparatively simple system. Very complicated companies will need as much as three years for this phase.

Selection and Acquisition

There are many methods of selecting the hardware and software for a computer installation. In private industry, especially in the smaller companies, sole-source procurement is often the method used. Under this method the requirements of the company are given to a selected vendor. He submits a statement as to the equipment and software needed to meet these requirements. Since the vendor and his hardware are known during the applications study phase, this often results in tailoring the system to the hardware rather than getting equipment to suit the system. This method is simple, quick, and not costly. The system may not be the best one for the company, since it is designed to fit the equipment, not vice versa, but without competitive vendors, the company is not in a position to get any concessions from the sale source. The selection, therefore, may not be the most economical.

Other methods involving competition between vendors are least cost, weighted scoring, cost effectiveness, and cost value. Under least cost, the computer selected will be only marginally able to do the job. As soon as the work to be done increases, additional components of a computer are needed. Under weighted scoring, weights are assigned to various factors. The computer with the highest weighted score is selected. Cost effectiveness is a similar method of selection. In this case the weighted score is divided by the cost. The computer with the highest result is selected. Under the cost-value method, each desirable factor is given credit in a dollar amount and each negative factor is charged in that amount. These credits and debits are applied to the dollar cost of the computer, and the one with the lowest net cost is selected.

Under any of the methods of selection involving competition, the information gathered in the applications-study phase is used to prepare an invitation for vendors to bid. This invitation is usually a rather lengthy document, giving the details of the applications to be run on the computer. The vendors submit bids that are evaluated, and the computer, its components, and software are selected on this basis.

Relatively few people have the knowledge and ability to validate the claims of various vendors and to select the optimal configuration. It is for this reason that experienced computer-selection technicians do this phase of the cycle.

After the computer is selected, a contract is negotiated with the vendor. Lawyers or procurement officers, using information furnished by computer managers, perform this function. If any concessions such as discount or extra services are to be granted by the vendor, this must be documented before the contract is signed. After it is signed, it is much more difficult to get further concessions. Once the contract is signed by responsible officers of both purchaser and vendor, the acquisition phase of the cycle is completed.

The selection and acquisition phase takes a minimum of six months and a maximum of a year. On the average, it takes about eight months.

Preparation for Installation

During the preparation-for-installation phase, systems analysts and programmers are hired and trained. The details of the system are finalized, and the applications are programmed and tested. A site is prepared for the computer. In the federal government, and often in the larger companies, there is a readiness review about two months before the computer is delivered. This is an examination to decide whether preparations are far enough along to make effective use of the computer on the scheduled delivery date. If at the time of the readiness review, these preparations are very much behind the planned point, the delivery of the computer is delayed.

Preparation for installation is normally under the direct control of the manager of data processing. He is responsible for planning and scheduling the entire operation. In the less complex organizations, he establishes milestones and controls the operation through Gantt charts. In complex preparations, either the Performance Review Evaluation Technique (PERT) or Critical Path Method (CPM) is used. Most of preparation for installation is done by technical people, and the manager or director of the preparation effort submits regular reports to top management or to the steering committee. These reports are reviewed and actions are taken to keep the preparations on schedule. In smaller companies, preparation for installation takes six months; in the more complex companies, it may take a year and a half. On the average, it takes a year for this phase.

Conversion

Conversion is the changeover from previous manual, EAM, or computer operations to the new computer. In a conversion from manual or EAM operations, the primary jobs are the establishment of new files, implementing new clerical procedures, and ensuring that the new system works accurately. For years this was done by operating both the old system and the new system for a period of time and comparing the results. This, of course, could be done only if the new system was the same as the old system. It was a costly method—more than twice the number of people were needed for the conversion. One crew ran the old system; another ran the new system; and a third compared the results and corrected the errors in the new system. It had the advantage, however, of satisfying the conservative managers that the new system was acceptable before stopping the old one. Often, when there were discrepancies, the error was in the old system instead of the new one. If proper controls are established and programs are checked thoroughly, the conversion can result in a new system at least as accurate as the old one. Dual operations will not be necessary, and the conversion will be completed at a far lower cost.

In converting from one computer to another, the change has been primarily one of emulating or simulating the old programs on the new computer. Emulation is the use of hardware and simulation the use of software to make the new computer act like the old one. These make possible the running of old programs without reprogramming. Although the old program usually runs faster on the new computer than on the old one, it can run still faster on the new computer if it is reprogrammed. As more and more companies convert to American National Standards Institute's (ANSI) COBOL, emulation and simulation are replaced by recompilation of the programs. This recompilation, of course, is done only once, after which the new computer is used in a much faster mode than that for emulation or simulation. Software packages are available to convert other levels of COBOL (e.g., COBOL F) to ANSI COBOL. This type of conversion usually means that it will be necessary to have a machine run for the initial conversion to ANSI COBOL, a comparatively small amount of reprogramming, and then a compilation of the new ANSI COBOL program on the new computer. This is much faster and more accurate than rewriting the entire program in ANSI COBOL before the compilation.

Technical and clerical personnel do most of the work of conversion, but middle management reviews the accuracy of their work. Milestones are established and regular reports are submitted to top management or the steering committee, whose function is to see that the effort proceeds on schedule and to give assistance if needed.

Conversion from manual or EAM operations takes 6 to 12 months, the average being 9. Conversion from one computer an another with a major change in system takes from three to six months, with an average of four. In going from one computer to another with no change of system and using emulation, simulation, or recompilation, the change can be made in minimal time with almost no break in operations.

Operation

Operation of data processing is no different from any other function of a company. Data processing managers have attempted for years to surround their operations with a cloud of mystery, using terms such as bits and bytes in talking to top management. It should be no surprise to them when top management is reluctant to give them all of the funds and support for which they ask. Data processing managers should report regularly to management, using nontechnical language. This will enable a normal evaluaation of their needs, and further support when justified.

As indicated in Table 4.2, it takes a minimum of two years to implement a comparatively small system. A large system takes almost seven years. The average system requires three and a half years. The average life of a system is five years. This means that after a minimal system is in operation

TABLE 4.2

MONTHS REQUIRED TO IMPLEMENT NEW SYSTEM

Phase	Minimum	Average	Maximum
Feasibility study	0	1	2
Applications study	6	12	36
Selection and acquisition	6	8	12
Preparation for installation	6	12	18
Conversion	6	9	12
Total	24	42	80

for three years, preparations should begin for its replacement. In the average system a wait of a year and a half will permit the replacement system to be ready when needed. In large systems, preparations for the next system should begin as soon as the prior system is implemented. Furthermore, the system just implemented must last almost seven years instead of five.

DESIGNING INFORMATION SYSTEMS

The product of a management information system is information. Such information may be produced for either immediate or later use. It is ineffi-cient, perhaps impossible, to satisfy all of a manager's informational needs. The emphasis, therefore, should be on prime information needs.

Analysis of an information system does not always indicate the necessity of either designing a new one or redesigning the old one—no change may be considered desirable, or it may suffice to replace current equipment with faster but compatible models. In that case it is not necessary to redesign the system, and this need not be considered further here.

The great majority of business data processing systems are designed and implemented from the bottom. Under this concept the first step is an examination of how the current data processing system operates. An analysis is made to see how it can be improved. The new system is designed with these improvements as a primary objective. The emphasis, therefore, is on how one can do what he is doing more efficiently and/or economically. In the top-down approach, the first step is a determination of the objectives of the system. A system is then designed to meet these objectives, in which the emphasis is on what should be done rather than on improving current opera-tions. A third possibility is a combination of the top-down and the bottom-up methods. This involves the overall design of a system to meet certain objectives. The current system is then implemented into the overall plan, application by application—an evolutionary approach. This section of the chapter discusses each of the three methods, describing them more in detail and giving the advantages and disadvantages of each.

Although an order of steps is given in each of the methods, it should not be inferred that there is a continual and orderly progression through the steps. Instead, information developed in one step may indicate the advisability of returning to an earlier step, possibly back to the first step. It may be a reconsideration as to the advisability of the design of a new system at this time. It may entail a redetermination of the objectives of the system.

Bottom-up Method

The bottom-up method is intended to improve the current system—to make it more effective and/or more economical. The order of steps is

1. Examination of the current system.
2. Analysis of information-user subsystem.
3. Analysis of data-supplier-and-conversion subsystem.
4. Design of the new system.
5. Preparation of the five-year plan.
6. Proposal of the new system.
7. Implementation of the new system.
8. Maintenance of list of possible improvements.

Examination of Current System

This is really a feasibility study to determine if it is worthwhile to design a new system at this time. It involves determinations of user satisfaction, data preparation and conversion efficiency and costs, new developmental possibilities of improvements, and relative priorities of personnel, funds, and/or equipment. The design effort can (and often does) end at this point. If, however, it is considered feasible to design a new system at this time, the next phase of the process is begun.

Analysis of Data-Supplier and Conversion Subsystem

This starts with an inventory of current reports and the users who receive them. The analyst talks with these users to determine the value of the reports and possibilities for their improvement. He also tries to find out if other reports are needed and how the system he is designing can furnish them.

Analysis of Data-Supplier and Conversion Subsystem

This involves an analysis of the data needed to supply the outputs and the current way the data is developed and converted to a machine-readable language. Which data is no longer needed? Is it possible to convert the data to a machine-readable medium earlier in the process? Can the data be converted to a machine-readable form as a by-product of another operation? What controls are needed to ensure the completeness and accuracy of this data? What improvements in the data-supplier and conversion subsystem are possible?

Design of New System

Once both input and output of a system are determined, system design is simply the best way of getting from the input to the output. Speed, accuracy, and resources needed are the major considerations. If possible, pieces of the current system should be integrated into the new system. This will result in savings. More than one design often is possible; therefore, alternative systems should be designed. Then, if the system proposed is not accepted by management, an alternative may be acceptable and it will not be necessary to go through the design effort again.

Preparation of Five-Year Plan

The preparation of a five-year plan was discussed in Chapter 1. For each application the following information is prepared:

1. What is to be accomplished.
2. Implications of delay in implementation.
3. Justification for its level of priority.
4. Resources needed.
5. Schedule of implementation and operation.

Proposal of New System

Unless the new system is accepted by those who make the decision whether it will be installed, the best system in the world is of little or no value. The proposal for it, therefore, should be prepared with great care. These proposals generally are made orally, with written recommendations as additional information.

The written proposal should be a literate, careful presentation of the elements an executive should consider in order to make a decision whether to accept the recommendations. The items included should be as follows:

1. Introduction
   (a) Mission, and description of activity
   (b) General description of the problem
   (c) Background in data processing
   (d) Qualifications of the study group

2. Objectives
   (a) The intended objectives of the data processing system
   (b) Measures of the achievement of these objectives
3. Problem definition
   (a) Scope of workload
   (b) System problems
   (c) Control problems
   (d) Performance problems
4. System and subsystems considered
5. System and subsystems recommended
6. Equipment and software considered
7. Equipment and software recommended
8. Evaluation
   (a) Performance
   (b) Financial
   (c) Personnel
9. Five-year installation plans
   (a) Organization
   (b) Personnel
   (c) Equipment
   (d) Physical facilities
   (e) Financial requirements
   (f) Training
   (g) Detailed subsystem design
   (h) Programming
   (i) Conversion
   (j) Operation

Oral presentations are frequently crucial in gaining acceptance of a proposal. As in all such presentations, a few basic rules must be followed. Considering the audience, the presentation should be pitched at the proper level of knowledge. It should be simple, basic, short, and organized. The proposal should be not more than 20 minutes in length, and should aim at impressing the listeners with just a few salient facts. Optner[1] recommends six flip charts as the suggested outline of a logical oral presentation.

Chart I: The Content of the Presentation
     A.   Statement of the Problem
     B.   Alternate Solutions to the Problem
     C.   Recommended Solution to the Problem
     D.   Benefits to Be Derived
Chart II: Problem Statement
     A.   Background Conditions and Method of Study

1. Stanford L. Optner, *Systems Analysis for Business Management*. Englewood Cliffs, N.J.: Prentice-Hall, Inc., 1960, pp. 154-155.

Other suggestions for the presentation are to practice the presentation and to use colors on the flip charts to stress the important points. The person making the presentation should outline what he is going to present, present it, and summarize what he said. Each person involved in making the decision should be furnished a handout summarizing the important points and recommending a specific decision.

Implementation of New System

The implementation of a computer system was discussed under the heading "System-Development Cycle" in this chapter. Further amplification is unnecessary.

Maintenance of List of Possible Improvements

Possible improvements are continually found during the design, implementation, and operation of any system. If one were to try to incorporate each of these possible improvements as they came up, it is possible that the system never would be implemented. At some time in the design it is necessary to establish a cutoff date for changes. Once that date arrives, the only action to be taken on newly discovered possible improvements is to enter them on the list. When the application is in operation, and enough improvements are needed, incorporating them in one improvement operation should be considered. Following this procedure will result in the original system's operating earlier and will lessen the cost and difficulty of making individual changes.

Top-down Method

The top-down method usually is the best method for designing a system when there is no ongoing system to be redesigned. Probably the most outstanding example of the top-down approach to system design is in the

Semi-Automatic Ground Environment (SAGE) system. This system was designed to detect and intercept possible air threats to the United States from over the Arctic Circle. Since there was no such system in existence, the bottom-up approach was not possible. The top-down approach, which was used, proved the feasibility of designing large computer-based systems by means of the top-down approach.

Contrary to the most prevalent practice, the first step should not be an examination of how the current data processing system operates. Instead, the order of steps might be as follows:

1. Examination of the objectives of the system.
2. Segregation of the system into the optimum number of subsystems.
3. Development of subsystem objectives consonant with system objectives.
4. Development of the hierarchy of output within each subsystem to obtain the objectives.
5. Determination of the input necessary to produce the output.
6. Analysis of the current system to ensure that no significant input or output has been omitted.
7. Development of concepts concerning ways in which the system can operate.
8. Selection of optimum means of operations.
9. Selection of the optimum equipment configuration and the output that will be produced.
10. Proposal of the new system.

Objectives of the System

This refers to the objectives of the system that the data processing system will serve, not to the objectives of the data processing system. These objectives are the purposes for which the company exists, and should be written clearly so as to be meaningful and specific enough to be understood by all who are involved. The degree to which they are to be fulfilled should be measurable. If the objectives are deficient in any of these areas, the weaknesses should be rectified prior to proceeding with the study. If such objectives are not written, proposed objectives should be prepared and given to top management for approval, amendment, or whatever action is desired. A frequent complaint is that top management will not furnish the objectives so that the system can be designed. However, failure to give management something specific from which it can proceed to optimal objectives is usually the reason for not supplying these company or system objectives.

If the objectives are not specific enough, they should be rewritten to indicate what those doing the study believe the objectives were intended to mean. Management's approval will indicate that the study group's understanding of the rewritten objectives is correct. If top management does not concur with the interpretation, the areas of misunderstanding will be highlighted and can then be clarified.

If there is no tangible measure by which the degree of objective fulfillment can be ascertained, there is no means of measuring the success of the system that serves the data processing system. In the final analysis, a data processing system's sole purpose is to promote the success of the system it serves. If the success of the system can be measured, it will be possible to decide factually whether to install the newly designed data processing system. When installed without measurable objectives, there will be no basis for making future decisions with regard to the data processing system.

Since the amounts of money spent on systems are so enormous, measures of performance no longer can be considered academic exercises. To evaluate such results, time and effort must be spent to delineate specific productivity desired from the system.

Segregation into Subsystems

As indicated earlier, the number of subsystems normally should not exceed five or six. The subsystems should be defined without considering organizational lines. They should encompass functions, regardless of where the operations are completed. For example, a department store may be segregated organizationally into men's furnishings, furniture, notions and accessories, etc. To arrange the subsystems in this manner would be following the organizational line, probably without considering sufficiently the functions that are being performed. It would seem to be more appropriate to propose as starting points such subsystems as purchasing, retail sales, warehousing, stock accounting, and delivery. The completed list should not be overly long and therefore it may be necessary to combine certain of the proposed subsystems. Once the subsystems are established, segregating them into sub-subsystems may begin. The entire system should be divided into a workable system, subsystems, sub-subsystems, and sub-sub-systems (if necessary).

When the segregation is completed, the process of establishing specific and meaningful boundaries begins. This process, although long and involving many major and minor decisions, is necessary. Complete redesign might be needed should boundaries be changed after systems have been designed. These boundaries should be meaningful and specific so that future redetermination will not be required.

Development of Subsystem Objectives

Although it is likely that there will be written objectives for the system, there is less likelihood that such objectives will be available for each subsystem. Since subsystems may not follow formal organizational lines, their objectives may not be in writing. Possibly they will be parts of the written objectives of various organizational entities if such objectives are documented. Their existence, however, does not mean that they are compatible with system objectives. If they are incompatible with the overall system objectives, they should be changed to contribute to the attainment of such objectives.

Subsystem objectives, on the other hand, need not harmonize with the objectives of other subsystems. It is entirely possible that the objectives of suborganizations conflict to some degree with those of other suborganizations. From a comptroller's point of view, the stock of goods on hand should be minimized. Then less money will be invested in stock and more will be available for other purposes. Conversely, from the salesman's viewpoint, it is preferable to have a large stock of goods on hand to fill all requests for goods. His primary interest is in increasing sales, not in keeping money on hand for purposes other than those that benefit him. Since the boundaries have been established for each subsystem, it should be possible to enumerate what the subsystem should accomplish. The development of objectives for the subsystem, therefore, should consider not only the objectives established for the system, but also suggestions made earlier in this chapter.

Hierarchy of Output

Once the objectives for each subsystem have been approved by management, it is possible to list the output necessary to achieve these objectives. It is suggested that the output be listed in the following order:

1. Required by law.
2. Required by higher authority, such as parent company or board of directors.
3. Needed to fulfill subsystem objectives.
4. Needed by other subsystems to fulfill their objectives.
5. Desired to fulfill subsystem objectives better.
6. Desired by other subsystems to fulfill their objectives better.
7. Nice to have in fulfilling subsystem objectives.
8. Nice to have in fulfilling the objectives of other subsystems.
9. Items of information requested by people outside the company, but for which there is no obligation to furnish.

In developing each item in this hierarchy of output it is not necessary to consider the way in which it will be accomplished or even if it is required only periodically. The major things to be considered are what information is to be furnished and the relative importance of such information. These will be the basis for determining the input necessary for the completion of the output. If all output listed cannot be produced, it will be helpful in deciding which will be furnished and which will be eliminated.

Determination of Input

Given an output list, the grid chart is an excellent tool in determining the necessary input. The output can be listed in order across the top of the chart. The input needed for the first output is listed down the side of the chart and a check mark is entered parallel with the input and under the output. The procedure is repeated for each output. Where an input is used for more than one output, it is not listed again. The multiple use is indicated by additional checks in the same row, each under the applicable output. This technique will aid in excluding the entry of data into the system when such data is not needed for any output. Furthermore, given the input and the output, the transformation from the former to the latter can be planned to minimize effort and cost.

Analysis of Current System

The first step in planning many data processing systems has been an analysis of current operations. The tendency here has been to plan a conversion of the current system to computer operation rather than to design the best possible system incorporating the computer as a tool. The design of integrated computer systems, therefore, has been more talked about than actually designed and implemented.

This is not to imply that the analysis of current system operations is unnecessary and that it should be discontinued. This analysis, however, should not be conducted until after the steps listed previously have been completed. The purposes of such an analysis should be to ensure that no required output has been omitted and to provide data to aid in recognizing possible undesirable side effects when the new system is installed.

System Operation Hypotheses

Probably the most interesting and creative part of system design is devising alternative ways in which the system can operate. With the possible exception of subsystem segregation, most of the work prior to hypothesis consists of gathering information, defining, and in other ways manipulating data. The problem is this: Given certain input and certain output, what are the ways in which the input can be converted to output? Although this is a creative effort, certain principles will help in the area of systm hypothesis:

1. Develop more than one way in which the system can operate.
2. Attempt to convert data to a machine-understandable form as early as possible and at the most logical point in the operation.
3. Simplify the system and steps as much as possible.
4. Exclude unnecessary steps and operations.
5. Provide information when it is needed, where it is needed, and in

the form in which it is needed. One need not be limited to formal periodic reports. Management can make better decisions with specific, incisive reports.

6. Control, but do not overcontrol.
7. Use feedback where possible to control system operation.
8. The system should be flexible to allow modifications as desired.
9. Use management-science techniques where they are advantageous.
10. Aim to improve rather than to devise a perfect system.

Multiple Hypotheses

Rarely must the design of a system be restricted to one possibility. On on the other hand, several methods are hypothesized, one is not limited to the factors leading to the selection of the best way may be quite subtle. If just one method is devised, the only choices are to accept it or reject it. If, on the other hand, several methods are hypothesized, one is not limited to the selection or rejection of each. Instead, alternatives combining the best features of different hypotheses may result in additional and better methods. Furthermore, the method selected by the designer may not be acceptable to top management. In this event, retreat can be made to the second-best hypothesis, instead of starting the design effort all over again.

Data Conversion. Years of experience in business data processing have shown that the conversion of hard copy to a machine-readable form is expensive. Machines normally are much more accurate than human beings. A strong attempt should be made early, therefore, to convert the information to a machine-readable form, and, if possible, to capture it as a by-product of other operations. Furthermore, more accuracy should result from the elimination of the human in this process.

An example of an application in which the human being is eliminated is the use of devices to ensure that the temperature of railroad-car wheel housings is within bounds. As the wheels pass the device, it looks for excessive heat. When discovered, the information is automatically relayed ahead so that the train may be stopped and action taken to prevent a hot box that otherwise would occur. An operation in which the human being is involved and the data is converted to a machine-readable form would be the prepaaration of bills of lading in a programmed Flexowriter. The machine types iterative data according to its program and stops at the point where the variable information is to be entered. As a by-product of the typing of the variable data, punched paper tape or punched cards are the normal machine-readable output.

Simplification. A sophisticated system sometimes is needed to yield optimal results. One of the items to guard against in systems hypothesis is the unnecessarily complicated procedure. As systems become more complex, opportunities for errors and unexpected detrimental side effects increase geometrically. The designer should examine every frill that he incorporates into his hypothesis. If it does not add measurably to the effectiveness of the system, it should be discarded. Even if it does add measurably, he should weigh the anticipated benefits against any added costs and also the possible losses due to the increased possibility of error. Where the benefits exceed the probable disadvantages, the more sophisticated method should be retained —otherwise it should be discarded.

Elimination of Steps. As noted in the preceding paragraph, the increased sophistication of a system primarily increases the probability of error. Secondarily, there is the probability of detrimental side effects. The elimination of unnecessary steps, however, is aimed at reduction in processing time and costs. Although it may reduce the possibility of error, this is not the prime aim of the reduction of unnecessary steps. A major reason for such reduction is that undesirable side effects will not be introduced. Before pruning a step, the designer should ensure that it will not result in such side effects.

Information Furnished. The basic purpose of a data processing system is to furnish information when it is needed, where it is needed, and in the form it is needed. Data may be valuable as information if it is timely enough to warrant the action needed. If, on the other hand, it is not timely, its value is merely historical and has deteriorated substantially. Information may be needed by a decision maker as a basis for his decision. If that information is not furnished where and when it is needed, it might just as well not exist. It is relatively easy for the system designer to determine the time and place that information is needed. His task is to devise a system that satisfies these criteria.

More difficult to establish are the information needed and the form in which it should be furnished. First, the decision maker may not know what information he will need. Second, he may not know what the computer can do to meet these needs and/or he may not be able to communicate his needs to data processing. It is up to the system designer, therefore, to make suggestions and to discuss information needs with potential users. In doing this, some of the things he must consider are:

1. The decisions to be made.
2. Who makes the decisions.
3. When decisions are made.
4. The information that will help in making the decision.
5. The way the information is to be used in making the decision.

6. Management sciences.
7. Exception reporting.
8. Levels of reporting.

Level of Control. If systems have no controls or are undercontrolled, the information furnished may be misleading. If, on the other hand, they are overcontrolled, the information should be more accurate, but the cost may be excessive. The decision whether to install a control should be based on a comparison of the cost of the control versus the probable loss if the control is not installed. In a warehouse, for example, the item number, the unit of issue, the number of units, and the identification number of the purchaser merit careful control. Conversely, the correct spelling of the purchaser's name and the name of the item do not need expensive controls. The requirements of the system should determine the level of control.

The only item discussed in the preceding paragraph is the level of control. Other principles of controlling systems will be discussed in Chapter 5.

Feedback as a Control. A system that is controlled internally is normally more reliable than one controlled externally. It depends upon itself to ensure that it operates properly and does not have to depend upon external events over which it may not have control. Feedback, according to the definition given earlier in this chapter, originates within the system and is used to control system operations. Since it does not cross a boundary, it is neither an input nor an output.

Criteria established to weed out inaccurate or suspect input should help considerably in reducing the number of inaccuracies in the system. Questionable items can be checked with the originators to prevent the system from being distorted by such input. Instead of getting reports of stock status each day, for example, and examining the listing to determine what to reorder, the computer can make comparisons automatically and initiate purchase orders or notices to the purchasing office as desired.

System Flexibility. In both industry and government, conditions are dynamic—change is apparently inevitable. For example, a social security deduction system is installed in a company. Congress passes a law tacking medical care onto the social security system. The company data processing system must be modified to incorporate the provisions of the new law. Product lines may change and new technical developments may alter completely the way in which the business operates. All these events indicate that a system should be flexible enough to allow for desired modifications.

The principle of flexibility is associated closely with the principle of simplification discussed previously. It is much easier to modify a simple system than a complicated one, principally because it is easier to recognize the possibility of detrimental side effects earlier. Another aid is the assumption that there will be changes after the system is installed. The operations should be planned in segments or modules. What affects each segment and is affected by other segments should be documented. If a change is necessary at a later date, the segment can be reprogrammed and consideration given to other segments that are affected.

Management Sciences. In certain instances, intuitive decisions might equal or surpass those made with the aid of operations research or other management sciences. In total, however, intuitive decisions should not be as good as scientific decisions. It is normally to the advantage of business to make use of scientific methods. In designing a system, the decision points should be examined. It can then be determined if the implementation of one or more of the techniques of management science may be of assistance. If this proves true and the probable value of the implementation exceeds the estimated cost, it should be installed. One should not, on the other hand, install a scientific method where it is not warranted. Oversophistication can be costly and can lead to detrimental side effects.

Aim to Improve. It has been said that the perfect system never will be devised. Even if it were devised, it would not be installed because it might not be satisfactory to top management. If not accepted, the most perfect system ever designed would be valueless. When the designer cannot get acceptance of the system as he designs it, he should consider the best design that will be accepted. His aim should be to improve the system measurably rather than design and install a perfect system.

Selection of Optimal Design

At this point the system designer should have more than one concept of the ways in which the system can operate. His problem is to narrow these hypothetical possibilities down to the best one or, if they are approximately equal, to two choice systems. In making this selection he should consider both the degree to which system objectives are satisfied and the approximate cost of the system. It is suggested that, prior to this evaluation, each of the objectives to be met be given a weight corresponding to its relative importance. Cost also should be assigned a weight. However, in certain systems, such as SAGE, cost is given little or no consideration. If that is the case, cost should be given little or no weight. To each of the calculated weights the percentage of achievement of the objective or the relative cost should be applied. An example of these calculations is given in Table 4.3. In this example, System 1 would be selected as the optimal one. It should be noted that this method considers factors such as real time versus batch processing and

TABLE 4.3

SELECTION OF OPTIMAL SYSTEM

Objective	Percentage Achieved	Ratio of Minimum System Cost to Cost of This System	Weight	Weighted Success Factor
System 1				
A	100		40	40
B	90		30	27
C	95		20	19
D	60		10	6
E	80		30	24
Cost		90	60	54
Total				170
System 2				
A	50		40	20
B	60		30	18
C	70		20	14
D	80		10	8
E	100		30	30
Cost		100	60	60
Total				150

the cost and size of computers as inherent parts of the weighting process. The former comparison is considered in the degree to which system objectives are achieved, whereas the size of the computer is included in the cost factor.

Selection of Equipment Configuration

In narrowing down the hypothetical systems to the one that appears to be best, the designer, in order to get approximate costs, will have selected the general size of the computer if one is included in the system. Most computers are modular in concept so that capacities can be increased or decreased by adding or deleting individual items in the basic configuration.

The designer should first select the minimum computer configuration that will produce all items in the hierarchy of output. Allowance should be made for predicted growth in the next two or three years. If this configuration is selected, the assumption is that all output in the hierarchy should be produced. In order to test the validity of this assumption, the configuration should be pared successively of individual items such as modules of memory, tape drives, speed of tape drives, and disk packs. As the capability is decreased, it will be necessary to drop individual outputs from the bottom of the list. The amount saved from each paring (including the programmer and operator costs as well as machine costs) should be compared with the value of the output eliminated. By trying various combinations, the optimal equipment configuration and a revised schedule of outputs should emerge.

Proposal of New System

While the oral and written presentations discussed earlier in this chapter appear to be aimed at a fragmented solution rather than at an integrated system, they are logically arranged and easily adapted to the presentation of an integrated system. The subject, therefore, will not be discussed further here.

Combination Method

Where systems have been in operation, it has been found that the bottom-up method results in comparatively minor improvements. The top-down method, although having the potential of yielding better results, takes too long to achieve. Management is not willing to invest money in a system and then wait a long time before getting a return on its investment. Furthermore, with the difficulties in getting competent analysts to design the system, there have been many failures in the implementation of a top-down approach. A combination method of designing and implementing major revisions in existing systems is emerging. Briefly, this method establishes what the total system should accomplish and what modules or subsystems are required. The existing systems are incorporated into the overall plan, constituting "islands of information." The various subsystems are then built from the bottom up, always keeping the ultimate system in mind. Under this method there is no breakdown in the current information system. New subsystems are implemented fairly rapidly. It takes longer than the top-down system to reach the ultimate objective, but there is a steady increase in the amount of information available. Furthermore, the problem of getting competent systems analysts and designers is decreased.

Under the combination method the first five steps are the same as the first five in the top-down approach. It is not necessary, therefore, to discuss them again. The remaining steps are:

1. Analysis of the current system to determine the capabilities of current subsystems.
2. Determination of further information requirements.
3. Selection of priority of subsystem implementation.

Analysis of Current System

The current system is analyzed to determine the characteristics of subsystems already automated. Since they probably are "stand-alone" systems, they may be called "islands of information." This analysis determines what has to be done to improve them and to fit them into the overall plan designed in the preceding steps. An integrated data base has been found to be difficult to plan and implement. Under the combination approach, the data base of each subsystem is maintained separately, but communications between data bases are implemented. This effectively reduces the complications of an integrated data base. Instead, channels of communication should be documented and implemented. Under this concept a glossary of standard terms will be developed so that all subsystems of the system use the same term in calling for or furnishing data. Each subsystem stands by itself. The areas of interface, however, are standard and documented so that one subsystem can get the data it needs from another subsystem. Also, each subsystem then will be able to furnish data desired by other subsystems.

Determination of Further Information Requirements

Forms, such as those illustrated in Chapter 1, can be used to determine the information requirements of the various echelons in the company. It is only by working closely with people in the various departments of a company that their requirements can be identified. Studies indicate that when management does not participate in the design of an information system, the results often are not used. All levels of management should be encouraged to participate as much as they can in stating their information requirements. Too often in data processing an attitude of, "I know what they need. Don't bother to ask them," has precipitated a poor system. The experience of this author is that the ideas of people in the organization—those who often have little or no knowledge about the systems or data processing—are far more valuable than those of the technical experts in data processing. The computer expert's role is one of synthesis rather than of origination. He is primarily responsible for putting the technical requirements together and for considering their potentials and problems from a technological standpoint.

Selection of Priority for Subsystem Implementation. It is suggested that priority allocations begin with the identification of current systems and applications that are working reasonably well, which can be eliminated from a high priority in the plan. Their areas of interface with current or planned subsystems, of course, will be considered, but only as they affect other subsystems. Both current and potential subsystems that merit consideration should be identified. Multiple hypotheses can be developed concerning the implementation and operation of each of these subsystems. It is better to increase islands of information than to start a new island. New subsystems contiguous to already established subsystems, therefore, merit consideration. The determination of priority is merely a sensible way to decide what, how, and when to do something. For determining the priority of subsystems, the cost/benefit process of analysis involves the following steps:

1. Determine the expected benefits of each alternative. What are the bases for these expectations?
2. What resources will be needed to develop, implement, and operate each hypothesis? What will these resources cost? In each case the basis for the estimates should be furnished.
3. Arrange the hypotheses in order of their net value to the company.
4. Present the list to management for approval.

SUMMARY

Computer hardware developments are significantly ahead of the systems designed to use them. There are few examples of management's taking advantage completely of the power of the computer. The fault is rightfully laid on management's doorstep. Although there are some examples of highly integrated systems that use a great proportion of the potential effectiveness computers provide, these examples are few and far between. The great majority of companies use the computer to run fragmented applications instead of integrated systems. Computers are used to better advantage when management takes an active hand in systems design. Management has three major responsibilities in this effort:

1. Establish the objectives of the system that data processing will support.
2. Establish the objectives of each subsystem of the overall system.
3. Give overt support to the establishment of an integrated data processing system.

There is a cycle in the development and implementation of an information system. The phases of this cycle are:

1. Feasibility study.
2. Applications study.
3. Selection and acquisition.
4. Preparation for installation.
5. Conversion.
6. Operation.
7. Review and evaluation.

The system-development cycle is a long one, ranging from two years for a small system to seven years for a large one. The development of a system to replace an ongoing system should start early enough for it to be implemented before the current system is completely outmoded.

Traditionally, the design of a system has started with an examination of the current system—the bottom-up approach. This approach often leads to computerizing a currently functioning system instead of designing an optimal one. The following steps are proposed in designing an integrated information system:

1. Examination of the objectives of the system.
2. Segregation of the system into the optimal number of subsystems.
3. Development of subsystem objectives consonant with system objectives.
4. Development of the hierarchy of output within each subsystem to attain the objectives.
5. Determination of the input necessary to produce the output.
6. Analysis of the current system to ensure that no significant input or output has been omitted.
7. Development of concepts concerning ways in which the system can operate.
8. Selection of optimum means of operation.
9. Selection of the optimum equipment configuration and the output that will be produced.
10. Proposal of the new system.

Although the top-down approach ultimately has the better chance of resulting in a completely satisfactory system, it is a long and difficult one. Management is not happy with the long·wait before getting a return on its investment. Furthermore, there is no guarantee that the system ultimately developed will be successful. Where the current system is computerized (at least in part) the combination approach has been successful. The first five steps are the same as in the top-down approach. The remaining steps are:

1. Analysis of the current system to determine the capabilities of current subsystems.
2. Determination of further information requirements.
3. Selection of priority of subsystem implementation.

Under this approach, the ultimate system is designed from the top but is built subsystem by subsystem from the bottom. This is done by expanding islands of information (current operational subsystems). Instead of establishing an integrated data base, separate data banks are maintained. Interfaces are standardized so that each subsystem can communicate with the others.

EXERCISES

1. Trace the development of computers and computer-based systems for the past 20 years. Project each for the next 5 years. Defend your projection.
2. What factors led to the comparatively slow development of computer-based systems? What would you recommend to correct this problem?
3. Differentiate between integrated and fragmented systems. What is a total system?
4. Give the advantages and disadvantages of integrated systems as compared with fragmented systems. Which are better? Why?
5. What is a real-time system? Is a computer needed for a real-time system? What are the essential elements of a computer-based real-time system?
6. Describe three examples of computer-based real-time systems in government and/or industry.
7. Illustrate in chart form the elements of a system.
8. The system involved is an information counter in a railroad station. What are the elements of this system?
9. What problems are involved when there are too many subsystems in a system? How does one take corrective action if a potential system has too many subsystems?
10. What is the formula for the number of areas of input and output for a system with subsystems? Is there a limit beyond which one should not have more subsystems. If not, why not? If so, what is the limit? Why?
11. What are the functions of the different levels of management in each phase of the system-development cycle.
12. What are the phases of the system-development cycle? How long does each phase normally last?
13. Compare and contrast three methods of designing systems.
14. Discuss the steps of the top-down approach to designing computer-based information systems.
15. When would you use the bottom-up method of designing systems? The top-down? The combination? What factors would influence your choice of methods?
16. Discuss the principles of developing system hypotheses.
17. Describe some methods of selecting the optimal hypothesis from several system hypotheses.

5 ◀ CONTROLLING INFORMATION SYSTEMS

In designing an information system, a safe assumption is that any error than can occur will occur—and usually at the most inopportune moment. Aside from inadvertent error, people may falsify records deliberately—whether to gain fraudulently or to get revenge. Furthermore, data processing equipment is not infallible. Although the electronic parts of a computer have extremely low error rates, they depend upon people and peripheral units that are largely mechanical. Thus, they are more prone to error than is the computer itself.

Despite controls built into computer-based systems, news reports of grotesque errors continually appear. Customers are charged too much or too little. Refunds or payments are too large or too small. These are the results of errors, whether mechanical or by people. But what about people using computers to defraud? In one week, newspapers reported the embezzlement of millions of dollars from a bank and the theft of freight cars from a major railroad. In both cases the computer was alleged to have been the tool of the thief.

If one leaves money lying around with no protection, sooner or later it will disappear, whether by theft or by accident. On the other hand, it would be equally foolish to build and use a $100,000 vault to protect an item worth $10. Somewhere between no protection and overprotection is an appropriate level of control. It varies for each system. The problem for any analyst is to determine which controls to use so that the system is controlled but not overcontrolled.

This chapter discusses the various controls that should be considered in designing a computer-based system. For purposes of discussion they are segregated into four areas: input controls, computer controls, noncomputer controls, and preservation of assets. Within each area, batch controls will be covered first, followed by controls for on-line systems. Guidelines will then be offered for deciding which controls to implement.

INPUT CONTROLS

Purposes

One of the most overused acronyms in data processing is GIGO (garbage in, garbage out). If the input data is wrong, one should expect a wrong answer. Input controls are intended to ensure correct input to the computer. Their purposes are to assure that:

1. All data are received on time.
2. All data are converted accurately and completely to a machine-readable language.
3. All data enter the computer for processing.

When in court a witness swears to tell the truth, the whole truth, and nothing but the truth. Input controls should be treated similarly. The preceding three purposes cover the "truth" and the "whole truth" parts, but not the "nothing but the truth." The last area is taken care of in the subsequent section of this chapter, "Computer Controls." Most input controls for computer systems stem from electric accounting-machine practices—item counts, batch totals, control totals, and logs. The growth of on-line systems, however, has required extension of these practices.

Batching

In a batch system the purpose of assuring that data is received on time implies a cutoff date. At a particular time (such as payroll-running time) the program is run. All input not received on time are excluded from the run. Sometimes one knows that a specific number of batches must be received. At other times he either runs what has come in by run time, or is informed when no more batches are forthcoming.

Specified Number of Batches

An inventory system is an example of a system in which number of returns to be received is known and a certain number of installations must report stock status as of the end of the month. These reports are due at data processing by the tenth of the following month. Data processing can keep a log and check off returns as they are received. As soon as all returns are received, the data can be converted to a machine-readable language and the computer program can be run. Telephones, radio, or other means can be used to request the data, if any returns are not received by the cutoff date.

The degree of precision needed determines the degree of control. If the run is done for statistical purposes, the degree of accuracy required may not be as great as if it were a payroll run. In the former case, the analyst might examine the individual submissions. He might find that the ten largest returns constitute 90 percent of the dollar value of inventory and that one missing from this group would justify delay of the run. For the remaining returns, the data for the past month might be substituted. If necessary, when all returns came in, the substitute data could be replaced by the late return. If the file was not to be used again until the next month, and a corrected report was not needed, this deletion of the substitute data and insertion of the proper data could be done as a part of the next month's run.

Varying Number of Batches

A method used quite often when items are sent from the source to data processing in small batches is for the originator to indicate which is the last batch before the cutoff date. Usually, such a system includes batch and control totals. Batches are numbered sequentially. The final batch indicator gives the number of batches, the total number of items, and the total value of the items. If the converted data checks with the totals supplied, the computer run can start. If a batch is missing, it can be identified easily by the numbering system.

Item Counts and Control Totals

Item counts and control totals are standard methods of ensuring that all data are converted accurately and completely to machine language and that all data enter the computer for processing. In a card operation the cards can be run through an electric accounting statistical machine to ensure that card counts and such control totals as dollar amounts agree. Further, the computer program should compare the actual number of cards entering the computer for processing and the total value of the times, to ensure that they agree with the controls. These control totals at times are hash totals— totals that in themselves have no meaning, but ensure that all items are entered correctly. Examples are the sum of all part numbers in an inventory system and the total of all employee numbers in a payroll system. In case of disagreement, both the control total and the actually calculated total should be printed so that a correction can be made.

On-line Input Controls

On-line systems present particular problems. Data in such systems normally is converted to a machine-readable form as close to the source of the data as possible. The data then is transmitted, usually by wire, to the computers. Despite the added possibility of error introduced by the remoteness of the terminal and the possibility of transmission errors, a well-designed on-line system can be more accurate than a batch system. Examples of techniques that can be used are discussed below:

Sequential Numbering

Messages may be numbered sequentially, either by the operator of the terminal or by the terminal itself. If, at any time, the sequence is broken, the computer can initiate a query to the terminal concerning the missing number. This control helps ensure that all data enters the computer for processing.

Checkpoint

A checkpoint is the terminal equivalent of the batch total. As messages are sent, the terminal keeps a control total of the number of messages sent and of the total dollars or some other quantifiable unit in the messages. As messages are received, the computer maintains cumulative totals for each terminal. During slack periods (at least once a day), cumulative totals are transmitted to the computer for verification. If in balance, the controls are reset to zero, both in the computer and at the terminal. Any differences between control totals can be corrected at the time of verification. If the terminal will not keep such totals, the terminal operator can maintain them manually. Mechanically kept totals, of course, are less susceptible to error.

Batch Totals

In some quasi real-time systems, items are not transmitted as they occur. Instead they are sent in small batches. The normal method of control here is an item count and dollar or unit transmittal totals. These figures are sent at the end of each batch. Any discrepancy can be located by the computer and correction procedures can be started.

Undecipherable Messages

Undecipherable messages are defined as messages that do not fit the patterns established in the computer. Here, because the computer cannot contextualize, it is not as good as human operators. A variation of one character can make a message undecipherable to a computer. Requesting retransmission each time might increase the number of transmissions too much. The console operator or a clerk should try to clean up messages that are undecipherable to the computer. Retransmission should be requested only if personnel are unsuccessful in their efforts.

Parity Checking

Bits are transmitted serially rather than in parallel on a wire. If more bits must be transmitted, more time will be needed. Any check bits that involve extra transmission will take more line time and cost money. Some systems add a bit position in each character for horizontal parity checking. In certain machines the parity bit is used to ensure an odd number of bits for each character. In others, there must be an even number of bits. If a bit is dropped in transmission, the computer will signal a parity error and request retransmission. Some systems also have longitudinal parity checks. After a certain number of characters, a row of vertical parity bits is entered, ensuring that parity across and down are maintained. If there is only one error, it can be located automatically and corrected, but for more than one, retransmission is requested.

Transmission-Line Error Rates

It is possible to calculate the error rate with a reasonable degree of accuracy for each line. If the error is high, as compared with the requirements of the system, more controls should be implemented. If it is low, less control need be used.

COMPUTER CONTROLS

Purposes

A computer-based system relies upon human performance, peripheral units, and a computer for accuracy. The human being, of course, usually is the most error-prone of the three. Peripheral units are largely mechanical and have a much higher error rate than computers. Because the computer is primarily electronic, it has the lowest error rate of the three. Although its error rate is low, the computer does make errors. There have been many well-publicized examples of computer errors, resulting in wrong bills or payments because operators have lost cards. Less known, perhaps, are the problems with peripheral units. Tape drives, for example, may start below normal speed, may stop and/or backspace improperly, and may signal incorrectly at terminals such as load points or end of reel. The possible results of such malfunctions are the duplication or the loss of data on a tape or the failure to process some data.

The purposes of computer controls are to assure that:

1. Only valid data is processed.
2. Unacceptable data is flagged for correction or removal.
3. All data are processed through each program in an application.
4. Hardware controls operate satisfactorily.

The first two purposes refer to the validity of data—the "nothing but the truth" check that was not discussed under "Input Controls." The last two purposes may be classified under run-to-run controls.

Validity Checking

Character Mode Tests

A character mode test is a check to ensure that the data in a field is alphabetic or numeric. In certain cases it may be completely alphabetic or completely numeric. In others, it may be alphabetic in certain parts of the field and numeric in others. For example, a units-order field may be completely numeric. In a license-plate number field, the first two characters might be designated as alphabetic and the last four characters as numerals. A word of caution, however—names of people cannot be presumed to be solely alphabetic. This author has seen names such as "Willie ⅝ Jones."

Self-checking Numbers

This method of checking is also called redundant-digit checking. Under either title, a nine-digit number, for example, has a tenth digit appended. This digit is derived mathematically from the original nine numbers. When the ten digits enter the computer, the mathematical calculations are made on the first nine digits. If the tenth digit and the results of the calculations are identical, it is presumed that the number is correct. If they disagree, however, there is an error. The best known system is Modulo 11, an IBM system based on the differences between the digits and 11. There are many similar systems.

Reasonableness Check

This check ensures that amounts fall within predetermined limits. A payroll check may not, for example, be larger than the gross calculated pay of the highest paid person in the company. A refund check may not exceed a certain amount. A person's dependents may not exceed 12. An order for 20-gallon garbage cans may not exceed 200. It is possible that there will be valid cases where certain transactions will exceed the established parameters. The purpose of this control is to highlight the exception for human verification. If it is valid, the transaction is reinstated. If not, it is corrected or removed. This type of control can save a lot of money and/or embarrassment. One must be careful, however, in establishing the limits. If set too stringently, a lot of time and effort will be spent in checking valid transactions. If set too loosely, costly errors will be undetected.

Consistency

Certain items of information are needed for particular transactions. A change in account number, for example, should include both the old and the new numbers and the name. On the other hand, if it is a change in name, the items required will be number, old name, and new name. If the data and the transaction code do not agree, this check segregates it for correction or removal.

Comparison

This check is usually done by comparing items against a table of legitimate items. Tables of legitimate transaction numbers, customer numbers, and part numbers, for example, are maintained in the computer. Data on incoming transactions is compared against the appropriate table(s) to ensure that it is legitimate. Anything that is not in the table is rejected for correction.

Run-to-Run Controls

File Identity Verification

Each file should have a header record (internal file identification label). At at minimum, this header record should include file identification information, creation date, and disposal date. Whenever files are used, the computer can check to ensure that the proper file is mounted. Furthermore, it can ensure that the file is the latest updated version prior to the present run. A master file catalog can be maintained on disk or drum. Whenever a file is updated, it is checked against the catalog; if the file is the proper one, the computer run is made. After the run is completed the master file catalog is updated to this (the latest) run.

Record Counts

A control (that is, number of records in file) should be maintained and updated prior to or immediately after a run. The control comprises

> (Opening number of records) + (additions − deletions)
> = closing number of records

The computer counts as each record is written onto tape. If the computer count and the calculated count do not agree, both figures should be printed in the error message. Personnel will be needed to find the error and make the appropriate corrections.

Control Totals

Control totals should be maintained immediately prior to or after a file is updated. For example,

> (Amount receivable at beginning) − (payments + new charges) ± (adjustments—as applicable) = amount receivable at end

As the accounts are written onto tape, the computer accumulates closing balances and checks the sum against the calculated control total. Again, in case of error, both figures should be written in the error message so that people can make the proper corrections.

Sequence Checks

Even though input data has been sorted, there may be errors in order. Sorted input data should be sequence-checked to ensure proper sequence for processing. Similarly, master files should be checked during up-dating runs to make sure that the sequence has not been disrupted.

On-Line Computer Controls

If the computer fails during a batch run, the operator can go back to the preceding restart point and complete the job. With entries coming from many remote terminals in an on-line system, a computer failure creates several problems. New entries should be accumulated while the computer is down, and these entries should be processed when the computer is back in operation. There should be provisions to ensure that the exact status of all transactions at the time of the failure is known. Which transactions were completed? Which were waiting to be processed? Which were being processed at the time of the failure, and how far had they been processed? Some of the needed controls are discussed below.

Transaction Log

All transactions should be logged and given a serial number before being processed. The log entry should include the terminal of origin, the date, and the time. This information will enable a restart without much difficulty.

Checkpoint

Occasionally the computer should establish a checkpoint for each terminal. This checkpoint, usally maintained on drum or disk, and is very helpful in restarting a system. The transaction log procedure provides better control and requires less transmission than the checkpoint procedure. On the other hand, it uses more channel and computer time.

Return Message

After the transaction has been processed completely, a message should be sent by the computer to the terminal. This has two purposes. It guides the input operator and expedites validity checks. From a psychological standpoint, the inputter is satisfied. He knows his transaction has been processed, and does not feel the frustration of uncertainty. Furthermore, if the computer goes down, he knows which items have been completed and can restart by transmitting all items that have not been completed.

All validity checks mentioned previously can be made as soon as the transmission is received in the computer. If an apparent error is discovered, an error message can be sent as soon as is feasible to the terminal. The operator can make the correction while the transaction is still fresh in his memory.

Terminal Limitation

A system can be designed so that orders are permitted only from certain terminals. Payments are limited to specific other terminals. Change notices can originate from only certain terminals. The computer may be programmed to accept only transactions that are legitimate for the terminal being used. All others are rejected. This type of control helps eliminate unauthorized entries.

Daily Listing

One of the necessities of an on-line system is the provision of measures for graceful degradation. Even if the computer is down, there should be some provision for carrying on the work. The service may not be as complete or as rapid, but it continues. During the night, a listing of current status of each account can be sent to each terminal. If the computer fails the next day, the terminal operators can enter transactions manually on the listing. When the computer is operating again, the manually entered transactions can be sent to the computer.

File Dump

Periodically, files should be dumped and the date and time of the dump recorded. In case the computer goes down or malfunctions occur, the erroneous accounts can be reconstructed.

File Scan

During slack periods the computer can scan accounts in the file. Apparent errors can be traced back to the appropriate terminal by means of the log. This procedure tends to maintain a comparatively high level of accuracy in the files. Without such a control, there is a tendency for errors to accumulate in files until eventually a massive correction run is needed. Individual entries may appear to be in line. An examination of many such apparently correct items may indicate that something is wrong. For example, one order of tires on a gasoline card account, or even two, might be all right. Several orders for tires, batteries, and other accessories in a short time would indicate the possibility that the card had been lost and that the finder was using it to purchase items illegally. File-scan checks will locate such things.

Hard Copy at Terminals

The safest procedure is to maintain hard copy of all transactions at each terminal. It is preferable if one copy of all transmissions goes directly into a locked container to which the operator does not have access. This will provide an audit trail and will help deter thefts and frauds.

NONCOMPUTER CONTROLS

A data processing system is not limited to the data processing department. On the contrary, practically all data originates outside of data processing. Furthermore, the output is used throughout the company. In order to have an effective data processing system, the entire system should be treated as a cohesive entity—from input preparation to report delivery. This implies that controls are needed both within and without the data processing department. The purposes of noncomputer controls are (1.) to promote the effective use of people and equipment, and (2.) to provide for continuity of operations.

Data Control External to Data Processing

Written, formal procedures should be established for the capture of data, as close to the source as possible, and for the transmission of such data processing. A control group may be needed to make sure that the flow of data adheres to these procedures. The functions of this group are to receive control information, reconcile all discrepancies, and ensure reprocessing or proper disposal of questionable transactions.

Data Control Internal to Data Processing

Clear-cut documented operator procedures are necessary to prevent operator intervention. These are particularly necessary on programmed computer halts. Operator entries should be via the console typewriter. Where available, there should be two copies of the console typewriter output. The original can be used for operational purposes. The carbon should go directly into a container to which the operator does not have access. A responsible person (not the operator) should analyze this log daily. Without prior warning, this review function should be assigned to a different person. These reviews have three major functions:

1. To monitor how well the operator is following established rules.
2. To review how effectively the computer is being operated.

3. To prevent frauds. (Ways in which fraud can be deterred are discussed more fully, under "Preservation of Assets.")

Clear-cut conventions should be established for the use of rings on reels of magnetic tape and for the manual depression of appropriate control buttons on the computer. To ensure compliance, computer programs should check that control devices have been set properly before continuing with the computer run.

Input/output documents should be preserved according to their importance. Data processing managers may know how long such documents should be retained for operating purposes. The auditor, however, should establish the length of retention. He is responsible for compliance with law, audit trails, and safety. Bringing the auditor in for consultation during the system design will forestall a lot of problems in this area.

With regard to the computer, preventive maintenance schedules should be followed quite rigorously. A detailed log of errors and machine time should be maintained and analyzed. This will enable location of recurring difficulties so that remedial action can be taken.

Supervision and Training

It will be noted that, throughout this area, guidelines indicate the establishment of documented rules. Strong supervision leads to observance of the rules. Review and analysis "after the fact" ensure that clerks and operators know that strict adherence to the rules is required and that they will be called to account for transgressions or omissions. If the actions of clerks and operators are to be reviewed critically, it follows that they should be well trained before doing the work. If analysis shows that they continue making errors, the need for retraining may be indicated. If, after such retraining, the errors and/or omissions continue, possibly those who persist in making them should be replaced by employees who are amenable to supervisory correction.

On-Line Noncomputer Controls

Here again the controls are essentially the same for both batch and on-line systems. The manner of application, however, differs. As discussed previously, when the computer in an on-line system uncovers an error in transmission, it notifies the sender so that the correction can be made immediately. Also, after processing is completed, a notification is sent to the terminal. Documentation of procedures both internally and externally to data processing is essential. Furthermore, the computer can check the degree to which many of these rules are followed. The system should be programmed so that a log of all errors is kept, and every week or so a report should be sent to the appropriate supervisors. Thereafter, steps to ensure compliance are the same as in batch processing. Both within and without data processing, operator instructions with regard to actions, especially when there is an outage, should be rigorous. One of the prime supervisory tasks is to be sure that operators follow these instructions to the letter. In both cases a strong effort to fight an "it doesn't matter" attitude is needed.

PRESERVATION OF ASSETS

Purpose

The computer is the Achilles heel of modern business. In many cases the firm has lost the ability to revert to manual or electric accounting-machine operations. As time passes, more and more applications are put on the computer. People who knew how to do the work before it was taken over by the computer leave for other positions, retire, or die.

Management has paid little attention to this problem. Ignoring it, however, will not cause it to go away. There is a well-known saying that lightning only strikes once in the same place. After it strikes, there is nothing left to strike again. A catastrophe in the computer room can be just as devastating. Without adequate countermeasures, there may be no company left to suffer another catastrophe. Managers can no longer ignore the risk involved in using computers. It is too vital. The hazards in using computers should be analyzed and treated as any other business risk.

Newspapers continually report computer-related thefts. In England the accounts of a grocer were on the computer. A dishonest employee established an account for one of his relatives. Fictitious purchases were recorded, and large payments were made by the grocer before a curious clerk accidentally uncovered the fraud. Computer-related frauds have ranged from raises in pay, sold by computer operators, to millions of dollars misappropriated from banks and stockbrokers. How many such frauds have not been detected or, being detected, have not been publicized? The major purpose of these controls as data is processed is to safeguard the assets of the firm.

Operating Procedures

One of the most basic safeguarding procedures is to assign duties so that the work of one person acts as a check on the work of another. A corollary to this is that no person should have control over transactions from start to finish when such tranactions involve the assets of the company. Having more than one person involved will not eliminate the possibility of fraud, but it will lessen the probability considerably.

Some frauds are accomplished by unauthorized program changes. Others are done by computer operators running a job such as payroll when no one else is in the computer room. To reduce the probability of such frauds, all computer programs and program changes should be approved by responsible personnel. Computer operators should get only the details of a program necessary to operate the computer. Operator access to output documents should be carefully defined. In a payroll run, checks should be prenumbered. The computer should not be the means of numbering checks during such a run. After the run is completed, the operator should be required to account for all checks, including those filled in, those spoiled, and those not used. Rigorous procedures, accompanied by enforcement measures, are excellent deterrents to fraud.

The growth of on-line systems has injected another chink in the protective armor of computer-based systems. No longer is limited access to the computer complete protection. The current risks related to computer-based systems are so pervasive that they will be evaluated individually. Both preventive and ameliorative measures will be suggested in the next section and a rational method for deciding which measures to adopt will be outlined.

Hazards

Catastrophes

Fire. In 1959 a fire in the Pentagon destroyed a large computer installation. The fire started in a light fixture and spread quickly through the area. Flames, heat, and smoke destroyed computers valued in the millons. This, however, was the only visible part of the iceberg. Losses in programs and data far exceeded the cost of replacing the computers. It took years for the Air Force to recover completely from this fire. Few businesses would have been able to resume operations after such damage. Shortly after the Pentagon fire, another computer a half-mile away caught fire. A guard ruined the computer by using a fire hose on it. There have been so many fires in data processing installations since 1959 that they no longer are worthy of headlines. They appear as small items in the middle of the newspaper and/or in bankruptcy, dissolution, or merger statements.

Explosion. Although not as common as fire, explosions are another hazard to data processing. Gas, chemicals, or explosive materials have resulted in accidental damage to buildings. A computer in the building is at least as vulnerable as the building and its other contents.

Natural Disasters. Floods, hurricanes, cyclones, tidal waves, and earthquakes have caused much destruction in computer installations. Hurricane Celia in 1970, for example, tore power lines, flooded computer centers with salt water, and wrecked buildings housing computer installations. In 1971 an earthquake in California disrupted power and ravaged computer centers.

Sabotage

Deliberate sabotage of computer installations may be categorized into two areas: protests based on social considerations, and revenge. Examples of the former are peace demonstrations and those for civil rights, the fighting of poverty, and those attempting to safeguard the ecology. Disgruntled employees and customers recognize that the greatest damage can be wrought in the computer system with the least effort and least danger of apprehension. A humanities course offered at Syracuse University was reported to be a workshop on the nonviolent sabotage of computer installations.

Social Protests. The right to personal property—to use it in any way you desire—is no longer sacrosanct. Bombs in universities in Wisconsin, California, and Kansas attest to this. Welfare recipients occupied the Welfare Department's computer center to protest the withholding of their checks. Students in Massachusetts took over the college data processing center. They did no overt damage, but held the installation as ransom to force the college administration to accept a number of demands. This installation was particularly vulnerable, because there were no backup files. Furthermore, no data could be processed until the students released the center.

Revenge. Many companies bill customers on prepunched cards, which are to be returned with the payment. Most of these systems anticipate only a small number of exceptions. It doesn't take very many customers spindling, folding, or stepping on the return card with spiked golf shoes to swamp those handling exceptions. A concerted effort by customers protesting a company policy could completely disrupt the system.

Environmental Problems

Only in a minority of cases is the computer installation a part of the original plans of a building. More often the computer installation is built within an occupied building. Compromises with the existing structure are necessary. It is fairly common to see water pipes or steam pipes running through such computer installations. Leakage or bursting of these pipes could cause great damage. Newspapers quite often report damage to a seemingly impervious installation. In at least two occurrences, completely fireproof computer installations were damaged severely by fires on contiguous floors. In one case, water to put out the fire on the floor above the installation deluged the computer. In another case a fire on the floor below resulted in the computer's falling into the basement. Elsewhere a computer was installed above a bank vault. Yeggs dynamited the vault, seriously damaging the computer above it.

Power Difficulties

Most managers recognize the possibility of power failure. Since such disruptions normally are of short duration and comparatively rare, they are usually treated as calculated risks. When such failures last for hours, or even days, the ramifications can be great. Many computers in England were "off the air" for long periods of time in 1970 because of power stoppage.

More insidious than power failure is damage from power brownouts or temporary surges or drops in power. Many computers can tolerate power variances of $\pm$ 10 percent. The brownouts of 1970 were reported to be decreases of 5 to 8 percent. It does not take much of a temporary drop at these times to exceed the 10 percent tolerance. Furthermore, it is possible that in coming years it may be necessary to reduce power more than 10 percent in order to prevent a complete blackout. Surges or drops in electric power are fairly common and are expected at particular times of the day. A sudden storm or change in temperature or cloud coverage can result in such surges or drops. The damage to the computer from such variations in power can be recognized and corrected. Damage to programs, files, and reports may not be discovered until much later, if ever. Power variations have resulted in the updating of wrong records in a vendor master file. In another case, data when read from disk was written erroneously in core. Drops in power have caused disk drives to go out of operating status, aborting the run and necessitating a rerun.

Other Hazards

Loss of Programs and/or Data. Earlier in this chapter reference was made to programs or data lost in fires. Not as well publicized, but more often occurring, are such losses because of misoperation or environmental difficulties. An installation experienced data damage on tapes, which at first could not be explained. It was noticed that this damage was only on tapes stored on the bottom shelves of the tape library. Eventually the trouble was traced to a floor buffer, which set up a magnetic field and distorted the patterns of the magnetically stored bits on the tape. Similarly, tapes containing data and programs were damaged by magnetic fields from a hand vacuum cleaner. Operator errors have resulted in writing data on tapes over the only copies of master files or programs. Also, data stored on disks has been lost. At best, if other copies are available, such loss results in the use of extra machine time. If backup copies or data dumps are not kept, reconstruction costs and time used can be a considerable, if not an impossible, task.

If a time-sharing company is used for running programs, there is another possible loss of data or programs often not recognized. If the time-sharing company were to go bankrupt, as has occurred, how does one get his property back? He might have a difficult time convincing an officer of the court that although the tape or disk belongs to the time-sharing company, the data belongs to the customer.

External Radiation. Even tapes stored normally within computer installations are not safe from external radiation unless special precautions are taken. A computer was installed in the basement of a building. A large electric motor outside the computer installation created a magnetic field, wiping out tapes shelved on the adjacent wall outside the tape-storage area. Tapes have been erased while being shipped from one installation to another. Motors with enough power to damage tapes in a computer installation are comparatively rare. Short circuits, however, are not unknown, and do have such power. Reports of damage of data on tapes from radar have not been verified. Tests in 1972 showed that tapes more than 18 inches from the radar source will not be damaged. Radar, however, can affect the operations of a computer, thus resulting in incorrect results and aborted runs.

Mechanical or Electronic Breakdown. Outright failure or intermittent malfunction of computer equipment is another hazard. The former usually results in a small amount of time lost, necessitating reruns. If, however, a replacement part is not available locally, the installation may be down for days. Intermittent failures, however, are more dangerous because one may not realize they have occurred. In short interval of malfunction, wrong accounts may have been updated. Files may contain erroneous data. If the malfunction is not located quickly and the tapes with errors corrected, the backup tapes may be released for other purposes. In this event, recovery may be difficult and costly, if not impossible.

For example, in a large computer installation an operator got a read-error signal on a disk drive. The problem really was a faulty read head, which in fact was ruining the data on the disk. Thinking that the problem was with the disk, he removed it and substituted the backup disk. By the time the real problem was discovered, recovery had become time consuming and expensive because it involved punching cards from the last printing of the files and then doing all subsequent runs. This could have been a catastrophe if the complete file had not been printed.

Operator Error. As long ago as the early 1940s, when Mark II was running at Harvard University, operators have been mounting wrong tapes. To this day they use tape rings improperly, forget to set switches, or damage cards. These are only a few of the many ways that operator errors occur. The results range from loss of time for reruns to loss of customers' good will because of wrong billings. In some cases, recovery is made within the hour. At other times it takes weeks of costly effort.

Data Theft. Newspapers are continually reporting individual thefts of data from computer installations. According to such reports, an encyclopedia publisher allegedly found that former employees were selling his mailing list even to the company's competitors. An airline "lost" information worth millions. Policemen in New York were convicted of using computer output files, maintained manually, to sell information to detective agencies and airlines. In Sweden, employees in a service bureau "borrowed" tapes with population registry information. Among buyers of the data were a private statistics office and a political party. When the tapes were found missing prior to a special run, this theft was discovered.

On-line time-shared installations are particularly vulnerable to data and/or program theft. FBI agents arrested an 18-year-old youth for using leased telephone lines to steal data. According to the agents, the youth was close to bypassing completely the file security programs. About a month later, another man was charged with grand theft—the stealing of proprietary programs from the computer of a time-sharing company. It was reputed to be the first theft committed by plucking the brains of a computer.

One of the top computer software experts in the world said that any enterprising person can get through the security of any time-sharing system. Furthermore, it is comparatively easy to copy data sent over wires. Computers have been wiretapped with portable recorders. An unshielded line may be tapped without others knowing that it has occurred. It is possible to record input and output from outside the building, without those within the installation being aware it is being done.

Other Thefts. Computer time and equipment are also prime targets for thieves. In Chicago, five employees were accused of using their employer's equipment during slow hours to set up their own data processing firm. In an encyclopedia company the employees were said to have used the company's equipment to copy the tapes. A government employee used time on the night shift to run jobs for his own clients. He did this for some time before he was discovered and discharged. He then set up his own service bureau to continue servicing his clients from the spurious operation. Since he now had to pay for machine rental, he had to raise prices considerably. At costs ranging into the hundreds of dollars per hour, computer installations may be paying a great deal of extra rental and other costs for such illicit use. These are only a few examples where the culprits were caught. How many others have not been detected?

In some instances, programmers have learned company secrets or the details of sophisticated programs. Competitors have enticed such programmers to transfer to their employ, and the programmers have frequently made the secrets and/or program details known to their new employers.

Computerized larceny has one great advantage over other forms of larceny—it is seldom discovered. When it is discovered, it is hard to prosecute. There has always been a good market for stolen cards, tapes, or disks. With the miniaturization of computers, the theft of computers themselves can be expected.

Fraud. A bank was victimized by a systems analyst who was alleged to have funneled deposits of various customers into his account. A city employee was charged with selling raises in pay to other employees. These raises were made during night computer runs. In Los Angeles a swindle netted about $50,000 in false welfare payments. A stockbroker was reported to have been bankrupted by fraudulent manipulations of the computerized accounts. An accounts clerk was convicted of defrauding his employer of almost $120,000.

Law Suits. Newspapers are replete with reports of cars repossessed because of "computer error" or credit reputations damaged for the same reason. Increasingly the damaged party seeks recourse through suit. A retail-store owner admitted he blamed errors on the computer, even though he did not have a computer. With the bad press they are getting, computers and computer systems do not rank very high in the average man's opinion. Juries increasingly rule against the computer user in such suits. In these cases the verdict should depend upon whether or not all prudent precautions were taken to ensure against such errors. This loss of repute should recall to managers the saying about Caesar's wife having to be above reproach.

In New Orleans a company was in a dispute with the computer manufacturer over renegotiating an expired contract. It withheld rent and maintenance payments. The manufacturer sued, and the judge granted a writ of sequestration, ordering the federal marshal to seize the computer.

Suits by computer users against vendors of hardware and/or software are increasing. In addition, thousands of users have settled out of court or have absorbed the loss without recourse. At the writing of this chapter, at least three major suits had not yet been settled in court. A verdict in favor of the plaintiff could result in a large increase in such suits. Win or lose, such suits are expensive, especially where the lawyer is not thoroughly grounded in computer technology and its related jargon.

At first glance, these suits may appear to be a potential benefit, not a hazard, of data processing installations. The vendor ultimately must pass these costs down to the consumer in the form of increased prices. Furthermore, at best, the user can only hope to break even. Often the lawyer will be the only one with a profit. If the suit is lost, the user will have to absorb the additional legal fees and, possibly, court costs.

Looking at this from the other standpoint, many computer installations sell or rent hardware time, software, and/or operating services. In these cases they are vendors, just as much as the hardware and software vendors mentioned previously. As such, they easily could be defendants in similar suits.

Company officers can be sued by stockholders for poor management. The many examples of poor management of computer installations and recent surveys attest to this. Such derivative suits for mismanagement can readily exceed the total assets of the managers involved. The law is developing rapidly to reflect social changes. The citizen's right to call officials to account is being extended. It appears to be logical to extend this trend to computer managers, even in private companies.

Preventive Measures

Few, if any, data processing installations have the funds and need to take all available protective measures. Those discussed below furnish reference points for deciding which measures to employ. The possibilities are segregated into five categories: location, site construction, operating procedures, data protection, and legal protection.

Location

It may not be possible to choose the building into which the computer installation will be built, since the company may have only one building. If such choice is possible, one should consider possible catastrophes. If the area is subject to hurricanes and/or floods, the building should not be on the waterfront. A higher, more protected location might be selected instead. The building should not be over a geologic fault. There might not be an earthquake but, if there were one, damage would be much greater over the fault. The building to be selected or built should be strong, fireproof, and in a safe location. It would, for example, be rash to have such a building at the end of a busy airport runway or next to an explosives plant. Similarly, sharing a building with a firm that houses volatile materials would increase the danger of a catastrophic fire.

Location within the building should also be considered. The safest location is as close to the center of the building as possible, and on the lower floors. In a multibasement building it might be on the first floor below street level. This would provide the best protection from sabotage and radar. Of course, if it were necessary to put the computer in a building close to a waterfront subject to floods, a second- or third-floor location might be preferable. The lower the computer is in the building, the less will be the danger of earthquake damage. Aside from these precautions, one should select a location away from the regular stream of pedestrians, out of sight, and not contiguous to sources of danger. For example, the computer center should not be next to

Selective Service or a munitions manufacturer's offices, since these often are objects for group protests. In these disorders, the innocent bystander often gets injured.

Site Construction

Fireproof computer sites constructed in fireproof buildings provide the best protection against fire. To prevent damage from leaks, no wet pipes should be in the computer installation. Carbon dioxide fire extinguishers are dangerous to people, and sprinkler systems can damage the computer severely. Halon 1301 costs more than carbon dioxide or water, and is as effective as carbon dioxide, but is not dangerous to people.

Most sprinkler systems have wet pipes, which have the ever-present danger of leakage. There is, however, a dry-pipe sprinkler system. If the temperature below the sprinkler rises to 140 degrees, a solenoid allows water to flow into the pipe. If the temperature below the sprinkler rises to 212 degrees, water is released. When the temperature drops below 140 degrees, the sprinkler turns off.

Faraday cages or radio-frequency shielding provides the best protection against electrical emanations from external sources. These preventive measures, however, are costly, and it is possible that simple grounding of the equipment will divert stray transmissions from such sources.

A voltage regulator with a flywheel should keep power fluctuations within the ± 10 percent range. In case of power lapses, it will enable a "slow stop," thus preserving data. Temperature and humidity controls will prevent many computer malfunctions.

Carpeting on the floor normally should be avoided. Carpets cause static electricity to build up when humidity is low. When the IBM 360/30 first came out, a chemical manufacturer had a great deal of trouble with failing programs because of static electricity generated from plastic-covered chairs and from carts being pushed near the computer.

Locked maximum-security doors provide the best protection against undesired intrusion. A plain lock, which can be opened easily from inside the installation, is preferable. Under normal conditions, locks opened by specially treated cards work very well. If for any reason, such as fire, the electricity is cut off, these locks do not work. Unless optional means also are available, people cannot get in or out of the installation. For example, in an Air Force base with a tube computer, a card identification lock was used. A power failure shut down the computer and the air-conditioning system, and personnel could not get out for hours. Had the power been cut by fire, a tragedy might have resulted. In the 1970 California earthquake, the door to a computer could be opened only by the guard outside the door. He fled, leaving a man imprisoned in the computer room.

To protect against both unwarranted intrusion and the carrying of metals into the computer room, a double-door system with a scanning zone can be used. The first door, opened by a key, must be closed and locked before the person entering is able to pass between the electronic metal scanners. Thus, he can open the inside door only if he passes inspection. If he does not, he must telephone for assistance.

For protection against theft, unauthorized use of the computer, and sabotage during off-hours, closed-circuit TV provides comparatively inexpensive protection. A continuous picture of the computer installation is relayed to the guard's station. If the danger is great enough, an ultrasonic detector system with alarms to both the guard's station and to a central point will supply added protection.

Operating Procedures

The first defense is a perimeter defense. There should, if possible, be only one entrance used into the building, with a guard stationed there at all times. All windows and doors should have alarm devices. Any attempt to get into the building by other than the main door should trigger an alarm to the guard and/or to a central point. The guard should inspect all packages, to ensure against explosives or firearms being carried into the building.

Access to the computer facility should be limited to those whose presence is needed. The day of the computer as a showpiece is gone. Visitors should be limited and always accompanied by a supervisor. In addition to the security equipment previously detailed under "Site Construction," employees could wear color-coded badges. One color would provide entry for the wearer to all parts of the data processing department except the computer room. Another color would enable the wearer to go into the computer room. In addition to card colors, face recognition or introduction by the supervisor of a new employee helps control unwanted visitors. Any visitor permitted to take anything from the computer room or tape vault should be required to sign a receipt.

The tape room should be locked and under the control of a tape librarian. A tape log should be maintained, with a complete record of tape withdrawals, returns, times, purposes, and the person involved. Access to this room should be severely limited. No one, and that includes cleaning personnel, should be allowed into the tape room without the express permission of the supervisor. If, for any purpose, someone other than the tape librarian is allowed to enter, he should be watched closely at all times during his stay in the tape room. Tapes are comparatively small and easily damaged. Backup tapes for necessary programs and data should be maintained in a safe room, preferably in another building. As programs are changed or files updated, the current program of file should be substituted for the backup file or program that is outdated. This is a comparatively inexpensive means of ensuring safety of programs and data.

Regardless of how good a security system is, undependable employees can negate it. Computer-room employees should be checked carefully before employment. Furthermore, a buddy system should be used. There must never be only one person in the computer room.

Good control procedures are a key protection. Examples of such procedures follow. The run of a key program by an unauthorized employee might result in loss or embarrassment to the company. A changeable key word required before the program can be run will help make sure that there are no unauthorized runs. All error messages should be clear, and no computer run should be considered completed, unless there is a specific End of Job message. A separate console in a locked room is a good means of monitoring all changes and instructions entering the computer, all uses, and all outgoing messages. If this is not possible, two-part console paper, with the carbon going directly into a locked container, provides some protection—though not as much as an isolated console.

Operating procedures, no matter how carefully devised, quickly become ineffective without good supervision. Good procedures should be established and employees should be trained to follow them. Even this is not enough. Continual inspections and audits should be carried out to ensure that these procedures are followed faithfully. People have a tendency to bypass safety devices or procedures they consider to be unnecessarily restrictive. It is only by following the suggestions given above that a safe, well-run computer installation will result.

Data Protection

If it does not matter who sees anything that comes out of a computer installation, the following suggestions need not be followed. The degree of protection depends upon the amount of secrecy needed. Overprotection of computer records can be a very costly matter. The computer manager cannot normally make the determination. His job is to specify the risks, the possibilities of the data's being stolen, his estimate of the possible consequences, and the costs of the protection. He should give these, with his recommendations, to management, which makes the final decision concerning the precautions to be taken.

Unless proper precautions are taken, almost all input to or output from a computer can be read from outside the computer room without the knowledge or consent of those inside. Also, data transmissions over a wire or by radio can be tapped. For complete safety, the computer room should be enclosed in lead shielding and all outlets should be grounded. These are very expensive measures and are not used in any but the most secret installations.

Without them, sensitive jobs should not be run on a fixed schedule. Running them in the mornings, with a lot of outside noise, will deter stealing of data. Input/output gear should be located as close to the center of the computer room as possible. This will make reading them from outside more difficult. When a sensitive job is run (one where secrecy is important), either there should be no telephone in the computer room or it should be unplugged. All unused wiring should be removed from the computer room. Pipes, heating ducts, and similar conductors should be grounded as close to the computer as possible.

Ability to read disks, tapes, platens, and core after secret jobs are run is possible. In order to prevent such readings after programs are run, at least three streams of random characters should be written over these devices. Waste material, such as carbon paper and typewriter ribbons, should be destroyed. Procedures should be designed to prevent unauthorized persons from gaining access to this waste prior to disposal.

Growth in the use of telecommunications, on-line systems, time-sharing, and remote terminals for access to the computer has raised an entire new crop of security problems. That anything going over a wire can be read is a good assumption. To preclude such reading, encrypting all messages and decoding them at the receipt point will help. However, any code can be broken. Multiconductor cable with more than one circuit used at the same time will make reading more difficult. A rather expensive means, normally restricted to short-distance transmission, is the use of dry-air jackets around cables. Sensors note any penetration of the cable and trigger an alarm.

The ability of the computer to distinguish between different users of remote terminals and to limit their access to files accordingly is of importance in today's on-line and time-sharing systems. Fingerprint and voiceprint recognition devices are not yet practicable. A feasible sophisticated device is one that measures the hand and fingers of the user. This device is reported to be almost 100 percent accurate, but is fairly costly. Most systems depend upon key words, special numbers, and person-terminal coordination for recognition. They should ensure that unauthorized people cannot read the recognition term when it is used. Key words or numbers can be changed as often as desired. The computer can contain a table listing the files the user is permitted to use. This will help protect the files of other users. Key words or numbers should never be given over the telephone; they are too vulnerable to outside reading.

As mentioned previously, no software system is 100 percent safe. Assuming that all the methods discussed have been employed, a log of all users, their queries, and the files obtained should be kept where the user cannot control what goes into the log or read or change what is in there. Regular and continual audit of this file should reveal any attempted acquisition of sensitive files before the purloiner has accomplished his purpose.

Legal Protection

With the number of suits by users against software houses, service bureaus and manufacturers increasing, the computer manager must pay attention to this possibility. In dealing with a computer manufacturer, thousands (perhaps millions) of dollars are at stake. Even though it is a "standard contract," a lawyer who has experience with computer contracts should be retained. Otherwise, many of the caveats of these one-sided standard contracts may not be enforceable in court.

To bind a computer vendor, the written word of an officer of the company may be necessary. If the manufacturer decides not to keep the salesman, all the potential buyer has is the promise of a former employee of the vendor. One should not depend upon memory. After every meeting, a memorandum for the file, with copies to the individuals involved, should be prepared. Advertisements and brochures should be included in this file. Such a file might be extremely helpful in case of legal action years later.

Software houses or service bureaus should be careful of promises and assurances to customers. The honeymoon, where all errors or nonperformances were excused, is over. Failure to produce what is promised, when it is promised, and with the quality promised can result in a law suit. Even if the suit is won, the cost of defending it can be extremely high.

For internal operating purposes, when a person is hired or when a program is loaned or released for rental, one should insist upon a nondisclosure statement at the outset. An experienced lawyer can help in deciding how to protect software. Copyright, patent, and trade secret, or a combination thereof are possible. In order to protect against derivitive suits by stockholders, files should be kept. These files should give details and should cost-out possible alternatives that were considered in making decisions. Escape routes, in case things go wrong, also should be included. With such documentation, charges are commensurate with the worth of the decision, not to alternatives that were not considered.

Ameliorative Measures

Many of the preventive procedures discussed previously also act as ameliorative measures if the event they were designed to prevent occurs. For example, a fire-protection system should lessen the effects of the fire, if one occurs. The measures treated in the preceeding section will not be repeated here. Instead, this section is limited to additional procedures and expansions of preventive steps taken before.

The computers of a multicomputer company can be decentralized so that if anything should put a computer installation out of operation, the complete data processing capability of the company will not be destroyed. Another possibility would be to have a redundant installation in a remote location. Few companies, however, can afford or should accept this expense.

Almost as much protection, but with far less cost, is the use of a backup facility. The agreement with the furnisher of the backup capability should be in writing. Knowledge that the same model of the computer is used is not enough. Extra or missing capabilities or different versions of operating systems may cause programs to fail when run on the backup computer. Periodically, some jobs should be run at the backup facility. Despite the agreement and the complete compatibility of hardware and software, the backup computer may be in operation 100 percent of the time so that no time is available to run the backup work immediately. Arrangements should be made for a reasonable time allocation. The knowledge that the backup plan works or that adequate time is available to implement a new backup plan is worth a great deal more than the cost involved. A workable plan, of course, depends on an adequate supply of current programs and files maintained in a location other than the user's computer installation.

Although installation of fire- or heatproof safes will not prevent fire, they will lessen damage if a fire occurs. Safes protect only to a limited degree. If the fire is not too bad, damage will not be too great. Procedures should be established concerning actions employees are to take in case of an emergency. Periodic drills will make these procedures automatic.

If a time-sharing system is used, a tape should be sent to the central location. The files of the program should be dumped on this tape, ensuring that it is clearly marked as to ownership. If the time-sharing company goes bankrupt, recovery of both tape and data will be possible.

Business insurance is another ameliorative measure. Employees should be bonded if they have access to company assets subject to fraudulent seizure. Fire insurance may be purchased, not only for hardware and the premises but also for software. Thus indemnification will cover the expenses involved in continuing operations in a backup site until the computer facility is restored. Insurance covering errors or omissions is available also. For almost any of the risks detailed previously, some form of insurance can be bought.

Choice of Countermeasures

A computer installation probably should not take every precaution discussed. Overprotection can be very expensive. Furthermore, the ultimate decision rests with top management and not with the computer manager.

What can the computer manager do? What should he do? First, must identify the potential dangers. After these dangers have been pinpointed, he should prepare a cost/value analysis. At least the following elements should be considered: hazard, degree of damage, probability of occurrence, consequences, possible dollar loss, measures recommended, alternative measures considered, and costs of alternative measures. The following case problem illustrates how such analyses can be made. A data processing manager, after completing such an analysis, will have quantified the major elements of hazards and countermeasures considered and will be ready to make specific recommendations to management.

Case Problem

Situation. The company is completely wedded to computers as a means of operation. All records are maintained on magnetic tape and disk. For audit purposes the backup documents are held in central files, which is adjacent to data processing. Input documents are punched or entered by a key-to-tape process. The cards are maintained in data processing until the annual audit. Upon release by auditing, the cards are destroyed. Backup documents are kept in central files for three years before disposal.

The tapes and disks are held in an unlocked, nonfireproof room in data processing. All backup tapes are held in the same room. There is no backup to data kept on disks. When these disks are removed, they also are kept in the tape room. There is no tape or disk librarian. When tapes and/or disks are needed for a computer run, the operator gets the appropriate tapes, disks, programs, and working tapes from the tape room. After the computer run, the tapes and disks are filed in the tape room.

Problems. The greatest problems facing management are the interruptions to, or even stoppage of, company operations. Fire, error, and theft and fraud are serious occurrences.

1. Serious fire: If there were a serious fire, which included data processing and central files, there would be no way of reconstructing accounts receivable, accounts payable, or other computer records, and the company probably could not continue as a viable enterprise.

2. Minor fire: A minor fire in the tape room, sabotage by a disgruntled employee, or similar occurrences can wipe out the original and backup tapes and disks and all programs. It would be necessary to keypunch or do a key-to-tape process for backup documents and programs. Remedial computer runs would be needed. It would be at least two months before data processing could operate effectively again.

3. Error: Employees might take the wrong tapes or disks. In some cases they might write on these tapes and/or disks, destroying what was stored on them. If both the original and the backup tapes were destroyed, repunching or key-to-tape operations and remedial runs would be needed. If only the original tape were destroyed, a short computer run would correct the situation. If a disk were involved,

keypunching and remedial computer runs would be necessary.

4. Theft and fraud: The tapes in this company are not protected from theft or fraudulent changes. For example, programs can be manipulated to indicate payments by customers when such payments were never made. A list of customers could be sold to competitors. These are only two of the possible fraudulent opportunities. A list of company customers and details of their purchases could be sold to competitors. The company could be cheated out of amounts due. Employees could be overpaid fraudulently. Thefts of merchandise could be concealed. These are only a few examples of the many fraudulent opportunities.

Cost/Value Analysis

One particular action a data processing manager should initiate is a comparison of the costs involved in installing various preventive and/or ameliorative measures and the value of such measures. Table 5.1 is an example of such a cost/value analysis for the case problem. In this particular case, the data processing manager would recommend the storing of backup tapes at a remote location, the installation of security procedures, making backup copies of disks on tape, and the addition of a tape librarian. He would not recommend the construction of a fireproof tape vault, although it had been suggested. This would have cost $20,000, which would take a hundred years of probable loss to amortize.

Principles of Control

Fixed control rules cannot be established, but are dependent upon individual situations. The concentration, therefore, should be on analyzing specific situations and then recommending the installation of certain controls. Two rules should help:

1. The degree of control is directly proportional to the importance of the data.
2. The volume of transactions directly affects the degree and type of controls that can be established.

Controls for any system, therefore, cannot be designed arbitrarily. The importance and the volume of transactions must be considered. The greater the importance of the data, the more rigorous should be the controls. As the volume of transactions increases, the degree and type of controls should be modified; otherwise, extra machine time may cost more than the value of the controls.

The integrity of any data processing system can be maintained only if rigorous controls are established. Furthermore, after establishment they

TABLE 5.1   COST/VALUE ANALYSIS

Hazard	Cost of Loss, $	Annual Prob-ability of Occurrence, %	Annual Cost of Loss, $ (Col. 2) × (Col. 3)	Net Savings, $
Serious fire	5,000,000	0.01	500	
Minor fire or malicious damage	200,000	0.1	200	
Subtotal			700	
Annual cost of remote backup tapes			200	
				500
Error				
One tape	20	100 times a year	2,000	
Both tapes	1,000	5	50	
Theft and fraud	500,000	1	5,000	
Subtotal			7,050	
Annual cost of installing security procedures and adding tape librarian			6,000	
				1,050
Accidental damage to disk	1,000	5 times a year	5,000	
Copy disks on tape			2,000	
				3,000
Total				4,550

should be used constantly. The campaign against human error, machine error, system breakdown, theft, and fraud is continual. Only through diligen attention to controls can systems survive.

The perfect system would have controls that provide 100 percent protection, but cost nothing. Since this is impossible, there is a continual compromise in designing and installing controls. The quest should be for the maximum degree of control at the least cost.

SUMMARY

The purpose of input controls is to eliminate as far as possible input errors—the most usual source of errors in a data processing system. In a batch system, the normal means of such control are logs, item counts, control totals, and hash totals. In an on-line system, examples are sequential numbering, check points, batch totals, reconstruction of undecipherable messages by human beings, and parity checking.

The purposes of computer controls are to validate input data, to ensure that such data goes through each program, and to check hardware controls. Validity checking is done through character mode tests, self-checking numbers, checks to determine reasonableness and consistency, and comparison with tables of legitimate items. Examples of run-to-run checks are file identity verification, record counts, control totals, and sequence checks. In on-line systems these controls are transaction log, check point, return message, terminal limitation, daily listing, file dump, file scan, and hard copy at terminals.

The data processing department is only one segment of any data processing system. Controls are needed, therefore, both outside and inside data processing. These controls should provide for continuity of operations and for the effective use of people and equipment. Control groups and written procedures are needed outside data processing to reconcile discrepancies. Within data processing, clearly documented procedures are needed. After such procedures are installed, supervision and training are needed to ensure that they are followed. Whether it is a batch or an on-line system, the noncomputer controls are essentially the same. In both cases, a strong effort against an "it doesn't matter" attitude is needed.

It is probable that many companies are most vulnerable in the data processing department. A catastrophe there could put the company out of business unless proper measures are taken. This risk has been too often ignored by management. Catastrophes such as fire, explosion, floods, hurricanes, tidal waves, and eathquakes have razed computer installations. There has been sabotage; damage due to environmental conditions; and loss because of power difficulties, ruined programs and/or data, external radiation, mechanical or electronic breakdown, operator error, data theft, and fraud. The possibility of loss is very real, and legal action against data processing managers and company officials is becoming more common.

Preventive measures to be considered include location of the computer center, site construction, limited access to computer center and data, and strict observance of good operating procedures. On-line systems are particularly vulnerable to theft of programs and data. Some ameliorative measures are decentralization of computer facilities, backup installations, safes, and insurance.

It is probable that no computer installation can afford to employ all possible preventive and ameliorative measures. The computer manager should do a cost/value analysis in which he compares the cost of various controls against the probable loss if they are not installed. He should then recommend only those controls where the probability of loss exceeds the cost of installing the controls.

Fixed controls rules cannot be established. Both the numebr of transactions and the importance of the data should be considered. When controls are established, the data processing manager should ensure that they are always followed—without exception.

EXERCISES

1. Controls in data processing systems have been segregated into input controls, computer controls, noncomputer controls, and preservation of assets. Within each area, give the purposes of such controls and examples of specific controls to be considered.

2. Discuss the similarities of, and the differences between, on-line and batch system controls. How is it possible to make an on-line system as safe, if not more safe, than a batch system? If it is not possible, why?

3. What are the purposes of input controls? What measures for ensuring the accuracy and completeness of input data should be considered in a batch system? In an on-line system? What is each measure designed to accomplish?

4. What are the purposes of computer controls? What measures of computer controls should be considered in an on-line system? In a batch system? What is each measure designed to accomplish?

5. What are the purposes of noncomputer controls? Why is it necessary to have such controls both within and without data processing? What are the differences between, and the similarities of, such controls in on-line and batch systems?

6. What are the potential hazards of data processing to a company? What preventive and ameliorative measures should be considered as means of lessening the possible effects of such hazards?

7. The cost/value method of deciding which controls to recommend

has been discussed in this chapter. Discuss this method and evaluate it. What other methods can you devise for deciding which controls to recommend?

8. The number of items of information and the value of the information are two factors that influence the choice of controls to be recommended. What other factors should be considered? Why?

6 ◀ EXTERNAL RELATIONS

It is recognized that the emphasis in the United States today is on replacing or expanding computers currently in use rather than on getting new and larger computers. For organizations with such plans this chapter will not be too relevant. Nevertheless, there are thousands of new installations each year in this country. Furthermore, in developing countries, first installations of computers predominate. This chapter is aimed primarily at organizations installing computers for the first time.

A data processing installation does not operate in a vacuum. On the contrary, it influences and is influenced by its environment. In order to optimize these influences, a positive effort is necessary in the external relations of data processing. External relations are defined as relationships with people and organizations outside data processing. These people and organizations may be in or may be outside the same department or company.

The purposes of good external relations of data processing may be divided into four areas, to:

1. Influence decisions.
2. Instigate cooperation.
3. Allay fears.
4. Educate people so that they can
   (a) furnish better input data to the computer, and
   (b) make more effective use of data processing.

This chapter, therefore, has been separated into four sections: influencing decisions, instigating cooperation, allaying fears, educating people.

INFLUENCING DECISIONS

The Conservative Approach

An early contact of the data processing analyst with top management is desirable, to influence the latter's decision to approve the installation of a computer. In trying to get this approval, a major tendency has been to oversell rather than to understate the advantages to the company. If a computer is ordered because the advantages are exaggerated, top management expects more than it should. When its expectations are not fulfilled, it may take action to realize them. This action could take the form of bringing in new people to run the computer or, as sometimes happens, a retrenchment in data processing operations.

Management should be aware of the limitations of the computer, and these limitations should be considered in establishing the objectives for data processing. It is not enough to assume that management understands these limitations—misunderstandings have led to costly reprogramming.

Even with the best of intentions, estimates of the time and cost to "get on the air" with a computer have been far too low. An example of this is the often-repeated advice to a manager estimating the man-months necessary to program applications for a new computer: Make allowances for everything that can go wrong; include everything necessary to complete the works; be liberal; and then double the estimate.

Although top management may have been told, as honestly and completely as possible, what the costs of installing the system were estimated to be, it subsequently may be appalled at the heavy initial investment, the continuing high level of costs, and the length of time before a return is earned on the investment. In presenting figures to management for the approval of a computer, one should allow for contingencies: exaggerate expenses, personnel, and the time needed, but minimize profit and savings.

Progress Reports

With the many pitfalls in the installation of a computer, management should receive regular reports. These should start with the beginning of the feasibility study and continue until the new system is in full operation. Once the system is operative, data processing should report to management just as any operating department reports. Perhaps the objective of these reports is to "stamp out" surprises. One method is a regularly submitted written report. Another way to keep management informed of the progress in installing a data processing system is to appoint a steering committee. Those installing the system can make regular reports to the committee and enlist its aid to determine where the computer can be used.

Data for Management Decisions

Another connection of data processing with management is the furnishing of data to enable optimal decisions. This data should be timely and reliable. If there is a probability that a report will be delayed, those who are scheduled to receive the report should be informed as quickly as possible. This gives them time to plan alternative courses of action. Waiting until the scheduled date and then telling the manager he will not get the report on time, or merely not delivering it, may delay or nullify possible alternatives.

If data processing has an indication that a figure on the report may not be reliable, the user should be informed. This may stop him from taking hasty action based on the incorrect report. Furthermore, it will enhance his reliance on other data furnished him, without warning of possible unreliability. If such warnings become relatively frequent, however, the report user may tend to believe that all reports from this source are unreliable. The appearance of any such questionable data should instigate an analysis to remove the basic cause of the incorrect data.

People, in general, like to deride mistakes in computer output. Newspapers never print stories about the millions of correct bills or checks. Only the grotesque mistakes are considered to be newsworthy. No mention is made of the thousands of successful computerized payroll systems. A large company experienced many mistakes in wage payments. The employees went on strike because of this, and the company was forced to revert to a manually produced payroll. This story appeared in many newspapers.

INSTIGATING COOPERATION

Middle Management

A data processing system has little chance of success without the cooperation of middle management, which can express unacceptance in subtle ways. Applications in which the computer can be used to advantage may not be disclosed. Input data may not be accurate and on time. Every error that data processing makes will be magnified, while the successes will be minimized. Middle management influences the cooperation that data processing gets from practically every level within the organization. Data processing should, therefore, make every effort to enlist middle management throughout the company into the data processing "team." Data processing failures have been attributed to the failure of supervisory personnel to comply with the detailed new procedures.

The installation of a computer-based data processing system may require breaking departmental walls that have been many years in the making. It might sweep out whole ranks of supervisors and middle management. Even if these do not occur, changes in workload must be correlated with changes in budget and personnel: otherwise, inequities will appear. "Foot dragging" and semideliberate failures often plague the system after new procedures are installed.

The computer may become the center of a power struggle between those who built the old system and those who designed the new one. It may become the prize in a struggle by departmental heads for its control. If such struggles are not settled equitably and without rancor, the loser might try to neutralize the decision by demanding a computer for his department, since "the service of the central computer is not adequate." Such struggles, regardless of how they are solved, damage an organization, and therefore they must be foreseen and handled properly to be avoided.

Few managers are afraid that the computer will put them out of a job. Younger managers surely have welcomed the computer more than older managers. The older managers often have changed their attitudes when reliable information furnished by data processing has helped them. Optimistic predictions that are not fulfilled, however, often lead to negative reactions.

In order to get the cooperation of middle management, it is suggested that, once the decision is made to conduct a feasibility study, managers be notified as rapidly as possible. They should be told how the anticipated effects of the computer will relate to them. Furthermore, their ideas should be considered carefully in the systems analysis, design, and installation phases. If at all possible, their ideas should be included in the new system and they should be given credit for these ideas. The effectiveness of any system depends upon how well systems designers and managers communicate. It is the responsibility of these designers to relate to the managers and understand their functions and responsibilities. Before scheduling a talk with a manager, the systems designer should do his "homework." This involves examining all available material of staffing, objectives, functions, and other company data. It is presumptuous for a designer to schedule a talk with a manager prior to having done this.

Other Personnel within the Company

Those who will be affected by the computer are a vital target of the external relations of data processing. Unless they are included on the " computer team," they may interfere with the efficient operation of the data processing system. These acts can be of both omission and commission. In the former category is the failure to volunteer information concerning better ways of doing things. Other examples are withholding knowledge of exceptions to general procedures in the current system, and of impending discrepancies that are still at a stage where they can be averted. On the commission side, "foot dragging" may result in data's reaching the data processing division after deadlines. Even if the data arrives on time, it may contain errors. A relatively small number of errors has the capability, if not discovered, of negating the efforts of a team that carefully planned and installed a data processing system. Even if discovered, corrections of such errors may result in reports being delayed beyond the time they were required.

The planning, installing, and using of the products of data processing require and affect people. Ignoring this fact can result in failure. Furthermore, the full cooperation of all personnel in a company is essential to the success of its data processing system. The attitudes of people throughout the company can be one of the most critical factors affecting the success or failure of a computer system. Human beings plan and design adequate programs. They must be relied upon to furnish accurate input at the proper time. Resentment may cause employees to withhold information during the system-design stage with regard to the job to be done. This, of course, increases the difficulties of system design. After installation, tardy, erroneous, or missing data can disrupt the system.

Relationships External to the Company

It pays to maintain good relations with other computer users. If the other users have the same make and model of computer, they can provide backup. In case of a major malfunction, a local source that will lend or rent computer time helps. High-priority applications can be run there while one's own computer is being repaired. The major problems in this area are the timing of use and the compatibility of equipment and operating systems.

A clear understanding is needed in advance with regard to priorities and when the backup computer can be used. Most of these backup agreements are invoked only during the night or on weekends. Even when the backup system is larger than the computer it backs up, programs should be run when there is no emergency. This will prove that the computer is really available for backup services. Furthermore, if this practice is followed, one is sure that the operating system on the backup computer does not impinge on program operations. In some cases it has been necessary to write special programs so that particular applications can be run on backup equipment. This is especially true for backup computers with smaller configurations than those of the computers they are backing up.

Users associations are valuable sources of routines, programming aids, management techniques, and maintenance procedures that have proved successful in other installations. Computer users can share experiences and inform manufacturers of types of difficulties they have encountered.

Professional associations, such as the Data Processing Management Association and the Association for Computing Machinery, are beneficial to data processing managers. The monthly and annual meetings provide educational information. Informal lines of communication established there can be valuable. These contacts can provide access to similar installations. In some cases their programs can be used with only small changes. Furthermore, these meetings generate backup agreements and are a source of experienced personnel. In the case of electric accounting machinery, which is often operated in conjunction with computers, permission to use another's equipment has helped installations to complete peak workloads on time.

The saving of rental can be effected for a machine used only one or two days a month.

ALLAYING FEARS

Even though they may not be conscious of it, many employees fear the introduction of a computer into the company. Whether or not the computer will result in some adverse effects on them, the fears should be allayed. Otherwise these psychological reactions can be detrimental to a smoothly running company. In order to take the best action, careful study of what causes such fears should be made.

Reasons for Fear

Reasons why an employee is afraid of a computer include the following:

1. He may be afraid of things about which he has little or no knowledge—fear of the unknown.
2. He may fear loss of his job.
3. He may fear loss of his current skills and fear the need to learn new skills so that he can remain useful. In learning these new skills, he may fear having to do things beyond his ability or those he does not like to do.
4. He may fear routine, repetitive work, which increases the gap between clerks and administrative positions. The possibility of advancement thus will be lessened.
5. He may be forced to take a reduction in salary.
6. His role in the company may be downgraded. The "kingdom" of duties and subordinates he built up may be destroyed.
7. He may resist change. This factor, and to varying degrees the preceding ones, are more pronounced with older people than with younger ones.

Palliatives

Fears and uncertainty can be minimized only by a vigorous, positive program for orienting personnel. The feasibility study should be accompanied by an announcement from top management through planned conferences, meetings, directives, briefings, and articles in newspapers. All personnel should be told why the study is being made, what might happen, and how they will be affected. Furthermore, they should receive periodic progress reports. All attempts should be made to minimize displacements. If relocation and/or training is necessary, plans should be made as early as possible. In such planning, one normally assures that any necessary personnel reductions will be taken care of by attrition or by reassignment to suitable work. Those displaced by the computer should be given opportunities to qualify for jobs created by the computer. Adequate monetary and intangible compensation should be assured for all personnel.

Studies show that resistance to the introduction of a computer is prevalent and that it takes many forms. Loss of social acceptance and status and of economic or psychological security predominate. Resistance comes mainly from experienced employees with years of service in the company. These employees mainly are middle managers or clerical workers.

One of three approaches is generally used to overcome resistance to the computer. Sometimes nothing is done. This assumes that, after a period of time, those who are resisting will become resigned to the situation. At other times, the use of authority is the major weapon. Either employees stop their resistance or they are dismissed or relocated. A combination of education and patience is used in other firms.

Most of the fears mentioned previously have a common panacea—education. Learning what a computer is, how it will be used, and how it will affect the worker should reduce this fear of the unknown.

Many different media can be used in educating employees to accept the computer. As soon as management determines that a feasibility study will be made, someone, preferably the head of the company, should make an announcement. Company newspapers, special leaflets, or meetings with supervisors, but preferably directly with all employees, are the normal means of such announcements. They should express company policies concerning the impact of the computer (if one ultimately is ordered) on both the company and the employees. Normally, the policy is that new hirings will be on a temporary basis until those displaced by the computer have transferred to new positions. No employee should be lowered in grade or in salary. Those whose jobs are preempted by the computer will be trained for comparable positions. In decentralized companies, if a geographical transfer is needed, moving and relocation expenses will be paid for by the company.

Most problems can be solved if management sincerely believes that employees are among the most valuable resources of the company, and is concerned with employee welfare. The program, however, should be planned and timed properly. Before rumors start, company policy should be determined. This policy and the anticipated impact of the computer on all employees should be explained to those who may be affected.

People are the most important part of a system. Computers only help a system work well. Without the part that the people play, almost any system fails. Each person is an individual. His status and authority are important to him, as is his on-and-off-the-job life. All decisions, therefore, should consider their effects on individuals.

EDUCATING PEOPLE

Suppliers of Input Data

A computer system is no more accurate than its input data. It may be possible to program the computer to locate every significant inaccuracy and to correct the data automatically. If not, human effort in correcting the errors, and later in correcting errors in the corrections, will delay the output until it virtually becomes historical data rather than current information.

During the analysis and design phases, data processing should not concentrate on errors, since this might cause resistance to the new system. Instead, the new system should be installed. The effort should be toward correcting the error sources during the conversion period. Error-detecting devices can be included in the new system. Whenever an error of significance is detected, it should be corrected by the computer or the person who made the error. A record of errors should be kept so that corrective measures may be installed. Correcting unimportant errors will waste time and cause resentment of the new system.

Suppliers of data should know how a computer works and the kinds of errors it can locate. They should also understand the problems caused by errors not isolated by the computer. Furthermore, they should be informed of the uses made of the data they supply, the best ways of supplying the data, and the impact on the company of nonreliable input data. In order to accomplish these educational aims and to enlist the suppliers of data on the "computer team," an education program should be designed to orient them toward the new system. It should show them better methods of doing their work, and should allay their fears.

Report Users

Top Management. The data processing system may have been fragmented when it was a manual or an electric accounting machine operation. As such, each division may have decided the form in which its data should be maintained and the reports to be prepared from this data. In such systems it is common to find the same data in slightly different form in more than one of these fragmented systems. An educational program will inform managers about the additional possibilities of an integrated data processing system or of one system accessing the data maintained in another one. In such cases, managers have to concede that the form in which the data is maintained is not inviolable. The problem of ensuring that the data is the same in all systems is obviated. An educational program will help in achieving this purpose.

To forestall unreasonable expectations, management should be educated in the effective use of computers. Teaching them the rudiments of programming and having them write and debug a minor program should diminish the feeling that all they have to do is tell data processing what is desired. Results will be immediately forthcoming.

It is the exception rather than the rule that managers are fully aware of the possibilities of operations-research techniques. The amount of data that can be stored and the speed of calculation enables the computer to use such techniques in normal business operations. On occasions, decisions based on intuition will be better than those predicated on operations-research techniques. Overall, however, better decisions will result from the use of operations research. It is imperative that management be made fully aware of operations-research techniques.

Middle Management. If middle management knows little or nothing concerning computers and what they can achieve, there is no hope of expecting it to use the computer to advantage. A course should be designed for middle-level managers in order to increase the probability that the computer will be used well. This course should show how the computer accomplishes its functions. It might also help give abbreviated courses in machine-language programming and in higher-level languages, such as FORTRAN or COBOL, whichever is more appropriate. Once they have this knowledge, they can be introduced to the principles of systems analysis and design and the potentials of real-time operations. Examples of uses in other companies, whether or not similar, will lead them into new and better uses of computers for themselves.

If managers do not know the capabilities of computers, they may overlook places where they can be used to advantage. Managers who have received long reports for years and whose personnel have analyzed them manually for exceptions may be distrustful of exception reports. They may feel that the computer will miss some of the exceptions that human workers would have found. Data processing should educate them in the advantages of exception reports and should enlist their aid in determining what constitutes an exception.

One technique that has achieved some success is to continue giving managers the long report. Exceptions the computer locates are indicated by several asterisks preceding and/or following the exception. Any exceptions located manually should be analyzed so that the manual technique that located the exception can be included in the computer program. As the number of these additional exceptions decreases toward insignificance, it has been common for a manager to suggest to data processing that he will be satisfied thereafter with the exception report. If this occurs, he should be furnished only the exception reports. The possibility of giving him the full report with the asterisks at a later data should be maintained. Thus, an occasional manual analysis either will assure him or will uncover additional exceptions to be used as the basis for improving the program.

Nonsupervisory Users of Computer Output. A one- or two-day course can be designed for those who will use the computer output. The purpose would be the same as that described earlier but, for nonsupervisory potential users of computer ouput, it probably will not be necessary to go into the amount of detail given middle management. It should be helpful, however, to educate these users in the potentials of exception reporting. Sometimes they fear that the computer will not uncover exceptions that they would have found. Furthermore, it is not at all uncommon to find these people re-adding computer tabulations to make sure the computer did not make a mistake. In the former example, the complete listing with the exceptions indicated (as described previously) will help. In the latter, sooner or later they will find (if the programming is sufficiently accurate) that human beings make far more errors than computers do.

SUMMARY

In getting management to approve the installation of a computer, the data processing analyst should be very conservative in his estimates. The attempt should be to undersell, rather than to oversell, the computer so that management will not expect too much from its investment. Regular progress reports should be submitted to management during and after the installation of the system.

Strong efforts should be made to enlist middle management on the "computer team." The computer should be kept out of any power struggle for its control. Once the decision is made to do a feasibility study, middle management should be kept informed and involved in the design of the system. They, too, should extend cooperation outside of the company, for it will be to their advantage to have good relationships with other users and professional associations.

Current information concerning company plans and a policy of treating personnel fairly are significant factors in allaying fears. Top management, middle management, suppliers of input data, and users of data processing output should design training courses to improve the effects of data processing on the company and to encourage computer-oriented attitudes among personnel.

EXERCISES

1. Some managers of data processing use computer jargon in discussing their problems with top management and in requesting funds. Others translate their requirements into a language that management understands. Discuss these two approaches.

2. What are the advantages and disadvantages of using a conservative approach in predicting accomplishments of, and of getting funds from management for, data processing?

3. Discuss the problems that have emerged between middle management and data processing when a computer-based system is installed. What can be done to minimize these problems?

4. What are some of the difficulties that nonsupervisory employees can cause in a data processing system? What steps should be taken to obviate these problems?

5. How can relationships of data processing with outside organizations help the efficient operation of data processing? What should the manager of data processing do to foster good relationships with outside organizations?

6. What are some of the reasons why people often fear computers? What actions should a company take to allay these fears?

7. Discuss educational programs that a company can initiate to improve the use of the computer by the various echelons of non-computer personnel. Why are such programs needed? What should they include? What are they designed to accomplish?

7 ◀ TRAINING

Ever since computers were first introduced to the business world, the literature has pointed out continually that education and training are necessary if computers are to be used better. Like the weather—everyone complains about it, but nobody does anything about it. Neither industry nor state or local government have extensive programs for sending executives to school full time to get the needed education. Many, however, have paid for evening courses for their employees. The federal government has a fairly extensive program of part- and full-time education for employees.

On the other hand, colleges and universities have been particularly non-responsive to industry's needs. A series of articles in 1971 and 1972 claimed greatly improved college curriculums—but improved in what? To the individual writer's own ideas of what should be taught? Independent research in late 1971 found that most often the computer-related courses depend primarily upon the interests and abilities of the faculty. As the result of this chasm between the educators and the real world of industry, it is not surprising to note the minimal impact of college data processing education on business.

This chapter differentiates between education and training, and discusses how training rather than education is particularly applicable to computer systems. The discussion is separated into two categories: outside data processing and within it. In each of these areas, training is related to each of the major types of personnel involved.

EDUCATION VERSUS TRAINING

Definitions

Education and training are differentiated according to their purpose and the duration of the period of instruction. Education is considered to be comparatively long-range instruction intended generally to broaden the knowledge of the student. Training, on the other hand, is comparatively short-range instruction, designed to increase the knowledge of the student in a specific area. The data processing professional associations evidently consider them to be distinct for the Association for Computing Machinery has one national committee for education and another for digital computer programmer training. Many local chapters of the Data Processing Management Association have separate education and training committees.

Advantages and Disadvantages of Education

There are advantages and disadvantages in educating employees. From the long-range point of view, the major advantage is that the employee, having broadened his scope, will be able to operate at a higher level. Since he has learned new techniques, such as management science, he is in a better position to improve existing systems, both by means of automation and by better methods. Although his value to the company has increased, the disadvantage is that his acquired knowledge also makes him more valuable to another company. In government, when an employee is educated at government expense, he is usually committed to continue for a specified period in the employment of the organization that financed his education. His employer, however, does not exact such a promise and must find ways and means of retaining him after education is completed.

From a short-range standpoint, the company has additional expense and replacement problems when an employee is sent to a college or university for full-time educational purposes. Presumably, the function he was performing will still have to be done, and a replacement will be needed. Thus, there is a duplication of salary, since the salaries for two individuals must be paid while the original employee is being educated and while the replacement is being trained. An additional expense is the educational costs, which often are assumed by the company or agency. A large majority of companies pay all or a part of the costs of computer-related courses for employees.

Advantages and Disadvantages of Training

The primary advantage of training, as contrasted with education, is that the period of training is shorter. Thus, the expense to the company is minimized. Further, there is a longer lapse of time than is the case in education before the employee will be valuable enough for another company to recruit him. Usually, training is oriented to the function the employee will be, or is, performing. The company benefits by the work accomplished as a result of this training. The major disadvantage is that the employee's training is restricted to a particular area. Normally his scope will not be broadened sufficiently for him to operate at a higher level than the one for which he is trained.

TRAINING OUTSIDE DATA PROCESSING

Executives

Probably the most fundamental data processing problem is the need for managerial officials to acquire the knowledge that will enable them to comprehend and use automatic data processing (ADP) to optimal advantage. Orientation of executives is a responsibility of those installing and/or using a computer. This formidable problem deserves the serious attention of top management. Executives must gain a better understanding of the true potential of integrated systems and management by exception, if the company is to achieve anything near optimal use of the computer. The federal government has an interagency training program consisting of executive seminars in ADP; executive seminars in operations research, ADP, and personnel management; ADP and financial management; and ADP orientation courses. The Department of Defense Computer Institute (DODCI) was established to orient DOD flag and general officers and supergrade employees to computer and related subjects, to lessen their dependence on contractors. Within a year after its inception, another course was established for the next lower echelon of officers and civilians. A class was introduced to a course there by an Army executive's statement that the modern manager did not have to be a computer technician, but did have to understand the fundamental opportunities, limitations, and cost and time factors in using computers.

Recognition that executive training is vitally needed, however, is not limited to the federal government. The Data Processing Management Association and the American Management Association have established and are conducting seminars in data processing for executives. In the past five years a new educational medium has emerged—companies established to provide courses for managers and for other levels of employees. Every month, executives in a large manufacturing concern were given 2-hour seminars in the optimal use of computers and in the management sciences. A public utility, in conjunction with a new computer installation, insisted that all executives take an orientation course in data processing. These are only a few of the many examples that can be cited to show the recognition of the problem and the actions taken to solve it.

Training of executives is considered in two categories: informal and formal. The former consists of reading and day-by-day contacts with data processing at work. By its very nature this type of training is unstructured, and reading tends to be postponed because of the pressure of other duties. Although the results may be excellent in some areas, other subjects of extreme importance may be overlooked or treated superficially. Expecting top management to educate itself often fails because of lack of time and uneven training.

If the knowledge and ability to teach are available within the company or agency, it can run its own executive orientation courses, or it can run them with the assistance of the manufacturer or consultants. An advantage of in-house executive orientation courses, in addition to the financial savings, is that the courses can be tailored to the company. Examples used may be specific ones drawn from daily problems. Hours of class can be adjusted to periods when the executive's time is most available. Time lost going from the office to the classroom is minimized. The most apparent disadvantages of this provincial training are the absence of new ideas from external sources and the tendency to withdraw executives from particular sessions for "emergencies" that occur suddenly.

The suggestion that the manufacturer's assistance be accepted in this course is predicated on the assumption that the computer has been ordered and possibly delivered. If the manufacturer does not charge for the course, it should be less expensive than using outside consultants or commercial training companies. To lay the groundwork for future sales, it is to the manufacturer's advantage to have the computer installation used well. His assistance, therefore, will tend to be more objective than if the computer had not been ordered. Another suggestion is that, for effectiveness, the ADP presentation to top management should be made so that possibilities and problems will be known. Someone from data processing can make this presentation, since he will be familiar with these possibilities and problems. If no person in the company has the capacity to make the presentation, an outside consultant or commercial training company can be engaged. Time will be needed, however, for these instructors to study operations and to prepare material for the presentation. This approach gives the maximum orientation in the least possible time. The consultant or the commercial training firm probably has more ADP knowledge than is available "in-house." Furthermore, it avoids the problem of executives being oriented by their subordinates.

Most executives need greater depth and broader, more extensive knowledge of data processing areas. When acquired, this knowledge corrects the fairly common inability of executives to state their information specifications in any but the most general terms. Executives need to learn principles, not current practices, so that they can be applied to the various problems confronted in work.

Executives should learn that by using simulation techniques on a computer, different plans of action can be considered under almost any number of varying circumstances before the pragmatic test. Companies reporting good acceptance and useful results from operation-research applications tend to follow simultaneous application and training programs. Some companies use rigorous, comprehensive in-plant training sessions conducted by company operations-research personnel and/or competent outside specialists. One company put on a "road show" for personnel and departments concerned. They were shown how the model worked, the input data required, and what the output was, the role of the computer, and how the results could be used. Understanding, cooperation, and a real sense of participation were the products of the exhibit. Another training method uses computerized management games to introduce executives to the concepts and potentials of simulation. This can be a fairly useful training device in bringing out the basic interactions within a company.

Current orientation for executives in ADP is largely supplied by the manufacturers of computers. Although there is comparatively little expense in sending executives to such courses, and although the instruction usually is of high caliber, it is understandable that such instruction is oriented toward one manufacturer. The emphasis is on making the user's system fit the hardware rather than on developing a system and selecting hardware to fit the system.

In order to overcome the provincialism of manufacturer orientation, some companies contract with universities, consultants, and/or commercial educational companies for such courses. While this is more expensive than sending their executives to "free" manufacturer's orientation courses, such companies believe that the broadened orientation pays off later in more nearly optimal systems. Another widely used solution is to send executives to institutes, symposiums, workshops, and classes run by universities, professional organizations, consultants, and commercial educational companies.

Individual industries run executive schools for the computer industry, some of them in cooperation with a manufacturer. In general, these courses are fairly successful, since they combine the latest planning and thinking by representatives of other companies and the ideas and approaches of the manufacturers. Courses or symposiums in ADP have been sponsored by banks, certified public accountants, lawyers, and home builders.

A 5-day course involving about 40 hours is suggested. The first 2 days can be devoted to the more basic details of hardware and programming. These should enable the executive to understand better how the computer operates and what must be done in order to write a computer program. The writing of one or two minor programs in machine language or in an assembler language might be beneficial. This, however, is controversial. A survey of executives who had such orientation indicated that they found little or no benefit from such programming experience. The exclusion of programming practice would shorten the course by one day. The last three days should include the determination of requirements and the design of a system that will satisfy these requirements. The systems area should include real-time systems, time-sharing, information storage and retrieval. It should also cover the entire cycle, from the gathering of data at, or close to, the source through its storage, retrieval, and processing, and to its ultimate use in making optimum decisions by means of exception reports and management sciences. Some time may be used to acquaint the executives with the pitfalls of ADP and steps that may be taken to avoid them. The emphasis of the course should be on having the executives learn principles, not practices. Examples of carefully selected applications from various data processing systems, however, should be sprinkled liberally through the latter part of the course.

Middle Management

Not so evident as in the case of the executive group is the very real need for ADP training of middle management. This is aimed primarily to ensure the cooperation of this group and its contribution of new ideas to the system. Regardless of how good the computer is, and how complete and valuable the system may be, uncooperative people can ruin nearly all possibilities of success. Personnel responsible for the operations may be ignorant of the capabilities of the computer and may be unable to evaluate how they will be affected. They may, through fear, take courses of action detrimental to the success of the system.

The problems of informal training of middle management are substantially identical to those of executives. Additional elaboration is not needed. orientation courses, such as those for executives, plus a little more depth in systems analysis and design, have been beneficial for middle management. The added depth in systems work furnishes them background information for suggesting system changes that benefit their work. A little programming instruction enables them to understand how long it takes to write and machine-test a program and what difficulties can be caused by changes after the program is completed. Possibly, this understanding might motivate them to request computer programs when lead time is sufficient to write and test the programs prior to deadline dates. Also, it may temper their requests for minor improvements or changes in the product.

A 2-week course of about 80 hours is suggested. All topics for executives are applicable to midddle management. In addition there is sufficient time to write one or two minor programs in a higher-level language, and laboratories can be used to solve case problems in systems design and the management of data processing.

Personnel Indirectly Connected with ADP

People who will be affected by the computer or who think they will be affected should be told as early as possible about:

1. Company plans for the computer.
2. Company policies concerning personnel moving into the computer division.
3. Policies concerning personnel displaced by the computer.

This is an orientation course concerning computer policies, and therefore the personnel or industrial-relations department of the company should be in charge of the course. Policies concerning the personnel should be authenticated by the president or director of the company.

Regular sessions can be held for 1 or 2 hours, not more than once a month, during the period of the feasibility and applications studies, conversion, and initial operation of the computer. The purpose of the course is to promote understanding and acceptance of the computer. The instructor, therefore, should have teaching capability and an understanding of the overall system, data processing techniques, and the company and its policies.

Some companies do not conduct seminars or meetings at which these items are discussed. Instead, they use company periodicals, bulletin boards, or fliers to ensure that the information is disseminated. The means is not important, as long as the news is issued from authoritative sources rather than being distorted by gossip.

Retraining is more readily accepted when it is at the company's expense and on company time. Some employees, however, will anticipate the effects of changes and will take night courses on their own in order to improve their qualifications and advance with the changes brought about by the computer. Others, unfortunately, seek new jobs, even though their own positions are not in danger. Those being transferred should be regarded as promoted, not displaced, and their training should be considered as training for a promotion. Since the success or failure of this program depends on the attitudes of management and the instructor, this is of special importance. If an employee is not transferred, but the job content of his position changes, he needs retraining to assure his technical knowledge of the new system. If he cannot be won over, it may be necessary to transfer the supervisor or the subordinates before commencing retraining.

Personnel Providing Input for the Computer

Regardless of how good a computer program is, its value is limited by the accuracy and completeness of its input. If the error can be corrected by the computer and the computer is programmed to make the correction, the only loss is computer time. If it cannot be corrected automatically, but is discovered by the computer in accordance with the program controls, the input may be rejected for manual correction. The output will probably be incorrect to some degree if the error is not discovered.

In order to limit the amount of input errors, personnel providing input to the computer should be trained in practical methods of error elimination. Although this training normally is sponsored by the department providing the data, the data processing department has at least the collateral responsibility of producing educational material as a by-product of its work. Also, it can perform part of the teaching. A number of other methods has been used. For example, a company that installed a large computer reported a successful program during which a cadre of data suppliers was trained. They, in turn, trained other data suppliers in their home departments. A bank prepared a special instruction film to bring home to data-originating departments the importance of accuracy.

Personnel providing input should be given the broad aspects of the entire system and specific details of the part in which they are involved. They should be shown the consequences of incorrect or incomplete input, examples of common errors, and the means of avoiding or correcting such errors before input to the computer. The importance of "selling" this program is great. Incorrect input can sabotage a system. Failure of the program can result in disenchantment of management and possibly in the elimination of the entire program.

TRAINING WITHIN DATA PROCESSING

Manager of ADP

Success or lack of success of the ADP installation may be focused on the ability of its manager. Although it is not essential that he be an expert in systems analysis and design, programming, and computers and/or electric accounting machines (EAM), general knowledge of these areas helps. Therefore, if he lacks this background, he should take a general computer-orientation course, such as that for executives. One given by the computer manufacturer and directed toward the computer selected will be helpful.

Management of the ADP installation is a full-time position, and if the manager spends his time writing and machine checking programs, this probably will be done at the expense of his other and more important duties. Nevertheless, some knowledge of ADP difficulties will help him to review estimates of programming time more effectively. The manager should take a course on the machine selected and in the programming language that most normally will be used in the installation. He should write and test a fairly simple program. Thereafter, he can apply the knowledge gained in planning and directing but should not spend his time in writing programs.

Systems analysis and design are areas in which the advice of the computer manager can be extremely beneficial. It is, therefore, a type of training in which a fairly high degree of concentration will result in large benefits. Unfortunately, relatively few courses are truly beneficial in systems analysis and design. These will be discussed under training recommendations for systems analysts. The computer manager should take the same course conducted for his systems analysts. A possible substitution is one offered by a professional organization, such as the American Management Association, or a commercial firm. A state government reported success with a week-long course for computer managers and head systems-analysts, designed and taught by a consultant. The course was repeated several times until virtually all systems analysts in the department had received the benefits of the instruction.

If the data processing installation also has EAM, knowledge of the capabilities and relative speeds of each machine will be helpful. This information can be obtained from orientation courses given by the manufacturer or from on-the-job training.

Informal training of data processing managers too often is neglected. Visits to other data processing installations will pay large dividends, since supervisors will be in a position to benefit from the experiences of others. From the same standpoint, attendance at meetings and symposiums of professional organizations and universities will broaden the manager's knowledge. Also helpful are subscriptions to current professional periodicals and a library of professional books for everyone connected with data processing.

Systems Analysts

Reports are continually made that systems studies are conducted badly or not at all, and that higher degrees of sophistication are needed in the development of systems. Computer manufacturers provide little or no assistance here. Colleges and universities either do not recognize the need for such courses or, in general, have ignored the need. For years, the Association for Computing Machinery seemed to be more interested in the question of whether mathematics should be used for teaching the computer or whether the computer should be used for teaching mathematics. It was not until the end of 1972 that a curriculm recommendation of any real value in this area was published.[1] The recommendation as it appeared in *Curriculum Recommendations for Graduate Professional Programs in Information Systems,* copyright © 1972, Association for Computing Machinery, Inc., is as follows:

> Analysis of Organizational Systems
> > A1. Introduction to Systems Concepts
> > A2. Management Functions
> > A3. Information Systems for Management
> > A4. Social Implications of Information Systems
> Basic Tools for Systems Development
> > B1. Operations Analysis and Modeling
> > B2. Human and Organizational Behavior

1. R. L. Ashenhurst (Ed.), *Curriculum Recommendations for Graduate Professional Programs in Information Systems* (New York: Association for Computing Machinery, 1972), p. 373.

Computer and Information Technology
  C1.   Information Structures
  C2.   Computer Systems
  C3.   File and Communication Systems
  C4.   Software Engineering
Development of Information Systems
  D1.   Information System Analysis
  D2.   Information System Design
  D3.   Systems Development Projects

There is a long way between the proposal of such a curriculum and its implementation. An extensive examination of most university and college curriculums showed only a few of the listed courses actually being taught. Unfortunately, in most universities there is a comparatively long time between proposal of a course and its implementation. Protection of individual areas of interest is a strong deterrent to the installation of new and innovative courses of study. A school in one university was teaching seven of the recommended courses and had proposed (but had not yet approved) three more. The other three courses were taught at another school in the university. Another university was also teaching 7 of the 13 courses. At the time of writing of this chapter the author was unable to find any proposals for expansion.

The lack of adequately trained personnel continues to be a deterrent to adequate systems design. This deficiency is more noticeable in smaller companies that have no source of systems analysts upon which to draw. There are many training courses, but the implementation of high school and college courses should be encouraged.

Systems analysis courses have been run sporadically by companies for their own personnel. In general, they have not been very successful, owing to inadequate local ability in systems and/or lack of teaching ability of the lecturers. Other disadvantages of local courses are the limited horizons of those offering the courses and the lack of interplay between participants from various companies.

In the federal government the Civil Service Commission offers courses in systems analysis and design. The military services have attempted to solve the problem of systems analysis and design training by following the methods used in training computer programmers. Examples of such courses are those offered by the Army Management Engineering Training Agency (AMETA) at Fort Benjamin Harrison for the Army, at Sheppard Air Force Base for the Air Force, and by the Navy Command Systems Support Activity (NAVCOSSACT) for the Navy. The Department of Defense Computer Institute (DODCI) has the responsibility of training command and control systems personnel, regardless of the military service involved.

One computer manufacturer offered a systems analysis course that was considered by some to be quite valuable. General coverage of data processing and systems analysis was taught, followed by work on organization charts, classification documents, grid charts, analysis of end requirements, analysis of files maintained, analysis of source documents flow-process charting, and systems design.

Another manufacturer has a systems research institute, but enrollment in the vast majority of cases has been limited to selected employees of the manufacturer. Correspondence courses in systems work are offered by several organizations.

Panelists at a worldwide meeting of the International Federation of Information Processing Societies were asked what training they provided for systems analysts. With one exception, all replied that the problem was recognized but that little was being done to solve it. The exception, however, stated that his country had a 2-year program for training systems analysts for government work. The course included 6 months of classroom work and 18 months on-the-job training with competent systems analysts.

A systems analyst needs training in system analysis not oriented specifically to ADP, computer orientation, source-data information conversion media and principles, systems theory, systems design (as differentiated from systems analysis), computer programming, and management sciences. It helps to have the analyst take a programming course. After its completion he should write and test a fairly simple computer program. Thereafter he should concentrate on his systems analysis work. He will be in a position to do a better job because of his understanding of computer operations and programming problems, and because of his newly developed ability to communicate with programmers.

The shortage of systems analysts will increase rather than decrease at least through 1980. Facilities are available to train systems analysts, but not systems designers. The only foreseeable solutions lie in the courses offered by universities, consultants, commercial firms, and manufacturers. Perhaps some progressive university or commercial firm will recognize the need and offer an adequate course in systems design.

If a school should be established to train systems analysts, the course should last about six months and include systems analysis, computer orientation, source-data conversion media and principles, systems theory, systems design, computer programming, and the management sciences. Those who finish the course should be given practical training by experts. The trainees could help the experts in performing their functions, and at the same time learn their techniques.

Programmers

Programming schools provide only kindergarten training. Most programmer competence is acquired by experience. An employer should figure that training a beginner in computer programming will take at least six months. Approximately half of this time is spent in school. A month should be devoted to specialized programming techniques. The trainee should spend the balance of the time writing and machine checking a simple problem. The time, of course, varies, depending on the student's attitude and whether he has used data processing equipment previously.

The earliest computers were used by scientists who taught themselves to program. Since then, most programmer training has been done by computer manufacturers. Many companies, however, have their own programming courses. Those that run their own courses (usually with manufacturers' material) commonly do so because they feel that the courses can be adapted better to the specific needs of the company, and because they have better control over pacing the courses and motivating trainees. Usually, the course is a combination of classroom and laboratory work lasting a few weeks, after which the apprentice programmer goes to the programming department as a trainee. There he learns on-the-job local procedures and is given progressively more difficult problems. In the majority of cases it takes between six months and a year before the previously untrained individual is able to make a positive contribution to the programming effort of the company.

International Business Machines offers a basic course, designed to give the trainee an understanding of the principles of data processing and the operation of certain basic equipment such as punches, sorters, and calculating and printing machinery. The student is introduced also to block diagramming, flowcharting, and card and form design. Following this he is put into a computer programming course where he learns to program the machine selected. These courses vary in length, depending upon the computer and the language being taught. Instruction proceeds at a rapid pace and therefore the trainee must attend all sessions and work hard. On completion of those course the student knows the commands of the computer and how they can be used, but has not yet become a programmer. He needs further training in the more advanced techniques of programming, the programming customs of his company, and experience.

Heterogeneity of students in programming courses has limited the success of such courses to some degree. In a programming class there may be trainees with absolutely no knowledge of computers and others who have programmed different computers for years. If the course is taught at the speed at which the neophyte can proceed, the experienced programmers get little out of it. If, on the other hand, it keeps up with the abilities of the experienced programmers, the newcomers learn little. The course usually proceeds at a pace between these extremes.

Programmed textbooks, teaching machines, and computer-assisted instruction may present a solution to the problem of heterogeneity. Such teaching methods have been developed for several languages and have been incorporated into a manufacturer's programming course. The use of these books, however, opens the possibility of learning computer programming at home or from a correspondence school.

One company, in an effort to increase the knowledge gained by trainee programmers from the manufacturer's programming course, has contracted for a preprogramming course. The subjects covered include flowcharting, numeric systems, machine languages, input/output programming, verifying program accuracy, program languages, and steps in planning and programming computer applications, as well as accounting, auditing, and data protection. The trainees take this course prior to attending the manufacturer's basic and programming courses.

A large airline has reported more than anticipated benefits from in-house and third-party training courses. It has saved money by using video-taped instruction and in-house training. Furthermore, each trainee takes the right course when he is ready for it, not when a manufacturer's training center offers such a course. The results of this program indicate that a company training as few as five employees in one subject can recover the cost of the video equipment and a taped course. Although forced into such training by the unbundling of its computer manufacturer, the airline is completely pleased with the results.[2]

Many people anxious to get into the data processing field have seen television, newspaper, and magazine advertisements for commercial programming schools. Usually financed by G.I. program or their own money, they succumb to the promises of high-paying jobs without the necessity of a college education. A report by the American Federation of Information Processing Societies (AFIPS) estimated 15,000 programmer jobs opening up each year for noncollege educated applicants. About a third of these jobs are filled by transfers from within the company, leaving 10,000 for the 100,000 graduated from such schools each year. Furthermore, many of these 10,000 jobs are filled by college graduates not able to get better positions and those getting associate degrees from two-year colleges.

There are good commercial data processing schools and bad ones. At one extreme the student gets good training and the school places many of its students. At the other end are the schools that take the students' money and then go bankrupt. In between are schools that do not provide good training. Data processing managers recognize this, so they find it difficult to place such graduates. Others provide good training, but have difficulty in finding positions for those who complete the course. Still others provide good training and hire all graduates to work on contracts. In many cases, however, this work ends when the current contract is completed, and new graduates are

---

2. Edward J. Bride, "User Flexible, Efficient with Outside Training," *Computerworld* (July 7, 1971), pp. 1, 4.

used on later contracts. Studies indicate that the majority of commercial programming-school graduates either become computer operators or go into another field of work.

Console Operators

Many companies give the console operator either on-the-job training or a combination of a one-week course and on-the-job training. With either choice it is necessary to develop complicated self-sustaining trace routines or to allow the programmer time on the machine to test his program. Analyses show that it is much more economical to batch programs for machine testing, and to test them successively by the use of various routines. The programmer receives his output in the form of printed information, and can locate and correct errors at his desk. This is contrasted with debugging programs at the console of a machine that rents for hundreds of dollars per hour.

Console operators who also know programming can get better results in machine-testing programs than those who do not know programming. Therefore, many companies have their console operators take a programming course in addition to the console operator course. Although moving pictures have been reported as helpful in training computer operators, actual practice at the console has been more helpful.

In computers used for multiprogramming, it has been found that throughput can be increased by a skilled operator. Most of these operators have learned by rote the order in which to feed particular computer runs in order to increase throughput. On-the-job training and experiment appear to be the best methods of training operators to run multiprogramming computers effectively.

SUMMARY

Training is one of the more vital elements in the success or failure of data processing. This training should not be limited to personnel working in data processing, but should be extended to other employees whose work may interrelate with it.

Training should be provided for executives, middle management, those who will be affected by the computer, and those who provide input for the computer. No single course appears to be suitable for all groups. Instead, individual courses should be tailored to meet the needs of each group. In some cases, courses provided by the computer manufacturer, professional organizations, consultants, or commercial education and training companies will suffice. In others, in-house personnel or a combination of in-house people and instructors from outside the company may present a more beneficial course. Whichever is chosen, an optimal course should be based upon the specific needs of the group involved. Such training requirements should increase as direct communication and involvement of the executives with the equipment grows, and as their reliance on the system becomes firmer.

Training for personnel within the data processing activity is needed for managers, analysts, programmers, and operators. Such training may vary from a one-week course for computer operators to a two-year combination of a course and on-the-job training for systems analysts. Informal training has not been very successsful and normally is not recommended. The training for each category of personnel varies in length and content. The recommended courses, however, are needed if the data processing people are expected to develop and implement a system to meet the company's needs in dynamic situations.

EXERCISES

1. You are the director of training for an electronics supply firm with two locations in the same city. The firm is going directly from electric accounting machines to a rather sophisticated computer-based system. The system is a combination of real time for the inventory supply and of customer services work. Other operations, such as payroll, are batch processed. Develop a training program for the company.

2. Your company is going from one size of computer to a larger size, and intends to emulate during the early stages of the installation. What are the training requirements of this company? How would your answer change if the company were changing to the computer of another manufacturer? How would it change if it was decided to design a more sophisticated system instead of emulating?

3. Differentiate between education and training. What are the advantages and disadvantages of education as compared to training?

4. Discuss the training requirements of executives. In particular, include an answer to: You don't have to know how a car runs to drive it. Why should you have to know how a computer works to manage it?

5. Does a system analyst have to know how to program to be a good systems analyst? Discuss.

6. Compare the training requirements of analysts and programmers. In what ways do they differ and in what ways are they similar?

7. Commercial programmer-training schools are often advertised in newspapers. Discuss their value. Should they be licensed by the state? Should they be accredited by some such organization as a professional organization (education or computer)? What do you recommend? Justify your recommendation.

8 ◀ COSTS AND BUDGETING

Whether computers are profitable investments is a moot point, and has been argued time and time again. In the 1950s the challenge was to name one data processing installation that was saving money. While this author was lecturing in Paris, he was asked to name a computer installation in the United States that actually resulted in lower costs. A speaker at a Data Processing Management Association meeting said that only 40 percent of the data processing installations in the United States were successful. On the other hand, one can look at almost any current issue of a technical data processing publication and find one or more articles describing installations as extremely "successful."

What constitutes success of a data processing system? Is it the installation that costs least? Is it the one that produces the most lines of output? Is it the one in which the computer is productive the greatest percentage of the time? Is it the one that keeps its customers happiest? Is it the one that uses the most sophisticated methods? Is it the one that saves the most money, as contrasted to the one that has the greatest excess of value of products over its total costs? In analyzing success, this chapter considers both the cost of the installation and the value of its products. Methods of accumulatings costs are covered, followed by an analysis of items of cost in two major categories: one-time and continuing costs. The remainder of the chapter is devoted to methods of calculating the value of benefits, a comparison of costs versus such value, and budgeting for data processing.

COST CATEGORIES

One method of categorizing data processing costs is to use object-class accounts such as those used by the federal government. The four major categories under this system are personal services, contractual services, machine costs (including software), and other costs. Personal services include not only gross direct pay to individuals but also fringe benefits such as retirement payments, social security, health insurance, life insurance, paid vacations, and education and training. These fringe benefits constitute a significant per-

177

centage of gross wages and should not be eliminated from the costs of data processing. Contractual services include all payments under contract for data processing effort. They include not only payments for services of the contractor's personnel but also associated expenses such as per diem and travel costs. Machine and software costs include such expenses as rental, maintenance, purchase of spare parts, purchase price (if on a cash basis) or an amortized portion of the purchase price (if on an accrual basis), depreciation, and obsolescence. Software costs (whether rental or purchase) are also included in this category. If these costs are not combined, payments would be in different categories, depending upon the degree of unbundling of the vendor. Other costs include punch cards, paper, magnetic tape, wires, supplies, and communication services.

Another method of categorizing costs is the expenditure-account method. In this method each purpose of the expenditure is given a different expenditure-account number. If desired, the expenditure-account method can be combined with the object-class method, resulting in expenditures by purpose, by object class. Cost distributions, therefore, as treated in the rest of this chapter, are in accordance with the expenditure-account method.

ONE-TIME COSTS

Feasibility Study

There are conflicting views concerning whether the costs of the feasibility study should be included in the one-time costs of data processing. In evaluating the conflicting views, one should consider what would happen if the feasibility study concluded against the acquisition of a computer. The costs of the feasibility study could not be charged to a nonexistent process, but probably would be charged to general management improvement or some other overhead account. Furthermore, by the time the decision concerning whether to perform the applications study is made, all costs of the feasibility study will have been incurred. The costs of this study, therefore, should not affect the decision for acquiring or not acquiring a computer. For these reasons the costs of the feasibility study are excluded from the one-time costs of data processing. It is recommended instead that these costs be charged to a general management-improvement program.

Applications Study

There is substantial agreement, however, that once the decision is made to do the applications study, all costs of the gathering and analysis of the information and the designing of the data processing system should be charged as a one-time cost. The costs of an applications study include personal services (whether direct or for outside consultants), travel expenses, training for the study team, communications, and supplies. By far the largest proportion of these expenses is for personal services. The time of the systems analyst and the person with whom he talks are chargeable to the study. Travel expenses normally are for visits to other installations to look at systems in operation, trips to manufacturers' installations to look at equipment, and travel to seminars, meetings, and other training activities.

Original Programming

Programming costs include personal services (whether direct or for outside consultants) for flowcharting, coding (whether in machine language, assembler language, or a higher-level language), assembling and/or compiling, machine testing and program correction, documentation, and preparation of run books. These costs, however, are limited to the original programs, and do not include program changes or corrections after such programs are operative.

Although personal services usually constitute the major programming costs, machine time to assemble, compile, and machine-test the programs might amount to a considerable expense. Computer manufacturers often furnish machine time for these purposes without charge. If such free time is on a computer that is not on-site, the travel costs involved are chargeable to this function.

Data processing managers have more options than whether to write a software package or whether to use a package furnished by the vendor of the computer. Other places where packages of this sort are available include such sources as the public domain, user associations, other users, and software firms.

Some organizations have produced their own software packages. Either they felt they could not wait for the manufacturer of the computer to produce the software, or they felt they could do a superior job. The costs of producing such software may be very large. Those in the public domain are without charge, as are those supplied by many user organizations. Even if a package is purchased or rented from a software company, the developmental cost normally is spread over many other users. The cost of such a package usually will be less than that of writing it. On the negative side, however, it will probably be a generalized program and may require modification to suit the needs of any individual user. Furthermore, being a generalized program, it may not run very efficiently on the computer. Since the decision to write the package involves so much money, it is recommended that management review such decisions carefully. Also, the costs of software constitute an important part of the costs of a computer. They should be considered as a significant factor in the computer selection. Furthermore, the development of software packages often is time consuming and costly. If done by the user, it may disrupt the preinstallation schedule completely.

If the decision is made that the user will prepare a software package for a computer not yet delivered to any user, there is the possibility that the computer may not be delivered or may differ significantly from the original specifications. Southern Railroad ordered a new computer and commenced preparing its own software packages. When the computer ultimately was produced, it differed so significantly from the original specifications that the order was canceled. The costs of preparing the software packages produced no direct benefits for the railroad.

A large user felt that FORTRAN and COBOL did not provide the programming capability desired for a command-and-control system. A contract with a nonprofit software organization cost in excess of $500,000, but resulted in a language and a compiler considered better suited for the operations involved. This price furnishes an idea of the magnitude of costs in developing software packages.

Conversion

While conversion costs vary widely, depending upon the types of applications involved and the previous state and condition of the files, these costs are a major expenditure. Personal services and machine time are the major costs of conversion, although punch cards and magnetic tape costs may be considerable. Included in these costs are the expenses of establishing the files, whether it be merely a conversion from one machine-readable form to another, the location and correction of errors, and parallel operations if any are involved. In new systems the costs of correcting errors are attributed not so much to machine errors as they are to errors by people not used to producing input for computers and those not understanding computer output.

Also included in conversion costs are rental of conversion equipment, cards, salaries of keypunch operators, supervisors, programmers and analysts responsible for the transcription of records, and the programming of conversion routines. Careful planning and estimating can cut conversion costs. Possibly computer manufacturers can serve a useful purpose by confirming the user's estimates of conversion costs.

Often overlooked are losses due to changeover when such losses are caused by waste motion and duplication in learning a new system. As employees develop new skills, it can be expected that the installation of any new system, whether or not a computer is included, will result in a temporary loss of efficiency.

Site Preparation

Site preparation costs vary widely. Some companies desire showplaces, whereas others only want efficient, attractive, and comfortable quarters. The manufacturer's site preparation engineer can help in preparing a realistic budget for this function. Other sources of such information are consultants and people who have built similar installations. Such sources in the federal government are area public works offices and the General Services Administration.

Long check lists of items to be considered in planning an installation are available from many sources. They include such diverse items as additional power lines, wall outlets, transformers, air conditioning, false floors, sound-proofing, and equipment to move the computer into the building. Costs for architects' services and those involved in negotiating contracts and providing site inspection also should be included. Evaluations of case histories indicate a tendency to make other improvements while completing the computer installation. These "while we are at it" costs, which have nothing to do with the computer, should be charged to general building costs and not to the computer.

Training

Costs of training data processing personnel, those who prepare input to the system and those who use the output, are chargeable properly as one-time costs of data processing. Computer orientation courses for executives, supervisors, and people who will be affected or think they will be affected by the computer also should be charged to data processing. The costs include not only those for instructors, but also the time and expenses of the personnel being trained. Furthermore, during training periods, work may not be performed as efficiently because of disruptions and nonfamiliarity with new or changed operations.

Displaced Employees

Experience indicates that although the installation of a computer results in new and additional positions, almost inevitably some employees are displaced. The costs of maintaining and processing these displaced employees until they are reasigned or dismissed are chargeable to data processing. These costs include retraining, labor severance pay, and the costs of labor negotiations. Management may decide that no permanent employees will lose their positions because of the computer. The normal procedure in this case is to restrict hirings to temporary employees after the decision is made. Thus, fewer permanent employees will be displaced. Nevertheless, there may be a residue of permanent employees displaced. Once they are put on other work, regardless of whether or not it is a "make-work" project, their pay should not be charged to data processing. If employees are relocated, the costs of such relocation are chargeable to data processing.

Equipment

The price of purchased equipment, including transportation costs and taxes, is chargeable against data processing. If the equipment is rented, however, whether from the vendor or from a leasing company, the rental costs are chargeable as continuing costs. Examples of equipment are computers, EAM, peripheral devices, bursters, binders, degaussers, decollators, carts, repair equipment, splicers, clocks, files, and similar items.

Computer contracts are "alike but different." The data processing manager, therefore, should read and understand his contract thoroughly. Each manufacturer fits somewhere in the range from completely bundled to completely unbundled. The posture of each vendor in this regard should be examined carefully. Although many terms and conditions are similar, they differ in some important respects. Examples are standard working day, amounts of "use" time allowed for basic rental time, standards of acceptance performance, and amounts of time given for program testing and debugging, in what increments, when, and on what equipment. All these can have significant effects on both the preinstallation and postinstallation costs.

Supplies

The initial supplies for a computer installation also are chargeable as one-time costs to data processing. Included in this category are such items as magnetic tape, paper tape, control panels, punch cards, forms, programming sheets, and continuous printing forms. Once the computer installation is in full operation, however, added costs for such items should be charged as continuing costs. The costs of supplies cover not only the purchase price but also shipping costs and costs of design. The number of magnetic tape reels required is frequently underestimated, particularly where large quantities of data must be stored for long periods of time.

CONTINUING COSTS

There are many possible ways to categorize continuing costs. The ones that will be used in this section are input, amortization of investment, operating costs, taxes and insurance, output expenses, floor space, and other costs.

Input

The major operating cost is that of input preparation. Unless the system is overhauled comprehensively, this type of cost could be higher under the new system than it was under the old one. Included are such items as salaries of keypunch and equipment operators, supplies (forms and punch cards), and the rental or alteration of machines (keypunch, typewriters, and book-keeping and adding machines). In direct conversion, card punching usually continues, although key-to-tape, key-to-disk, and key-to-minicomputer have made substantial inroads. New equipment for recording data as a by-product of other operations, magnetic ink readers, and optical character readers are other alternatives in reducing keypunching costs. There is, how-ever, no substitute for bold thinking in system design.

The distinction between nondata processing costs and input costs on the one hand, and that between input and operating costs on the other, may not be defined clearly. For example, consider a system in which bills of lading are typed in field activities as a normal part of shipping materials from these installations. One of the multiple copies of the bill of lading is sent to a central location where it is keypunched and entered into a mechan-ical system for accounting and statistical purposes. There is little doubt that the transmission of the copy to the central point and the keypunching and verifying are a part of input preparations. But what about the effort involved in typing the bill of lading?

What are the effects of automating the preparation of the bills of lading and the use of a computer at a central location? A Flexowriter may be used to prepare the bills of lading, increasing greatly the production of the person doing the typing. A by-product of this operation can be punched paper tape or punch cards. There is more justification here for considering the prepara-tion of the bill of lading as an input cost. Even this, however, is based upon a comparatively tenuous line of reasoning. If the tapes or cards are mailed to the center, the mailing costs are probably best assigned to input. If the tapes or cards are converted to magnetic tape at the center, this might be con-sidered to be either input or operating costs. If the conversion is on special-purpose equipment, the tendency is to consider the function to be input. If, on the other hand, it is done on general-purpose equipment, it is often con-sidered to be an operating cost. Under multiprogramming or multiprocessing, with simultaneous conversion of cards to tape, tape to cards, tape to print, and the concurrent running of programs, it would be hard to segregate the costs adequately. In that case the costs might be charged as operating costs.

The problems of segregating input from operating and output costs are magnified in a real-time system, where data are generated in remote locations and transmitted without human intervention to a central computer. Replies are generated by the computer and sent to the appropriate remote locations.

Where the line of demarcation is drawn is not too important. These lines must, however, be specific enough to ease the problems of collecting cost data and to permit the determination of costs in these areas, both before and after conversion. If this is done and benefits are calculated similarly, it will be possible to assess the true value of data processing.

Amortization of Investment

This is normally the second largest expense in a data processing installation. Included in this category are investment in equipment, investment in the physical installation, and the remaining changeover costs. If equipment is purchased, the Internal Revenue Service allows 5 to 15 years for amortization, although it suggests 10 years. Rental costs include an allowance for obsolescence so that the user, not the manufacturer, usually pays for this obsolescence. Since the asset belongs to the manufacturer, he credits the depreciation and obsolescence allowance on his own tax return. There are three types of obsolescence: physical obsolescence, which is small for well-maintained electronic equipment; fashion obsolescence, although there are no evidences yet of an annual model change; and economic costs, which include other changeover costs and are difficult to estimate. Building improvements usually are amortized similarly to other building costs.

With software costs in many cases exceeding the hardware, the depreciating of such expenses is important. It was not until late 1969 that the Internal Revenue Service released a statement about the ways in which computer software costs could be treated for tax purposes. Software was defined as "all programs or routines used to cause a computer to perform a desired task or set of tasks, and the documentation required to describe and maintain these programs." Procedures external to operating the computer are specifically excluded. Thus, whether the software is developed internally, purchased, or leased, the associated costs are considered to be software costs. If the software is rented, it should be treated as current expense. If it is purchased or written internally and has a useful life of less than a year, it should be treated as a current expense. If the useful life is more than a year, it should be amortized. All such software costs can be capitalized and amortized over a period of at least five years from the date of completion. Where the useful life is clearly less than five years, it can be amortized over the useful life period. If the manufacturer is a bundled manufacturer, and the costs of the software are included in the price of the hardware, the software and the hardware costs are on the same straight-line depreciation schedule. Developmental costs for a new computer can be treated as current costs. To capitalize and depreciate them, it is necessary to get prior approval from the Internal Revenue Service.

After the computer is delivered, there may be a period of a few months during which very little productive work is accomplished. Some installations reach the point where the benefits and the costs of data processing are equalized in less than a year. Others, however, never attain the breakeven point. The breakeven point has been estimated to average about 18 months. The time to recover the investment in a computer, on the other hand, may be 4 or 5 years after the system is operating smoothly, which may be 10 years after the decision was made to get a computer.

In the federal government all one-time costs are calculated as described previously. Annual savings are compared with these costs. If the costs cannot be amortized in 4 to 6 years, approvals of computer selections are relatively scarce.

Operating Costs

Operating expense, which usually is the third largest cost, includes the labor of operating personnel as contrasted with people performing input and output functions. Examples of personnel whose salaries are included are the data processing manager, systems analysts, programmers, and clerks.

Salaries in this area often are underestimated, since there is a tendency to overlook the number of supplementary programs and revisions of original programs as circumstances change. Furthermore, salary increases are often necessary to retain the staff as they gain experience. There are other reasons why costs continue at a high level. After the major applications are on the computer, many small jobs may remain to be completed. Although the planned reduction in the junior staff may be achieved through attrition, a policy of continued employment for the senior staff may result in their performing nonessential work. Where part of an employee's time is saved, it may be difficult to reorganize the work to consolidate this partial savings. There is always the danger that additional work will be thought up to fill the spare time created by the computer.

Taxes and Insurance

The costs of taxes and insurance tend to vary widely. Since the federal government pays no taxes as such and insures itself, it has no allocations for these purposes. Contractors working for the federal government, however, pay taxes and insurance directly. If they work on a cost-plus basis, therefore, the federal payments cover taxes and insurance. If the contract is on a fixed-fee basis, such payments are included in the total contractual amount.

In 1972, California held hearings on a proposed tax on computer software. In 1971, Eastern Airlines won a tax reduction in another case in Florida by contending that software, services, and training were intangible assets without marketable value, and as such did not come under Florida's property tax law. At the writing of this book the situation is extremely fluid. Data processing managers are advised to see their attorneys concerning the taxability of computer software.

Output Expenses

The cost of producing output includes salaries, miscellaneous service charges, communication costs, and printed forms. The problems of segregating output expenses from operating expenses were discussed earlier in this chapter. In some computer installations these two items account for a relatively large portion of total annual costs.

Floor Space

A charge for floor space in lieu of a rental or burden charge usually is another operating cost. It has been recommended that it be charged at the maximum value of the space in its best alternative use. Another possibility is to charge data processing its relative share in proportion to the area it uses. For example, if rental, custodial services, and security services cost $100,000 for the business, and 10 percent of the total area is assigned to data processing, a charge of $10,000 to data processing would be equitable.

Other

Other costs, such as power, are relatively small. If the company policy is to charge each department its proportionate share of services, such as industrial relations and accounting, the charges should be included here.

VALUE OF DATA PROCESSING

Surveys continually find that reliable cost data for data processing installations is almost nonexistent. It is necessary for each computer manager to make his judgments in the light of his own experience, since individual case studies are not representative or meaningful. The uses to which computers are put and the experience with them varies from user to user. Applications that are profitable for one installation are not for another.

Data processing installations, in accumulating costs by application, use various methods of computation. One large governmental installation compiles total costs of the entire data processing installation and then allocates these costs to specific applications based upon percentages of total computer time. In another installation, costs are not actually kept, but are estimated for budgetary purposes. Idle time is not prorated. A national service center prices jobs three ways: an open-end contract, in which the customer may use the service center at any time with a specific charge for each hour of use; a fixed contract, with a quoted fee for each application; and a contractual rate per thousand cards or records.

Value of Data Processing

The value of data processing is not merely the cutting of expenses; it also enables management to make better decisions and results in higher profits. In measuring the effectiveness of data processing, it is necessary to consider both costs and benefits derived. The consideration of costs alone, without relating them to benefits, is short-sighted. If a policy of cutting real costs were to be carried to the ultimate, all data processing should be discontinued immediately. If these data processing efforts had cost $500,000 per year, the savings from such action would be that same $500,000. The modern company, however, might not be able to operate successfully without management information. In former times, decisions to acquire a computer were often based on the desire to cut clerical costs, as opposed to increasing the profits or giving better service, which is a common objective today.

A 1971 survey of the largest corporations in the United States showed savings to be the criterion most used in deciding whether to approve a proposed computer application. The objective of reducing direct data processing costs is worthwhile, since the funds saved may be added to profits or diverted to other uses. The most significant potential of data processing, however, is in providing better management information. This, in turn, enables better decisions and higher profits. The questions to be asked are: Will it furnish valuable management information not previously obtainable? Will the data be integrated with related information for optimum management decisions? What will be the impact of data processing on the overall effectiveness and economy of the company?

There appears to be a lack of appropriate criteria for evaluating and appraising data processing operations. Although management appears to be satisfied, is it satisfied with insufficient results? Should it demand a greater return? Both cost data and measures of effectiveness are of uncertain value. In order to assay the value of data processing, the cost of the operation before data processing took it over and the cost of the post-installation operation should be compared. If work is taken over by the computer, the work (and the workers involved) should be identified. Then the freed labor can be recaptured instead of disappearing when it is assigned to relatively less important work.

It is possible that the computer will provide services not previously furnished. To put a value on such services, an inventory of preinstallation services should be documented. There has been noted a tendency for the applications on a computer to increase to the capacity of the computer. In order to prevent this, there should be an orderly and regular comparison of cost versus value of all applications proposed for the computer. The importance of preinstallation services may be compared with that of post-installation services to evaluate changes made by the computer.

Managers who want information can place a value on it equal to the extra profits or savings resulting from better decisions based on better information. Although some companies use profitability for measuring applications, as mentioned before, this is not a prevalent practice.

While individual data processing installations maintain cost records, the validity of these records is questionable. The methods of obtaining the data may be valid, but many discrepancies are noted in the following of the prescribed methods. Records of savings are kept occasionally. Usually, however, they are informal and poorly documented.

Costs versus Value

Costs are most useful when compared with value. Management's acceptance and use of the information should be assessed so that the value of the benefits obtained can be estimated. One should attempt to express these in terms of dollars, although a more subjective evaluation may be needed. The subject of evaluating benefits was discussed in Chapter 1 and further treatment here is not warranted.

BUDGETING

Management Control

Management control may be defined as the process of assuring that the resources of a company are used effectively and efficiently in accomplishing the objectives of the company. The process is a closed loop. First, plans are made, followed by the completion of operations. Performance is measured and analyzed, resulting in information fed back for the next planning cycle.

A budget is an operating plan expressed in dollars. Although it is the principal formal means of stating the operating plans of a company, it is only one of a number of means circulating throughout a company as guides for company employees. Since management cannot actually control a product, it controls or tries to control those who manage or incur costs.

If the budget is expressed only in dollars, it becomes a negative control. Success is measured by the ability of the entity being budgeted to stay within the budgetary limits. Failure, of course, is when the organizational entity exceeds the budget. In order to be more meaningful, units to be produced and, possibly, man-hours should be included.

The principle of involvement also is an important factor. For effective control, a budget should not be imposed. Instead, the head of the entity for which the budget is being prepared should participate in its preparation. He can estimate his own needs, help in setting performance standards, and give rather specific guidance with respect to current trends in his department.

Budgets in themselves are not particularly effective as a management control device. They must be supplemented by progress reports. These reports should show budgeted dollars and other pertinent factors so that they can be assessed. The mere total of dollars spent is inadequate. An expense in excess of the budget limitation might easily be warranted. Expenditures, on the other hand, although within budgetary limits, might be excessive.

The final step in the management control cycle is the analysis of these progress reports so that new plans can be made. This use indicates how often progress reports should be made. Note the use of the words "analysis" and "new plans" in the sentence above. The time interval for progress reports should be the shortest period of time in which action can be taken to change performance. If it is too long, unwarranted expenditures and uneconomical practices could result in excessive loss. If the period is too short, random factors, which would average-out over a longer period of time, might have an inordinate effect. Only the experience of any particular company can show whether semimonthly, monthly, or bimonthly reports are best. These lengths of time, however, indicate the normal limits.

Cost Center versus Profit Center

As used in this context, a cost center is the organizational entity of a company. Costs of operating this entity are accumulative. Although such costs also are accumulated for subcenters (departments) of the profit center, the concept allows charges for entity services per se. As such, it is expected to show a profit on its operations. The difference between a cost center and a profit center, then, is that the former does not charge for its services and cannot show a profit. The latter charges for its services, and its profit or loss is the difference between its total charges and its total costs.

If its "customers" are within the company, and they must have their computing done by the company's data processing department, the profit center becomes a monopoly. It can raise prices and show a profit, regardless of the fact that it may have made many unwarranted expenditures. In order for a profit center to work well, the demand for its services should be flexible. Its customers should be free to go to an outside company for the service if they so desire.

For example, in one company, the data processing department was operated as a profit center. Prices were gradually raised until the charges were three times what such charges would have been if the work were done in a computer service center outside the company. Then word was "leaked" that if the customers wanted to, they could take their work to outside service centers. Despite the increased costs attendant with having the work done within the company, much of the work continued without change. Only a few departments of the company elected to take the work outside.

The preceding example indicates that the work of data processing is really not so flexible as one might think. Many customers are willing to pay more for the convenience of having the work done inside the company. Furthermore, since such charges are merely transfers of funds within the company, there is a tendency to consider such payments as "play money."

Treating data processing as a profit center, therefore, does not appear to be a valid procedure.

Data processing is a service organization. Unless the final product of the company is data, it exists solely to support the rest of the company in producing and marketing its products. Its workload varies directly and proportionately with the demands placed upon it, unless, to varying degrees, it is not responsive to these demands. It is recommended, therefore, that data processing be treated as a cost center and not a profit center.

Variable Budget

As indicated previously, data processing usually has little or no control over its workload. The normal means of budgeting for it is a fixed budget, which may or may not include overtime funds. If it includes overtime, data processing has the task of allocating overtime judiciously in an attempt to fill all demands. If data processing runs out of funds or demands are excessive, only three alternatives are available: it must request additional funds, substitute the new demand for a demand of lower priority, or refuse the new demand. If the fixed budget does not include overtime funds, whenever demands necessitate overtime a request for overtime must be made by data processing. This request will be approved by another echelon of management. None of the above methods of a fixed budget appears to be suitable for data processing.

It is suggested that a variable budget would be preferable for controlling data processing. This budget would recognize that data processing is a service organization and that it cannot control its workload. Table 8.1 is an example of a variable budget prepared for the keypunch section of the data processing department. It recognizes that the monthly workload might vary between 300,000 and 500,000 cards.

The table indicates that the keypunch section is staffed to punch 350,000 cards a month. A temporary drop in workload below that level, therefore, will not result in lower labor costs. Above the 350,000 card level, labor costs increase at a rate of $1,000 per additional 50,000 cards. Expenses for punch cards, on the other hand, vary directly and proportionately with the number of cards punched. The rate is $1.10 per 1000 cards. Since there are no overtime machine-rental costs when the work is done by the regular shift's working overtime, such charges remain stable regardless of the number of cards punched.

Overhead costs are segregated between controllable costs and other costs. Supervision, the first of the controllable costs, stabilizes until the workload reaches 450,000 cards. This indicates that overtime work is done without supervision until the workload reaches that level. When the 450,000 level is reached, however, overtime for a supervisor is needed. Supplies at

TABLE 8.1. VARIABLE BUDGET FOR KEYPUNCH OPERATION

	Number of Cards Punched				
	300,000	*350,000*	*400,000*	*450,000*	*500,000*
Labor, $	6,000	6,000	7,000	8,000	9,000
Punch cards	330	385	440	495	550
Machine rental, $	1,810	1,810	1,810	1,810	1,810
Overhead					
Controllable					
Supervision, $	1,500	1,500	1,500	1,800	1,800
Supplies, $	50	60	70	80	90
Other					
Allocated					
costs, $	1,000	1,000	1,000	1,000	1,000
Total	$10,690	$10,755	$11,820	$13,185	$14,250

the 300,000 level cost $50. They increase at the rate of $10 for each 50,000 increase in cards punched. Allocated costs are included to let the keypunch supervisor know that the completion of the work of that section is aided by others—that production is a team effort.

It will be noted that many different types of costs are pertinent: stable costs, direct and proportional costs, direct but not proportional costs, and costs that remain stable and then rise. It is a factual budget that will enable the keypunch operation to meet demands on it for services, with supplemental requests to management as workload varies. It also provides for lower costs if workload decreases below normal levels.

It is felt that this type of budget is optimal for a service type of organization. Since data processing generally provides services to the rest of the company, this type of budget is suggested.

Mention was made that expenditures, even though within the budget, may be excessive. Some costs in excess of the budget, on the other hand, may be warranted. The normal fixed budget, when compared against actual expenses, does not furnish enough tools to determine how well or how poorly the budgeted organization performed. The emphasis is on dollars, not performance. If the organization stays within the budgetary limits, everything is fine. If, on the other hand, it exceeds the budget, it did a poor job. This is a negative type of control, one that induces a service type of organization, such as data processing, to cut corners in order to save, even though it necessitates reduced services to accomplish such savings. Instead of "Can do!" the usual reply to a request for services is "Can't do!" The results, of course, are dissatisfaction of the potential users in the company and failure to use the computer to full advantage.

The analysis of variance is proposed as a tool for analyzing performance. This requires more effort when the budget is prepared. The writing of a computer program and a little machine time each month will produce the analysis. The results, however, are a better and more factual budgetary tool—one that stimulates better performance, not the desire to reduce services.

The budget cycle starts with the involvement of the budgeted organization in the preparation of the budget estimates. The example in Table 8.2

TABLE 8.2. ANALYSIS OF VARIANCE—PROGRAMMER DIVISION

Item	Budget	Actual
Projected budget		
Salaries	$2,500	$3,100
Keypunch charges	100	135
Computer usage charges	250	510
Total	$2,850	$3,745
Detailed distribution		
Instructions debugged	10,000	15,000
Keypunch charge per 1,000 cards, $	10	9
Programmer wage rate per hour, $	4.00	4.10
Programmer hours	625	756
Computer hours	1.25	2.00
Computer rate per hour, $	200	255
Analysis		
Labor Variation		
Volume variation budgeted: 625 @ $4.00	$2,500	
Correct base: 625 (15,000/10,000)		
@ $4.00	3,750	$1,250*
Labor usage variation		
Correct base:		
625 (15,000/10,000) @ $4.00	3,750	
Actually used: 756 @ $4.00	3,024	726
Wage rate variation: 756 ($4.00-$4.10)		76*
Subtotal		$ 600*
Keypunch variation		
Volume variation budget: 10 @ $10	100	
Correct base: 10 (15/10) @ $10	150	50*
Keypunch rate variation:		
15 ($10-$9)		15

TABLE 8.2—cont'd.

Item	Budget	Actual
Subtotal		35*
Computer usage variation		
Volume variation budgeted: 1.25 @ $200	250	
Correct base: 1.25 (15/10) @ $200	375	125*
Usage variation		
Correct base: 1.25 (15/10) @ $200	375	
Actually used: 2 @ $200	400	25*
Rate Variation: 2 (200-$255)		110*
Subtotal		260*
Total Variance		$895*

*Overspent.

shows the factors that should be considered in developing a realistic budget—one that will be useful in preparing an analysis of variance. The budget preparation starts with the estimate of workload. In this case the programmer division is used as an example. The workload of the division is debugged by machine instructions. Application of previous experience shows that approximately 625 programmer hours will be needed to complete the workload, and that the average cost is $4.00 per hour. To keypunch the cards at $10 per thousand, $100 will be needed. Similarly, 1.25 computer hours at $200 per hour will cost another $250, resulting in a budgeted total of $2,850.

In this example, instead of the budgeted $2,850, the programmer division spent $3,745. Under the normal budget analysis this overexpenditure of $895 would be considered to be poor performance. The facts that workload was up 50 percent, programmer hours up 21 percent, wage rates up 2.5 percent, computer hours up 60 percent, computer rate per hour up 27.5 percent, and keypunch charges per 1,000 cards down 10 percent are not easily established as criteria for performance analysis.

The analysis of variance, however, can be applied. The formulas have been included in Table 8.2. This will enable readers to apply this methodology to controlling and budgeting data processing. Table 8.2 shows that if there had not been an increase in instructions debugged per man-hour, $1,250 more than the budgeted $2,500 would have been needed for additional programmer pay. The 756 programmer hours at $4.00 per hour would have cost $3,024, so that $726 offsets more than half of the $1,250. Increased wage rates cost another $76, bringing the net labor variations to $600. In keypunch, similarly, the volume variation cost an additional $50, but lower rates per 1000 cards saves $15. In computer usage, higher volume cost $125, lower production per hour $25, higher charges per hour $110, for a total overexpenditure of $260 in this category.

From this analysis one can see that increased workload cost $1,250 plus $50 plus $125, a total of $1,425. Instead of doing a poor job, the programmer division did a very good job, since its net overexpenditure was $895 instead of $1,425.

In this particular example, a normal, fixed budget was used. If, on the other hand, a variable budget had been used, it would have been even more amenable to an analysis of variance. The variations due to volume changes would have been minimized, making the other variances more evident for analysis.

SUMMARY

In order to evaluate the success or lack of success of a data processing installation, it is necessary to compare the costs of producing the information against the value of the benefits derived from such information. These comparisons can be of definite value when making a decision as to whether to put an application on the computer.

In data processing, a heavy investment is incurred prior to the possibility of receiving any significant returns. The one-time costs of installing a computer must be calculated. If the activity is on a cash accounting basis, these costs are charged against income in the year in which incurred. When accounting is on an accrual basis, the amortization of the one-time costs constitutes a significant expense. The relative costs of software, as compared to those of hardware, continue to rise. Internal Revenue Service regulations give specific guidance concerning how these costs can be charged for tax purposes. The latest rulings should be examined to determine which allowable method is most advantageous to the company.

Records of data processing costs have not been very accurate. At the same time, records of the value of data processing have been practically nonexistent. In order to rectify this situation, it is necessary to establish procedures to keep such records. Furthermore, it is essential that these procedures be followed.

Since data processing is a service organization, the workload of which is not really flexible in relation to costs, it should be treated as a cost center, not a profit center. Using a variable budget and an analysis of variance to compare performance with the budget will control data processing effectively. Also, it will eliminate many of the negative responses to other parts of the company that request computer work. It will also reduce requests to management for approval of overtime. The result will be performance of data processing that contributes measurably to the success of the company.

EXERCISES

1. Discuss the one-time costs of establishing a data processing installation. How should such costs be treated in the cost accounting of
   the company?
2. Differentiate between the feasibility study and the applications study.
   Should the costs of these two areas be treated similarly? Discuss.
3. What factors should be considered in the decision whether to write
   a large programming package in the company or to procure it from
   outside sources? Discuss the impact these factors have on the decision.
4. Discuss the continuing costs of data processing. How can they be
   categorized? How should they be treated from an accounting standpoint?
5. It has been said that there are practically no records that indicate the
   value of data processing. What records would you establish to indicate such values? How would you determine these values for entry
   in the records?
6. Discuss the budgetary cycle as related to data processing. What are
   the functions of the various parts of the company in this cycle?
7. Discuss the advantages and disadvantages of treating data processing as a cost center as compared with treating it as a profit center.
   Select a company with which you are familiar. How would you treat
   data processing in this company? Why?
8. Compare variable budgets with fixed budgets. Establish a variable
   budget for the operations division of a company. The computer is
   rented and no electric accounting machines are involved.
9. Do an analysis of variance, including the recapitulation, for a programming division, based on the following data. Did this division
   do a good job in relation to its budget? Why or why not?

	Budget	*Actual*
Salaries	$8,000	$7,600
Keypunch charges	300	100
Computer usage charges	250	250
	$8,550	$7,950
Instructions debugged	30,000	29,000
Keypunch charge per 1000 cards, $	10	10
Programmer wage rate per hour, $	4.25	4.50
Programmer hours	1,882	1,691
Computer hours	2.00	2.00
Computer rate per hour, $	125	125

9 ◀ REVIEW AND EVALUATION

A study reported that 42 percent of the companies interviewed did not maintain accurate records of computer performance. Computers were operated only 64 percent of the available time, and 25 percent of all data processing man-hours were wasted. Furthermore, only 48 percent of the available computer time was used productively. Another study showed over an eight-year period, a decline of 30 percent to 20 percent[1] of computer time devoted to applications.

With an estimated $3.5 billion being wasted annually in EDP operations, more and more companies are reviewing and evaluating accomplishments in this area.[2] After such reviews, computer emphasis has been shifted from accounting to distribution, inventory management, and production. A transportation company completely reorganized its data processing department and changed the place in the company to which data processing reported. In the federal government, reviews of methods of calculating rental payments to computer manufacturers resulted in the collection of overpayments to manufacturers. A total of $207,000 was overpaid by selected military activities. Due to inadequate timekeeping procedures, a nonmilitary governmental agency overpaid its computer manufacturer $1 million. In at least two cases the computer was returned to the manufacturer and the company reverted to manual and/or electric accounting machine operations.

The foregoing examples are by no means the only ones available, but are presented because they are well documented. They illustrate some of the potential benefits of a review and evaluation. If the limited audits cited above were extended to cover all facets of computer use, the potential gains would far overshadow those listed above. Although the number of companies performing such reviews is pitifully low, it is increasing. Considering the $3.5

1. Robert M. McClure, *Trade-Off Between Software and Machine Size.* Paper presented at the Sixteenth Annual EDP Conference of the American Management Association, Feb. 24, 1970.

2. Dick H. Brandon, *Management Planning for Computers.* Princeton, N.J.: Brandon/Systems Press, Inc., 1970, p. 132.

197

billion wasted annually, a yearly audit of computer applications appears to be necessary.

In examining the subject of review and evaluation of data processing, this chapter analyzes who should be on the review team, the instruction that establishes the team, and the objectives of such a study. Individual areas of review are selected and, in each area, questions that the review team should look into are suggested.

SELECTING THE REVIEW COMMITTEE

Most companies use teams to audit data processing. In naming people to the team, objectivity is the primary criterion, since the review must be independent. Problems should be pinpointed, changes recommended, and the evaluation conducted without considering company politics. The individual committee members should have sufficient stature to deal effectively with department heads in face-to-face interviews and with top management in presentations. They need a thorough understanding of computers and their applications, and of the company's decision-making processes and information flow. Some members of the team should be articulate in written and/or oral communications so that group conclusions can be expressed clearly and convincingly.

There are various levels of such reviews in a decentralized company. An individual field component, such as a manufacturing plant, may review the effectiveness of its data processing operations. Headquarters might send a team to make the review. Individual parts of the system may be reviewed at several locations. For example, the comptroller might organize a team to examine computing and electric accounting machine applications in financial management, budgeting, and accounting. Furthermore, a headquarters team may audit all activities at an individual location. In such an audit, data processing is considered merely to be another of the many activities audited. No matter at what level the audit originates, an objective audit should be done by people with stature and knowledge.

IMPLEMENTING INSTRUCTIONS

When to Review

There is general agreement that a review and evaluation of data processing is necessary, but there is little agreement concerning when the review should take place. IBM recommends that it be held approximately 90 days after installation. In drafting its guidelines, a congressional subcommittee suggested that the first review be 6 to 12 months after installation, and that subsequent reviews be conducted as appropriate. Other authorities say that it should be after two, three, or four years of EDP experience. It is very possible that a major factor in these differences results from different concepts of the relationship of the reviewing team to the company, and of the nature and depth of the review.

The experience of this author is that holding the review from sources external to the activity prior to the end of a year's actual experience is premature. The director of data processing will not have time to recognize his almost inevitable errors and to take corrective action. Waiting too long, however, permits the perpetuation of costly decisions, especially when the director of data processing cannot recognize his errors and correct them. The first review should be made during the second year of operations, and subsequent reviews should be made every two years unless the first review indicates the desirability of an earlier subsequent review.

Charter

Top management should issue a companywide instruction authorizing the review committee. The announcement should give the purpose, scope, and background for the review; list the names of those on the committee; designate the chairman; establish a timetable showing the starting dates, times for intermittent reports, and the date and manner of the final report. The name of the person to whom the committee reports, a directive for all departments concerned to assist the efforts of the committee upon request, specific tasks that the team is to accomplish, and provisions for financial and clerical assistance also should be included. The authorization should be signed by top management.

Within the framework of the instruction, the team can establish a detailed calendar of actions required to accomplish its mission. An evaluation of this calendar and the personnel assigned to the task force will show whether the personnel, mission, and timetable of the authorizing instruction are compatible. If not, one or more of these will require revision for successful completion.

Objectives

It is necessary to reexamine data processing efforts to ensure proper priorities of effort and emphasis. The basic purpose of such a periodic evaluation is to detect areas for improvement, determine future development possibilities, and determine cost-benefit relationships. In the Department of the Army, the following objectives were established for the evaluation of automatic data processing systems:

1. Measures of effectiveness in meeting organizational objectives, e.g.: timeliness of shipments and increased revenue.

2. Usefulness and validity of data products: This involves a desk audit of the users of the system.
3. Data quality controls, e.g.: input processing and audit trails.
4. Recovery capability, e.g.: reconstruction plans, necessary redundancy, and adequacy of documentation.
5. Training of users and operators, e.g.: the understanding of users and operators of remote inquiry.
6. Management of system design and programming: the adequacy of automatic data processing project controls.
7. Machine-time utilization, e.g.: setup time, rerun time, and downtime.
8. Scheduling, e.g.: optimum job mix for multiprogramming.

Eleven areas are of prime importance in the review and evaluation of a computer installation. The rest of this chapter has been structured with these areas in mind:

1. Top management participation.
2. Objectives.
3. Organization.
4. Systems.
5. Planning.
6. Operations.
7. Hardware and associated vendors.
8. Software and associated vendors.
9. Personnel.
10. Controls and security provisions.
11. Economics.

REVIEW AREAS

Top Management Participation

For at least the past 20 years it has been pointed out that automatic data processing has little chance of success unless management participates actively in the design of the system. Studies in 1972 confirmed this viewpoint, finding that in many companies and government organizations the systems are designed by technical personnel from within the company or by outside consultants. In either case there is little or no participation by upper management. Research continually shows that the most successful systems result from the involvement of top, or at least upper, management in the system design phase. Like the weather—everybody complains about it, but nobody does anything to rectify the situation.

A Navy instruction stated:

> Automatic data processing has the ability to cut across organiza-
> tional lines. It provides an opportunity to make major changes in
> information processing systems. Only with top-level support can
> these changes be effected. Converting to automatic data processing is
> expensive and troublesome. Without the personal support of top
> management there can be little hope of success.[3]

This is not a lone cry in the wilderness. In 1963, Garrity wrote:

> Where top management plays its essential role, important conse-
> quences can follow: broad-scale use, significant intangible benefits,
> and high dollar return.[4]

In 1966, Garrity's lectures at the Department of Defense Computer
Institute reached substantially the same conclusions. Studies as late as 1972
continue to show extremely high correlations between the degree of top
management participation and the success of computer-based systems. Similar views have been expressed by highly regarded consultants and writers in
the information processing field. There are examples of computer installations that have failed because management was never entirely convinced that
it should support the data processing group completely. There also have
been cases where top management furnished such support originally but
withdrew such support when management became disenchanted later.

If an ADP installation is to furnish a service to a company, and if the
support of top management is desired, the active participation of top management should be solicited in establishing objectives.

In order to secure such participation, data processing should let management know what services can be furnished.

Cooperation of top management and ADP is a "two-way street." In
addition to the necessity for top management to cooperate with and support
ADP, the ADP group should, in turn, cooperate with and support top management completely. In order for this two-way cooperation to flourish, it
should be possible for the manager of data processing to discuss his significant problems with top management. He should be assured that these problems will receive ample consideration.

Some of the questions concerning top management participation are
listed below:

3. Department of the Navy, *Data Processing in Navy Management Information Systems.* Washington, D.C.: SecNavInst., P. 10462.7, 1959, p. V-1.
4. John T. Garrity, *Getting the Most Out of Your Computer.* New York:
McKinsey & Co., 1963, p. 20.

1. Did top management establish and document the goals for ADP and for the system that ADP supports?
2. What was the role of top management in the feasibility and application studies?
3. What is the extent of the orientation of top management in operations research? Has there been any formal orientation of top management in the management sciences? Are any benefits from operations research anticipated?
4. Are the decision criteria of the system valid?
5. What effects of the computer on items such as mission completion, profits, amount of inventory, and services are discernible? How valid are the indicators used to measure these effects? What has been the effect of the computer on these indicators?
6. Does top management recognize and support the need for high-caliber personnel in ADP?
7. Does the director of data processing get ample cooperation from top management? Does he have access to top management to discuss problems requiring a basic decision? Are these decisions given ample consideration?

Objectives

Self-evaluation by computer managers. A survey showed that the managers of many computer installations were not accurate judges of the degree of success of their computer operations. In manufacturing companies where data processing activities were rated as "less effective" in the analysis, 76 percent of the managers considered their operations to be better than the study rating. Of the installations rated in the more effective category, 37 percent considered themselves as above average; 5 percent did not feel capable of rating their operations. Many data processing managers have no quantitative or semiquantitative method of rating their own operations. Further, they are embroiled in an effort to get out the daily product, rather than to analyze its value. Appendix C is a Self-Evaluation Questionaire for managers of data processing. If a data processing manager will answer all questions in the questionnaire to the best of his ability, he will have gone a long way toward making a factual evaluation of his efforts. Glossing over the inadequacies that the self-evaluation reveals will make it an exercise in rationalization rather than evaluation.

Documentation of objectives. Objectives should be documented, both for data processing and for the system that it supports. If the objectives of ADP are not stated specifically, they can be inferred by studying the applications themselves. Lack of formal documentation of such objectives, however, may be indicative that management itself has not decided what it would like data

processing to accomplish. Installations that gain the agreement of management concerning the data processing objectives, and document these objectives, usually are more successful.

Measures of effectiveness. To measure effectiveness, it is necessary to
establish and define the desired results. Indicators should be selected to measure how well each objective is achieved, and measurement data should be
collected. The criteria for measuring effectiveness must be valid, must
measure what they are intended to measure, and must be expressed quantitatively. In establishing a measurement program, adjustments should be made
to the base as necessary, but each change should be documented and evaluated. Management needs a specific definition of computer effectiveness. It
should be pointed out that cost comparisons are not necessarily measures
of effectiveness.

In the more effective companies a large number of departments use the
data. Furthermore, the managers of these departments accept the computer
as a tool in filling their informational requirements. Possibly, then, the
extent to which the computer is used throughout the company is a criterion
of effectiveness. Also, the contribution the computer makes to company
profits would appear to be a better measure than cost-cutting. Samples of
questions that might be asked are:

1. Is the increased information from the computer actually used? If
   so, by which departments?
2. Is there a formal program for teaching managers how to use the
   new information?
3. Have there been any changes in the way in which management
   makes decisions? If not, why not?
4. What has been the effect of the computer on mission accomplishment or on profits?
5. What is the real value of getting information more rapidly?
6. Have horizontal and vertical communications within the company
   improved?
7. How do the output users rate data processing? Are their needs met?
8. Why aren't the nonusers making use of the computer?
9. Is each person getting the information he needs, when he needs it,
   with the necessary quality and in its most useful form?

Validity of objectives. The mere measurement concerning how well objectives are being met is not in itself an indication of the effectiveness of data
processing. Among other possibilities, the objectives may be out of date or
may not be significant. It is not enough to ask whether the computer is
accomplishing its intended purposes. The question should be whether it is
accomplishing all that it is capable of accomplishing.

Broad objectives, which are at the same time specific and measurable, may establish goals for data processing worthy of attainment. If these goals are achieved, the value of data processing to the management of the company is enhanced. If these goals become obsolete, however, they lose their value as guidelines to effective effort.

In a governmental agency, new laws or directives affecting the mission of the agency, a change in administration, or a reorganization may indicate that a review of the validity of objectives is needed. In industry, the counterparts of these indicators are changes in the product line, management changes, or reorganization. In both government and industry, technological breakthroughs in the hardware and software categories of computers might also indicate that the validity of data processing objectives should be reviewed. Some pertinent questions are:

1. Who participated in establishing the objectives?
2. When were the objectives established originally?
3. Have there been any revisions?
4. Is there any scheduled time for the revision of objectives?
5. Have the objectives been reviewed? By whom?
6. What changes should be made in the objectives? Why?

Organization

If the organizational placement of data processing was changed since the computer was installed, the reasons for the success or failure of the change will be available for analysis. Other information will be the internal organization of data processing, the degree to which systems analysts and programmers are assigned within data processing (as opposed to placement centrally elsewhere or with the individual customers of data processing), and the use of operations research in the planning and decision-making functions of the company. The review and evaluation team should determine if it might be advantageous to have data processing report elsewhere in the organizational hierarchy, to centralize or decentralize the system analysis and programming effort, or to reorganize data processing.

Although the review may not disclose a need for immediate organizational changes, it may indicate the type of future changes that may be needed. There is no standard against which to compare either the internal organization of data processing or where it should be in the organizational hierarchy, since these vary from installation to installation. The following questions should be asked:

1. To whom does the head of data processing report?
2. Organizationally, where is the person to whom data processing reports in relation to top management?
3. Has the organizational placement of data processing been changed

since its inauguration? If so, why? Did the change help? How?
4. Is the official to whom the head of data processing reports at least equal to the level of the highest user?
5. What criteria determined the organizational placement of data processing? How valid are these criteria today? Is ADP at the optimal organizational location?
6. What are the internal organization and functions of ADP?
7. Are large programming projects managed by the project manager method?
8. Are systems analysis and operations research within data processing? If not, are they directly under the person to whom the director of data processing reports?
9. What is the line of demarcation between systems analysis and programming? Is it clearly delineated?

Systems

A large proportion of the systems literature of the 1960s advocated integrated, or even total, systems and an integrated data base. At the writing of this book, computer procedures for handling large data bases are rudimentary. This author does not anticipate an effective and useful data base management system until the mid-1970s. Indeed, standards for such systems may not be available until then. The emphasis has shifted to planning integrated systems made up of individual subsystems that communicate with each other. The review, therefore, should consider both the plans for systems that have been made and the adequacy of the technology.

If it were planned to have a system integrated significantly, information should be sought about the current status of its installation. Is the plan being revised and improved in the light of current conditions?

In appraising the appropriateness of the applications now on the computer, one should determine how the applications were selected in the past, the criteria for selection, and the contributions each makes to the company? Have these criteria changed? To what extent is data flow between different departments interrelated? The use of data in various departments eliminates duplicate effort. When this procedure is carried to the ultimate, the results are a very highly integrated information system.

It is not enough to focus the attention of the review group on the past or even the current system effort. It should seek areas for corrective action and plan for their correction. If it does not appear that the changes will eliminate the weaknesses, the shortcomings should be determined specifically so that modifications necessary to correct them can be identified.

The following questions typify the kind of review suggested for evaluating information systems:

1. Was a thorough study concerning the feasibility of an integrated data processing system conducted? What were the recommendations of that study? What is the status of the implementation of these recommendations? Which ones have not been implemented? Why? Is there a schedule for their planned implementation?
2. If an integrated system was recommended, was it installed completely? If not, was it installed by subsystems? Will these subsystems fit into an integrated system when all subsystems are installed? What criteria were established to determine the order in which the subsystems should be implemented? How valid are these criteria?
3. Is the data maintained in a consolidated data base? If so, can the data be stored and/or retrieved expeditiously when needed? If not, do the individual data bases communicate with each other?
4. Does data enter the system more than once when used in different subsystems?
5. Does the system cut across organizational lines without undue difficulty? If there are difficulties, what are they? Are they solvable? Has the system replaced the old system completely? If not, why not? Is there a plan for such replacement?

In combining a telecommunications system and a computer into a working information system, the following questions should be asked:

1. Have the needs and objectives of all decision makers, from the line and staff supervision to the chairman of the board, been considered?
2. Will the information meet their needs with respect to time, content, and form?
3. Will they get the information they need and no more?
4. Is the information system designed to use the full capabilities of the computer?
5. Does the system take full advantage of the flexibility offered by communications?
6. Has the complete system—from input to output—been designed to eliminate duplication?
7. Is there the right mix of communications and dollars to get the best value per dollar?

Whether or not an integrated system was considered, the adequacy of the current system should be questioned:

1. Is there a current need for system modification and redesign? Are such modifications and redesigns always preceded by a thorough systems study? If not, why not?

2. Is the principle of management by exception used whenever feasible? Are source-data conversion media used whenever possible? Have all manual operations been automated where it is financially advantageous to do so? Does the system furnish management with new and improved information?
3. Have data transmission and electronic information display systems been included in the system? If not, is their feasibility being considered?
4. What are the relationships between the systems analysis staff and the programming staff?

Planning

Failures that have occurred in ADP, if traced to the source, can be attributed to deficiencies in planning. All too often the unanticipated comes to pass—unanticipated events with regard to the physical installation, people, programs, and systems. As examples: A steel manufacturer did not install a voltage regulator because of the stability of its power supply. When two blast furnaces were turned off at once, the resultant surge of power through the computer put it out of commission for several days. A computer was installed in a building at the end of a runway of an airport. One day an airplane lost power and hit the building, demolishing a computer installation.

A major military computer program was predicated on the assumption that not more than three officers of a particular flag rank would leave the service in one month. Because of a change in retirement provisions, more than 30 left in one month, thereby causing a delay while the program was rewritten. Another installation did not have a pipeline of personnel ready to fill in if key people left. Within a few months the director of data processing, the head of systems analysis, and several programmers left the company. More than a year later the positions of director of data processing and head of systems analysis were still vacant.

In an ADP installation a program was written to check the calculations on a 39-line, 32-column report. In order to conserve running time on the computer, it was programmed to punch after each 6 lines. The resulting program occupied practically all available internal storage locations in the computer. About 2 months after the program was in operation, the number of lines was increased to 54 and the program had to be completely rewritten. The new program was based upon the assumption that the user might change his requirements. It left more than a thousand memory locations unused, and assumed that either or both lines and columns might increase. Punching was done after each column, instead of after each 6 lines. The resulting program ran only 15 percent slower than the original program but took care of possible future changes.

In another company all programs were written in COBOL, taking advantage of the optional instructions the manufacturer offered. When the second-generation computer was replaced by a third-generation computer of another manufacturer, it was necessary to do quite a bit of extra programming to convert the programs to ANSI COBOL so that they would compile on the new computer.

It is not practical to list all areas of ADP where planning is needed. The foregoing examples and the following questions are illustrative of categories of planning into which the review and evaluation should go.

1. What provisions have been made for the continuation of data processing operations in case of:
   (a) Catastrophe?
   (b) External emergency?
   (c) Machine breakdown?
   (d) Loss of key personnel?
   (e) Peak loads?
2. What agreements have been made with users of similar equipment with regard to:
   (a) Use of equipment in case of emergency?
   (b) Exchange of routines and programs?
   (c) New techniques?
3. Have the agreements with regard to use of equipment in case of an emergency been tested by actually running some programs at the backup installation?
4. If a service bureau is being used, how stable is the service bureau company? Is your data at the service bureau on your tapes or your removable disks so that ownership of both device and data will be clearly established in case the company goes bankrupt?
5. Which programs were planned to be ready when the computer was turned over to the organization for use? Which ones were ready? What caused the deviations between those planned and those actually ready?
6. Is there a chronological plan for the completion of programming of computer applications? What are the differences between the plan and those actually completed? What caused the deviations?
7. Does planning take account of new technological developments? Is any organized analysis, such as a feasibility study, being conducted currently?

Operating

Priorities. Customer satisfaction is an important index of the performance of a computer installation. Such satisfaction is affected by scheduling, which enables the meeting of report deadlines. By interviewing department heads, supervisors, customers, distributors, and suppliers, the review should determine if reports are on schedule, if customer orders are filled rapidly, and if orders from suppliers primarily are normal reorders or emergency purchases.

Console procedures. Since a major portion of the costs of a data processing installation are those associated directly with the operation of the computer, the degree of efficiency of computer operations will be a significant factor in the success of an installation. The effectiveness of a review and evaluation of computer operations depends largely upon the knowledge and experience of the review group. If the reviewers do not recognize areas in which the computer is not being used well, their review will not bring these lapses and inefficiencies to light. Some examples of areas that teams have missed are use of relatively slow peripheral equipment on-line so that the central processing unit, which usually is the most expensive unit, operates only a small portion of the time; as the speed and capacity of data processing are increased, programs may be converted inefficiently by patching techniques; individual low usage of specific components, which may indicate excess equipment or poor system design; the proportion of time devoted to setup will be increased if there are many short computer runs; the proportion of time spent on reruns will be raised by improper programming, operator errors, and machine failure. Some rerun time is inevitable, but large amounts should be questioned.

Some questions that might be asked are:

1. Considering the capabilities of the equipment in terms of storage capacity, speed, sorting ability, and performance, is the equipment on site the best choice? Why or why not?
2. What actions should be taken to improve computer operations significantly? What changes, not within the purview of the computer department, should be taken to improve operations within the department?
3. Is the equipment used to its ultimate capacity? Is it used correctly? Can the work be done better or less expensively on another piece of equipment? Can the equipment be improved to handle the work more expeditiously and/or cheaply? Have probes been used to test the efficiency of computer operations? Are the channel assignments optimal? Should the computer be reconfigured?
4. After examining the computer log, what have been the downtimes for preventive maintenance and emergency maintenance? How much time has been lost due to computer malfunction? With regard to each component of the equipment, how do these downtimes compare with the experience of other companies using simi-

lar equipment? Have downtimes remained relatively stable, have they increased, or have they decreased? What, if anything, has been done to secure the assistance of the manufacturer in correcting persistent or increasing difficulties?

5. Is the manager of the computer department considering technological advancements? Is he considering advances by all companies, not just one? Is he considering future developments, such as those in optical scanning, random access, communications, and real-time systems?

6. What proportion of the computer time is spent for program testing and debugging? Is it too high? If so, a need might be indicated for better planning and/or programming. If it is too low, possibly not enough effort is being exerted to write new programs or to reprogram current applications to run faster.

7. What are the attitudes of report users toward the service they are getting from data processing? Are they satisfied? Do the customers make use of the reports as rapidly as the schedule indicates? Are the reports too voluminous? Do the users view data processing as an impartial company service, or do they associate it with a functional office?

8. To what degree does data processing cooperate with its customers? Speed? Flexibility? New reports? Changes? Constructive suggestions?

9. Who determines priorities for use of the computer? What are the criteria for the determinations? Are they followed? Are they valid? Is the schedule posted so that all who should know will know what it is? Where is it posted?

10. Is ample time set aside for testing of programs on the computer? Who does the testing? Are routines available so that the computer operators can test programs and provide memory dumps, trace routine output and other information, so that the programmer can correct the program at his desk? Are they used? Always?

11. By application, what is the schedule for the completion of programming? Is it met? How effective is the programming effort? Are completed programs continually improved? Is a routine and subroutine library maintained? What use is made of programs available from user associations or in the public domain? What is the degree of coordination between systems analysts, programmers, and auditors?

12. Are computer operational-run logs maintained? Accurate? Adequate? Are they used? For what purposes?

13. By application, what is the scheduled running time on the computer? Actual time? What causes the deviations? What attempts

have been made to smooth out peak loads? Considering all elements of cost, could the schedule have been planned better so that report deadlines would be met with lower costs? Is the installation cost-conscious? How do actual costs compare with estimated costs?

14. Are computer applications continually examined to ensure that it is worthwhile to keep them on the computer?

15. Has the equipment acquisition and release schedule been followed? To what degree?

Hardware and Associated Vendors

Prior to IBM's charging separately for hardware, programs, maintenance, and support, this vendor normally furnished both programs and hardware to the user. After this unbundling by IBM, other manufacturers followed these practices to some degree. It is therefore necessary to consider relationships with hardware vendors separately from those of other services. Accordingly, relationships with vendors are segregated into hardware and software, the latter including everything but the hardware.

Unbundling has opened up many new possibilities for computer managers. Previously, almost all equipment attached to the computer was furnished by one vendor. It is quite commonplace now to have split installations—those where equipment from different vendors is attached to the same main frame. Furthermore, companies have been established to maintain computers. Experience in their handling of split installations often has been very satisfactory. Managers of computers, therefore, must be aware of developments and of opportunities not from only one manufacturer, but also from many others, both large and small.

The following questions are suggested:

1. Month by month, what was the total time the computer was functioning properly? Malfunctioning? What were the causes of the downtime? What percentage of the total power on time each month was the computer functioning properly? Do the internal controls of the machine provide the required degree of accuracy?

2. Is there a schedule of times when the computer is to be available for preventive maintenance? To what degree is the schedule followed? Did the manufacturer comply fully with the terms of the contract?

3. By month and by component, what was the productive time? Idle time? Rerun time? Makeup time? Assembly time? Compiling time? Program-testing time? How were these times recorded? Are records maintained and available to the vendor's engineer for the resolution of discrepancies? Do the monthly billings agree with the utilization records? Does the data processing manager approve

billings before they are paid? Were the billings calculated to the best legal benefit of the user?

4. Was each item of equipment delivered on schedule? Was it turned over to the user on schedule? Did it operate as warranted? In the speeds promised? Were unforeseen items of equipment, such as voltage regulators, required? What were they? Had the vendor pointed out, before the contract was signed, the possibility of these items being needed? Does the equipment have adequate safeguards to minimize operator error? Does the card feed have a tendency to jam continuously? Do rises in temperature and/or humidity result in computer errors? At those times, are the room temperatures and/or humidity within the limits prescribed by the vendor?

5. Was a vendor's engineer always on hand when the computer was in operation? When the computer malfunctioned, was the engineer always on hand to repair it? How much time was lost waiting for the engineer to arrive? How much time was lost waiting for parts?

6. Have other vendors been considered for replacing and/or adding peripherals? Modules of memory?

7. Have maintenance personnel been requested unnecessarily from the vendor at times when the user paid a premium for such service?

Software and Associated Vendors

Computer managers have four major sources of software. They may rent or purchase it from a vendor other than the manufacturer of the computer. They may rent or purchase it from the manufacturer of the computer. They may get it without charge from the manufacturer of the computer, user associations, other users, or from the public domain. Finally, the programs may be written internally. In deciding which source to use, the manager should consider many variables, such as cost, time before the program becomes operational, documentation, maintenance of the program, computer time lost because of general characteristics of the program, skill of the internal programmers, quality of the program, and the stability of the vendor. With software involving a greater percentage of installation costs, this becomes an important area of review.

There have been times when the failure of a computer installation was attributed to the failure of the vendor to deliver the software he had promised. An installation ordered a large computer and, in accordance with the vendor's promise, commenced programming in a higher-level language. More than a year after the computer was delivered, the installation still was paying no rent on the computer, because no compiler had been completed for the higher-level language. In fact, no such compiler ever was completed for that computer. Another installation was unable to assemble and test its programs because the vendor had not completed the various computer programs promised. Another user ordered a large computer program from a software house. He made partial payments as certain milestones were reached. The vendor went out of business, and the documentation of the program was so poor that little of the completed effort could be salvaged. In each case the computer installation could only be considered a failure because money had been spent and time had passed with no productive results.

The following questions are suggested.

1. What support did the equipment manufacturer provide to the system analysis? Program writing and computer testing? Software? Advice and guidance? What was the caliber of his customers' representatives? Did he provide all of the support he promised?
2. How flexible is the operating system of the computer? Of the programs that were aborted, what percentage were stopped because of job-control language errors, as contrasted with those with program or data errors?
3. Are all COBOL programs written in ANSI COBOL?
4. Have any program packages been purchased or rented? How well are they documented? Has there been any trouble with these programs? Who maintains them? Is the vendor providing the necessary support for these programs? What percentage of computer time is devoted to overhead, as contrasted with productive time?

Personnel

Although machines, systems, and programs are important, without intelligent, well-trained, and highly motivated personnel, the data processing effort may fail. This is an area of review and evaluation that should not require deep probing, since the facts should be readily apparent. Probably the best indicator of personnel relationships is employee morale. If it is high, one expects to find good working conditions, equitable promotion policies, and a concerted effort to improve the education and training of employees. Turnover rates should not be skewed too much in any direction.

The questions that might be asked are:

1. How high is the morale of personnel in data processing? What are the causal factors? Are human aspects taken into account, and are positive steps taken to improve morale?
2. What criteria were used in selecting the manager of data processing? Systems analysts? Programmers? Other personnel? Were they valid? Are they valid now? Are any changes desirable?
3. What education and/or training was given the manager of data processing? Systems analysts? Programmers? Operators? Other

data processing personnel? Those whose jobs were affected by the computer? Suppliers of data? Users of reports? Executives? Middle management? Is there a continuing education and/or training program? What are future plans in this area? What orientation is given new employees? Is after-hours use of educational facilities encouraged and supported? Financially?

4. What is the turnover rate in each employee category in data processing? Why do people leave? Can these reasons be eliminated? Should they be eliminated? What are the recruiting practices in data processing? Can they be improved? Is there a pipeline of personnel ready to move up in each category of personnel?

5. What is the age distribution of data processing employees? Have any plans been made to replace key personnel who may retire or transfer? What are the educational levels of programmers, systems analysts, and the pipeline of replacements? What can be done to improve it?

Controls and Security Provisions

Input Controls. The purposes of input controls are to assure that:

1. All data are received on time.
2. All data are converted accurately and completely to a machine-readable language.
3. All data enter the computer for processing.

Some questions that should be asked in this area are:

1. Is a log of incoming data maintained?
2. What controls are maintained to ensure that data are received on time?
3. What actions result if data is not received when scheduled?
4. If data still is not received when processing must start to complete the report on time, what actions are taken?
5. Are item counts maintained and checked by the computer to ensure that all data is converted and enter the computer for processing? Control totals?
6. In case the item counts and/or control totals do not agree, are both figures printed so that they can be reconciled?
7. If data is submitted from remote locations directly into the computer, are messages numbered sequentially for each submitting location? Are check-point totals maintained? How are undecipherable messages handled?

Computer Controls. The purposes of computer controls are to assure that:

1. Only valid data is processed.
2. Unacceptable data is flagged for correction or removal.
3. All data is processed through each program in an application.
4. Hardware controls work satisfactorily.

Some questions that should be asked are:

1. In validity checking are the following controls used where practical: Character mode tests? Self-checking numbers? Tests of reasonableness and consistency? Are items compared against tables of legitimate items? On what basis are decisions made on which controls to install for validity checking?
2. In run-to-run controls, are file identities verified by the computer before programs are run? Are record counts and control totals maintained for each file? Are input data, files, and output data sequence-checked during computer runs?
3. If data is submitted from remote locations directly into the computer, is a transaction log maintained? Are check points maintained so that the system can be restarted after a malfunction? Are return messages to submitting terminals used? For both correct and incorrect items? Are terminals limited to particular types of transactions? Is a daily listing of all transactions maintained? Are files dumped periodically? Does the computer scan on-line files during slack periods for apparent errors?

Noncomputer Controls. The purposes of noncomputer controls are:

1. To promote the effective use of people and equipment.
2. To provide for the continuity of data processing.

Some questions are:

1. Are there written, formal procedures outside of data processing for the capture of data as close to the source as possible?
2. Is a control group established to receive control information, reconcile all discrepancies, and ensure reprocessing or proper disposal of all questionable transactions?
3. Are there clear-cut, documented operator procedures within data processing to prevent operator intervention?
4. Are operator entries restricted to the use of the console? Is a copy of the console typewriter output reviewed regularly by a responsible person? Is the review assignment changed without prior warning?
5. How are determinations made concerning the length of time documents are to be preserved? Who makes these determinations?

Security Provisions. The purpose of security provisions is the preservation of company assets. Questions to be asked are:

1. Is work assigned so that one person acts as a check on another? In transactions involving the assets of the company, does one person have control of such transactions from start to finish?
2. Is operator access to checks limited and controlled strictly? Must the operator account for each check? Are all checks prenumbered?
3. Is the computer installation in a safe location? Is the building itself safe?
4. Is the building fireproof? The computer site? What fire-preventive and corrective measures are used?
5. Is access to the computer installation limited to those with actual need for such access? How?
6. Are tapes in a locked location under specific and limited control? Who has access to this room? Where are backup tapes maintained?

Timeliness of Data Processing. Even though incoming data is received on time, the prompt completion of final reports is not assured. Especially in the large service-center type of data processing installation, unless proper precautions are taken, it is possible that the report deadline may be missed because of conflicting priorities; unexpected trouble in equipment, programs, or software; or human error.

1. What controls are established to ensure the timely completion of all reports?
2. Who monitors the timeliness?
3. What actions are taken if the processing falls behind schedule?

Output. The review group should prepare a report of the outputs of data processing. This report should contain a brief description of the methods by which reports are controlled. Each report should be identified, given a number, and the method of preparation should be described. The authority, frequency, purpose, and use should be assessed, along with reasons why it is produced automatically rather than by some other method.

1. Are requests for new reports screened? Are existing reports reviewed continually? Does the review consider the value of a report and its associated costs against the value of another report and its associated costs?
2. What is the user's evaluation of the advantages of the report? Considering only end products, not intermediate results, what is the frequency in changes in report content or format?

Run Books. The primary purpose of run books is to document the procedures to be followed in both computer and EAM data processing. Following the procedures in these run books insures that identical methods will be followed each time a report is processed. Furthermore, they furnish guidance for console operators. They constitute a safeguard against disrupted data processing even though operators leave the company. One of the measures of performance of a data processing installation is the availability of written procedures, of which run books are designated as complete guides to programs.

1. Have run books been prepared? For all applications? How many copies? Where is each copy maintained? To whom are the copies available?
2. Do the run books contain both EAM and computer procedures for the same application? What are the contents of the run books? Are all run books current?

Economics

Among the reasons for the review and evaluation is a comparison of both benefits and cost with what was anticipated in these categories—an analysis of comparative costs. This is the time to make a "trial balance" of both financial advantages and disadvantages of the computer. If the net costs are available, management will be able to make an informed judgement as to whether the benefits of the computer contrast favorably with the measurable costs. It is not necessary to use precise figures, since exact ones may be difficult to ascertain. This is especially true in defining and measuring savings and advantages, although costs of both capital investment and operating expenses are relatively easy to total.

1. Within the data processing installation, what have been the net reductions or increases in payroll, machine rental, software rental, and other expenses such as punch cards, printed forms, heating, and air conditioning? What were the net increases or decreases in computer-related costs outside the computer department? Have there been any changes in payroll in other departments because of the introduction of the computer? Have there been any other measurable savings, such as reduced investment in and carrying charges for inventory?
2. What has been the return on the investment of the computer? Has the initial investment been recovered? Do current operations represent a net gain or a loss? What future financial trends are estimated from the currently installed equipment? Has the question whether to lease or purchase the computer been given a recent and fair consideration? Have third-party leases been considered?

SUMMARY

Considering the percentage of total costs allocated to data processing and the tremendous potential for management benefits, a periodic review of data processing operations is essential. The members of such a review team should have stature and be knowledgeable and objective. The first review should be made during the second year of operation, and subsequent reviews should be made every two years thereafter. The charter should be issued by top management and should specify the areas to be reviewed. The areas normally to be reviewed are top management participation, objectives, organization, systems, planning, operations, hardware and associated vendors, software and associated vendors, personnel, controls and security provisions, and economics.

As systems get larger, more integrated, and real-time, the knowledge and ability of the review team must expand. The areas to be reviewed will not lessen, but will increase as geographically separate installations are linked into integrated systems.

EXERCISES

1. A computer-based information system has been established in one of your plants in California. Establish a plan for evaluating the effectiveness of the system, including when it should be evaluated, who should do the evaluating, and what elements should be evaluated.
2. What are the different levels of review and evaluation? Who should be on the review team from each of these levels?
3. Discuss the items to be included in an implementing instruction for a review and evaluation. What factors influence each of these items?
4. Select the three areas of review and evaluation that you consider to be most important. What questions would you ask in these areas?
5. Develop a detailed plan for the review and evaluation of one of the areas to be reviewed, including who is to be included on the team, whom each is to interview in the area, what questions will be asked, and how the results will be evaluated. Include a timetable of the estimated time to complete the review and evaluation.

APPENDIX A ◀ XYZ COMPANY

Washington, D.C., 20001
XYZ INTERNAL
NOTICE 4400
SA
December 11, 1972

XYZ INTERNAL NOTICE 4400
From: President, XYZ Company
To: All Offices and Divisions of XYZ
Subj: XYZ Automatic Data Processing Feasibility Study Committee; establishment of
Ref: (a) XYZINST 4400.16 of October 26, 1972

1. *Purpose.* To initiate a feasibility study of a possible automatic data processing system for use of the XYZ Company and to establish a full-time working committee to accomplish the study.

2. *Background.* The rapid developments in the capacities of computers and data communication facilities necessitate a review of present XYZ methods for handling business data processing problems. Since certain XYZ-managed activities have been making significant progress in the installation of computers in recent months, it becomes mandatory that the "home-office" keep abreast of its widespread family. The question is whether a computer is feasible for the headquarters office. If it is possible that a computer will be of assistance, this feasibility study will be followed by an applications study. Otherwise the installation of a computer in the headquarters office will not be considered further at this time.

3. *Establishment of a Working Committee*

a. The membership of the XYZ Automatic Data Processing System Feasibility Study Committee is as follows:

Member	Division
Mr. R. Harris (chairman)	DM
Mr. M. M. Martin	J1
Mr. J. J. Johnson	M3
Mrs. A. Chait	T1
Mr. E. Lohengrin	TX

b. The Chairman is charged with the overall responsibility for the completion of the study and for the submission of the report. Other members of the committee are assigned on a full-time basis until their tasks are accomplished. Throughout the period, the above-named personnel are assigned to the committee. They will, however, be attached administratively to their regular divisions.

c. The committee headquarters is established in Room 2423, Building B.

d. The committee is established effective December 11, 1972.

4. *Action*

a. *General*

(1) The Working Committee Chairman will report to the Vice-President (Code O) via the Director of Information (Code OS). The work will be done by full-time committee members with such part-time assistance by operating divisions and staff offices as is required.

(2) All vice-presidents and directors are directed to assist the efforts of the Working Committee as requested when their areas of work are under review.

(3) Code S16 will provide consultation assistance and service in the manner as is now provided to field activities.

(4) Code T will provide technical assistance as required.

(5) Funds approved by Code O for travel and per diem for the Working Committee will be provided by Code OD.

(6) Code OJ will provide clerical assistance as required.

b. *Specific*

(1) Reference (a) contains guidelines for XYZ-managed activities. While it is not pertinent to the establishment of this committee, it provides the current objectives of the company. Broadly speaking, the Working Committee will be concerned with the following:

(a) Examine the current information system of the company in terms of adequacy, timeliness, accuracy, form, and cost.

(b) In general terms postulate an information system in terms of adequacy, timeliness, accuracy, and cost that will better fill the needs of the company.

(c) On the basis of a comparison of the current and the postulated systems, recommend whether it is worthwhile for the company to do an applications study. This recommendation, whether affirmative or negative, will be made to the Vice-President (Code O) for approval no later than January 13, 1973.

(2) The tasks of the Working Committee are:

(a) Visit activities that already have installed a computer or may be investigating the requirements for a computer.

(b) Discuss present and proposed procedures with operating divisions concerned and solicit aid as necessary.

(c) Use existing data, after assuring its accuracy, in order to avoid time-consuming studies duplicating past efforts.

(d) Discuss with Code S16 the system that is postulated and derive the approximate monthly cost of the computer that is needed. All costs will be included.

5. *Completion date.* Target date for completion of the feasibility study is January 13, 1973. Any deviation from this date requires specific approval of the Vice-President (Code O) of the XYZ Company.

6. *Cancellation date.* This notice is cancelled on January 14, 1973, unless modified by action indicated in paragraph 5.

APPENDIX B ◀ XYZ COMPANY

Washington, D. C., 20001
XYZ INTERNAL
NOTICE 4410
SA
January 14, 1973

XYZ INTERNAL NOTICE 4410
From: President, XYZ Company
To: All Offices and Divisions of XYZ
Subj: XYZ Automatic Data Processing Applications Study
        Committee; establishment of
Ref: (a) XYZINST 4400.16 of October 26, 1972.

1. *Purpose.* To initiate an applications study of a possible automatic data processing system for the use of the XYZ Company and to establish a full-time working committee to accomplish the study.

2. *Background.* A January 6, 1973, report of the XYZ Automatic Data Processing Feasibility Study Committee recommended that the XYZ company could profitably use a computer at the headquarters office. It recommended also that an applications study committee be established to develop in necessary detail the specifications of the systems and subsystems that are desirable. This notice establishes the XYZ Company Automatic Data Processing Applications Study Committee to develop the specifications. If, in the opinion of the committee, however, a computer will not be of assistance, a recommendation to discontinue the study should be made.

3. *Establishment of a Working Committee*
   a. The membership of the XYZ Automatic Data Processing System Applications Study Committee is as follows:

Member	*Division*
Mr. R. Harris (Chairman)	DM
Mr. M. M. Martin	J1
Mr. J. J. Johnson	M3
Mrs. A. Chait	T1
Mr. C. Trujillo	T1
Mr. V. Bauer	T1
Miss E. O'Byrne	T1

b. The Chairman is charged with the overall responsibility for the completion of the study and for the submission of the report. Other members of the Committee are assigned on a full-time basis until their tasks are accomplished. Throughout the period, the above-named personnel are assigned to the Committee. They will, however, be attached administratively to their regular divisions.

c. The Committee's headquarters is established in Room 2423, Building B.

d. The Committee is established effective January 13, 1973.

4. *Action*

a. *General*

(1). The Working Committee Chairman will report to the Vice-President (Code O) via the Director of Information (Code OS). The work will be done by full-time committee members with such part-time assistance by operating divisions and staff offices as is required.

(2). All vice-presidents and directors are directed to assist the efforts of the Working Committee as requested when their areas of work are under review.

(3). Code S16 will provide consultation assistance and service in the same manner as is now provided to field activities.

(4). Code T will provide technical assistance as required.

(5). Funds approved by Code O for travel and per diem for the Working Committee will be provided by Code OD.

(6). Code OJ will provide clerical assistance as required.

b. *Specific*

(1). Reference (a) contains guidelines for XYZ-managed activities. While it is not pertinent to the establishment of this Committee, it provides the current objectives of the company. Broadly speaking, the Working Committee will be concerned with the following:

(a). Develop the necessary details of the system and all subsystems. This information ultimately will become a part of the Request for Proposal (RFP) which will be sent to vendors of computers.

(b). On the basis of a comparison of the current and the postulated systems recommend whether it is worthwhile for the company to select a computer. This recommendation, whether affirmative or negative, will be made to the Vice-President (Code O) for approval no later than December 29, 1973.

(2) The tasks of the Working Committee are:

(a). Visit activities that already have installed a computer or have completed the applications study for the installation of a computer.

(b). Discuss present and proposed procedures with operating divisions concerned and solicit aid as necessary.

(c). Use existing data, after assuring its accuracy, in order to avoid time-consuming studies duplicating past efforts.

(d). Prepare flow charts, block diagrams, and reports of present and proposed procedures selected for adoption in order to provide programming guides.

(e). Prepare details of the proposed computer input, including format, average and high workloads, input media, timing, and constraints.

(f). Prepare details of the proposed computer files to be maintained, including format, media on which to be maintained, and constraints. Data also will be furnished on the current size of each file and the anticipated growth rate.

(g). Prepare details of the means by which input data and file data will be manipulated in order to furnish the output, including editing procedures, conversion formulas, timing, and constraints.

(h). Prepare details of the proposed computer output, including format, media of output, timing, constraints, and whether output will be regularly scheduled and/or by request.

(i). Develop a long-range program outline for computer use covering the period through calendar year 1978.

(j). Discuss with Code S16 the system that is postulated and derive the approximate monthly cost of the computer that is needed. All costs will be included.

5. *Completion date.* Target date for completion of the applications study is December 29, 1973. Any deviation from this date requires specific approval of the Vice-President (Code O) of the XYZ Company.

6. *Cancellation date.* This notice is cancelled on December 30, 1973, unless modified by action indicated in paragraph 5.

APPENDIX C ◀ SELF-EVALUATION QUESTIONNAIRE

I. Objectives

    A. Have any data processing objectives been established?
    B. What are they?
    C. Are they written?
    D. Are all of them written?
    E. Who participated in establishing these objectives?
    F. When were these objectives first established?
    G. Have there been any revisions?
    H. Is there a schedule for a regular review of objectives?
    I. How often are the objectives reviewed? By whom?
    J. What changes should be made in the objectives?
    K. What has been especially advantageous or disadvantageous concerning these objectives?

II. Organization

    A. Feasibility and applications studies

        1. Were feasibility and applications studies conducted? By whom?

        2. If study groups were used, who selected those to be on the groups? What was the background of these members?

        3. Were the study groups given a written charter? By whom? Is a copy available?

        4. Were consultants used? If so, how?

        5. To whom did the study groups report?

        6. Organizationally, where were the persons to whom the study group reported in relation to top management?

        7. What has been especially advantageous or disadvantageous

concerning the study groups, the level of management to which they reported, and the background of the individuals in the groups?

B. Organizational placement of data processing

1. To whom does the head of data processing report?

2. Organizationally, where is the person to whom he reports?

3. Has the organizational placement of data processing been changed since its inauguration? If so, why? Did the change help? How?

4. What has been especially advantageous or disadvantageous concerning the organizational placement of data processing?

C. Internal organization of data processing

1. Sketch an organizational chart of the data processing group.

2. If systems analysts are included within data processing, what is the line of demarcation in duties, as contrasted with those of computer programmers?

3. If systems analysts are included in data processing, are there any systems analysts elsewhere in the organization? If so, where? What is the line of demarcation in the duties between the different groups of system analysts?

4. What has been especially advantageous or disadvantageous concerning locating systems analysts in multiple locations in the organization?

5. If systems analysts are not included in data processing:

a. Who made the decision not to include them in data processing? Why?

b. Where are the systems analysts? Sketch an organizational chart to show their placement.

c. What has been especially advantageous or disadvantageous concerning the lack of systems analysts in data processing?

6. Are all computer programmers within the data processing organization? If so, what has been especially advantageous or disadvantageous concerning this concentration of programmers?

7. If all computer programmers are not within the data processing organization:

a. In what parts of the organization are they?

b. Do these decentralized programmers prepare instructions

for all types of programs? If not, what do they program as contrasted with what the centralized programmers do?

c. What has been especially advantageous or disadvantageous concerning the decentralization of the programming effort?

8. Are any operations research personnel included within data processing?

a. If not, is operations research carried on elsewhere in the organization?

b. What is the line of demarcation between system analysts and operations research personnel?

c. What has been especially advantageous or disadvantageous concerning the placement of operations research personnel in the organization?

III. Selection of Personnel

A. Were any personnel selected for data processing before the various positions were defined? If so, for what positions?

B. Were complete position descriptions prepared before the remainder of the positions were filled?

C. How was the availability of data processing openings publicized? Was it effective?

D. What was especially advantageous or disadvantageous concerning this method of publication?

E. What was the "in-house" reaction to the announcement?

F. If "out-of-house" applicants were sought, what successes or difficulties were encountered?

G. Were written tests used in the selection process? If so, for what purpose?

1. What tests were used for each category of personnel?

2. Is the use of these tests considered to be advantageous or disadvantageous? Why?

3. To what degree did the written test enter into the selection process?

H. Was experience considered as an evaluation factor in the selection process?

    1. What importance was attached to experience (by type of position)?

    2. Who evaluated the experience?

    3. Were any formal criteria established for evaluating the experience?

I. Were personal interviews used in the selection process?

    1. For what types of personnel?

    2. Who did the interviewing?

    3. What weight was attached to the interview in the selection process?

    4. Were any particular characteristics sought? Located?

J. Were personnel selected for specific data processing positions or were they selected generally as "applicants with potential" to start at the lowest data processing positions so that they could progress through various positions? If neither, what policy was followed?

IV. System Design

A. Who designed the system for data processing? When?

B. What approach to system design was used? (For example: one-for-one changeover, one-for-one changeover with improvements, department-by-department, integrated system, or combination method.)

C. If the system was integrated to a significant degree, was the conversion done all at one time, or was it done subsystem by subsystem?

    1. How many subsystems are in the system?

    2. Have the boundaries between subsystems been defined specifically?

    3. Is there a list of all interfaces for each subsystem, together with a detailed description of each?

D. What percentage of the system design effort was devoted to improving areas already on the computer?

E. What percentage of the system design effort was devoted to developing an integrated system?

F. Is there now an active investigation of the advantages and disadvantages of revising the data processing system and/or changing the capacity and/or changing equipment?

G. What is the grade level or salary range of the "journeyman" systems analysts?

H. What has been especially advantageous or disadvantageous concerning the system-design effort?

V. Planning for Preconversion

A. Who did the planning for the preconversion effort?

B. Who approved this planning?

C. Were charts used in controlling the various elements of the preconversion effort? What type? How effective were they?

D. What controls were established to assure that all efforts were proceeding as planned?

E. What was the planned time between the decision to get a computer and the delivery of the computer? What was the actual time? If there was a deviation, what caused it?

F. In the light of experience in planning for the installation of a computer, if the same preconversion effort were now starting, would the lead time be the same? Earlier? Later? Why?

G. How many programmers were involved in the initial programming effort?

H. What was the role of the vendor in the initial programming? How well was this role filled?

I. Where and at what times of the day was a computer available for debugging programs? Was it always available and operative when desired? When promised? Was there enough debugging time? How much more was needed? Why was it not supplied?

J. Were debugging and utility routines promised by the vendor provided at the time promised? How effective were they?

K. Was there a file conversion? If so:

1. Were the old files converted to computer-readable files? If so:

a. What was the relative accuracy of the old files?

b. What was the relationship between the number of such

inaccuracies in the old file and the number created (temporarily) by the conversion process?

c. Were any files combined, expanded? To what degree? Why?

2. If the old files were not converted:
a. Were new files created from the original documents?
b. Was a new file started from the incoming documents without any effort to build a historical file?
c. If neither, what method was followed?

3. What was especially advantageous or disadvantageous about the file-conversion effort?

L. To what extent did personnel from outside data processing enter into the conversion or creation of new computer-readable files?

M. What controls were established or methods used to ensure accurate files? What degree of accuracy was desired? Achieved? In view of the errors corrected, was the control effort too great? Too little? Just about right? Why?

N. Were consultants used to any degree in the conversion effort? Service bureaus? To what extent? How effectively?

O. Were supplies, such as preprinted forms, magnetic tape, etc., available when needed, where needed, and in the quantity needed?

P. Was peripheral equipment available when, where, and in the quantity needed?

Q. Was the need of what supplies and/or peripheral equipment overlooked in the original planning? Why? Was it corrected in time, so that the preconversion or conversion effort was not hindered?

R. In general, was there fairly complete satisfaction with the preconversion effort? If it were repeated, what changes would be made?

VI. Planning for Conversion

A. Were there parallel operations during conversion? If so:

1. How long?

2. Were any errors found?

3. If so, what percentage were in the new system?

B. If parallel operations were not used during the conversion:

1. How was the cutover to the new system made?

2. What troubles were encountered?

3. How soon was the former equipment released?

C. What was especially advantageous or disadvantageous concerning the conversion method?

D. What were the more troublesome aspects of the conversion?

E. If the conversion were repeated, could the troubles be avoided? How?

F. How valid were the estimates of the time and cost to make conversion? What caused the difference?

G. What elements were not ready at the time scheduled for the conversion? Why? What corrective measures were taken?

H. If the conversion was from one computer to another:

1. Were any programs run in an emulation or a simulation mode on the new computer?

2. Who made the decision to continue in that mode? What was the basis for the decision?

3. Is there a schedule for reprogramming part or all of the programs run in emulation or simulation modes? Was it followed? Why or why not?

4. Were any programs written previously in the language of the earlier computer? Were they converted? If so, how?

5. Were any program packages purchased, rented, or obtained free to aid in the conversion? Who supplied them? How effective were they?

VII. Reports

A. During the feasibility and application studies

1. What reports were submitted by team members to the team leader?

2. How often?

3. Under what authority?

4. For what purposes were these reports used?

5. Were these reports the basis of reports to higher echelons?

B. During the preconversion effort

1. What reports were submitted to the director of the preconversion effort?

2. By whom? How often? Under what authority?

3. For what purposes were these reports used?

4. Were these reports the basis of reports to higher echelons?

5. What was reported? To whom? Under what authority?

C. During the conversion:

1. What reports were submitted to the director of the conversion?

2. By whom? How often? Under what authority?

3. For what purposes were these reports used?

4. Were these reports the basis of reports to higher echelons?

5. What was reported? To whom? Under what authority?

D. During operations

1. What reports are submitted to the director of data processing operations?

2. By whom? How often? Under what authority?

3. For what purposes are these reports used?

4. Are these reports the basis of reports to higher echelons?

5. What is reported? To whom? Under what authority?

VIII. Physical Facility

A. What problems were encountered in the planning for the physical facility? How were they met?

B. What problems were encountered in the building outside the data processing area? How were they met?

C. What problems were encountered in the data processing area? How were they met?

D. Is any part of the data processing area on a raised floor? What part(s)? Were there any problems with the raised floors?

E. Was this the first data processing installation that the builder or contractor ever constructed?

F. Draw a small diagram of the location of the various parts of the data processing division.

G. Is there anything especially good or bad about these locations?

H. What preparations (if any) were made for the possible growth of the data processing effort?

I. If the physical facility could be reconstructed, what changes would be beneficial?

IX. Operations

A. Priorities

1. Who makes decisions regarding priority of system analysis? Programming? Processing?

2. On what basis? By what authority?

3. What has been especially advantageous or disadvantageous concerning the handling of the assignment of priorities?

B. Controls of timeliness of data processing:

1. Is a log of incoming data maintained?

2. What controls are maintained to ensure data is received on time?

3. What actions result if data is not received when scheduled?

4. If data still is not received when processing must start to complete the report on time, what actions are taken?

5. What controls are established to ensure the timely completion of all reports?

6. Who monitors the timeliness?

7. What actions are taken if the processing falls behind schedule?

8. What has been especially advantageous or disadvantageous concerning the manner in which the timeliness of data processing is controlled?

C. Controls of the accuracy of data processing

1. What controls are established to ensure that all incoming data is received? That there are no duplicate submissions?

2. What controls are established to ensure that all data received

is converted accurately and completely to a machine-readable language?

3. What controls are established to ensure that all data is processed through each run of an application? That none is processed more than once?

4. What controls are established to ensure the accuracy and completeness of incoming data?

5. What controls are established to ensure the accuracy and completeness of the data processing?

6. Have inaccurate reports been released? If so, what caused the inaccuracies and were there any unfavorable effects?

7. Is a log kept of erroneous input data sent to data processing? Is this log segregated by source of the data? Is there a designated path by which the source of the errors is informed concerning them? Are the procedures for such reporting of errors in writing?

8. What has been particularly advantageous or disadvantageous concerning the manner in which the accuracy of data processing was controlled?

D. Controls of output

1. Is a log of report distribution maintained?

2. By whom? How effective is it?

3. Are reports delivered by data processing? Is a third party used for the delivery? Do the "customers" send for their data processing reports?

4. Is any review made of reports regarding:
   a. Excess information?
   b. Desirability of including additional information?
   c. Furnishing reports only where there is a need to know?
   d. Use of reports for valid purposes?
   e. Value of the reports in relation to their cost?

5. What has been especially advantageous or disadvantageous concerning the manner in which the reports are controlled?

E. Run books

1. Have run books been prepared? For all applications?

2. How many copies? Where is each copy maintained?

3. To whom are the copies available?

4. Do the run books contain both electric accounting machine and computer procedures for the same application?

5. What are the contents of the run books?

6. Are all run books current?

7. What has been particularly advantageous or disadvantageous concerning the manner in which run books are maintained and used?

F. Console procedures

1. Identify the computer used. How much memory? How many tape drives? How much disk space? What peripheral units? What operating system?

2. Is a computer log maintained?
   a. By the operating system or by some other means?
   b. Contents?
   c. What is the method of recording the time?
   d. Are the computer units metered? Which ones?
   e. Is the time on the computer log verified and reconciled with the customer engineer?

3. Do programmers debug their programs at the console? If so, what is the average monthly total debugging time?

4. If not, who makes the debugging runs? Are they debugged in a batch mode, or is the operating system available for serial debugging?

5. By category of operation, what is the average monthly time in use of the computer?

6. How many console operators are available?

7. Do personnel other than console operators ever operate the computer on production runs? If so:
   a. Who?
   b. Why?
   c. How often?

8. Is assistance, such as tape handlers, available to the console operators? If so, how much?

9. Are the console operators all of one sex? If so, which sex? Why?

10. If not, are both sexes equally satisfactory? If not, why not?

11. Who readies program decks or tapes and input decks or tapes for computer runs? Removable disk packs?

12. What procedures are followed to minimize the computer time between runs?

13. Are parallel operations (multiprogramming or multiprocessing) conducted on the computer?

    a. If not, is the computer capable of being programmed to do these operations?

    b. If capable of being so programmed, why has it not been done?

14. What has been especially advantageous or disadvantageous concerning the manner in which console procedures are handled?

G. Preservation of assets

1. If it was possible to choose the building where the computer installation is located:

    a. Is it in a site not susceptible to natural catastrophes such as storm, flood, and earthquake?

    b. Is the building in a dangerous place such as at the end of an airport runway or near volatile materials?

2. Where in the building is the installation located?

3. Is the building fireproof?

4. Is the installation fireproof?

    a. What type of fire-extinguishing system does the installation have?

    b. Do pipes with water or steam in them run through the installation?

5. What protections shield the installation from external emanations?

6. Is there any protection against variances in voltage? What is the protection?

7. Are there carpets on the floor of the computer room?

8. What provisions are there so that people who do not have to go into the computer room are kept out of it?

9. What protection is there against theft, unauthorized use, and sabotage during off-hours?

10. Is there a tape and/or removable-disk storage room?

    a. Is it locked and/or under the control of a tape librarian?

  b. Is there a withdrawal log? What are its contents? Is it current?

  c. Who has access to the tape/disk room?

11. Where are backup tapes and/or disks stored?

12. Is there ever only one person in the computer room?

13. What protection is there against unauthorized changes of programs and/or files?

14. What protection is there against an unauthorized reading or use of programs and/or files?

15. If telecommunications directly into the computer are used, what devices are there to prevent unauthorized use, theft, and sabotage?

16. Is a log of all queries and transactions maintained for the on-line system?

17. If time sharing is done on the computer of another company, how are the records you have on that computer protected?

18. What backup provisions are there if the computer fails? Have they acutally been used? Is the agreement in writing?

19. Is the company insured against risks for which no protective measures have been taken?

20. How are decisions made concerning which countermeasures to take? Who makes them?

H. Maintenance of equipment

  1. Is the equipment maintained by the vendor of such equipment? If so:

  a. Is there a charge for such services?

  b. Is the customer engineer on the premises at all times during production runs?

  c. If he is not there at all times, what has been the average time between the call for him and his arrival? The longest time?

  d. How cooperative has the customer engineer been?

  2. If not, who maintains the equipment? How well? What are the arrangements for maintenance services?

  3. What time of the day normally is scheduled for computer operations?

  4. Is preventive maintenance time regularly scheduled? At what day and time? Why?

5. What has been the average downtime per month? The longest period of downtime?

6. What units (if known) caused the downtime?

7. What has been especially advantageous or disadvantageous concerning the maintenance procedures for the computer?

I. Payments to vendor (if computer is rented)

1. Answer without consulting contract:
   a. What times are chargeable? What times are not chargeable?
   b. What are the provisions for averaging the time of multiple units?
   c. What are the provisions for overtime payments?
   d. What are the provisions concerning non-overtime, non-normally scheduled operations?
   e. What other charges can be assessed by the manufacturer?
   f. What services are available from the vendor without charge?

2. Is a copy of the contract available? If so, compare the previous answers item by item with the contractual provisions.

3. What steps have been taken to minimize rental payments to the vendor?

4. Have there been any disputes with the vendor's representatives regarding the amount of rental payments due? Why or why not?

5. In view of the experience to date, is the equipment on hand excessive to needs?

6. What has been particularly advantageous or disadvantageous concerning the manner in which payments for computer rental are handled?

J. Assistance by the vendor

1. What are the contractual provisions for assistance to be furnished without charge by the manufacturer?

2. Is there complete agreement concerning the meaning of these contractual provisions?

3. Has the contractual assistance been given?
   a. If so, to what degree?
   b. If not, why not?

    4. Of what value was the assistance furnished by the vendor? Why?

    5. What improvements should be or have been made to the vendor's software?

    6. What has · been especially advantageous or disadvantageous concerning the vendor's assistance?

X. Review and Evaluation

    A. Are regular reviews and evaluations made of the data processing operation? If so:

        1. By whom? How often? Under what authority?

        2. How soon after the initial conversion was the first review made?

        3. What items are covered in the review?

        4. Is the report in writing?

        5. To whom is the report made?

        6. What actions were instigated by the report?

    B. If regular reviews and evaluations of data processing operations are not made:

        1. Have any such reviews and evaluations of data processing operations been made?

        2. If so:

            a. By whom? How often? Under what authority?

            b. How soon after the initial conversion was the first review made?

            c. What items were covered in the review?
            d. Was the report in writing?
            e. To whom was the report made?
            f. What actions were instigated by the report?

        3. If a review and evaluation has not been made:
            a. Why not?
            b. Is it felt that such a review would be beneficial? Why or why not?

XI. Costs

    A. Are costs records of data processing maintained? By whom?

    B. What costs are included? Excluded? Why?

C. Are costs distributed to individual applications or subsystems?

    1. Direct costs only? If so, all such costs?

    2. Indirect costs? If so, what indirect costs? How are they pro-rated to individual applications or subsystems?

D. What uses are made of the record of data processing costs?

E. Are "customers" charged for the data processing services they receive? What costs?

F. Are "customers" informed of the costs of the data processing services they receive?

G. When requests for data processing services are received, are cost estimates prepared?

    1. If not, why not?

    2. If so:

        a. Is the estimate used as an aid in deciding whether to comply with or to refuse the request?

        b. Is the "customer" informed of the cost estimate?

H. What is the basis for assessing particular applications with direct costs?

I. Are samples available of records kept and of reports made?

J. Is there anything especially advantageous or disadvantageous concerning the system of recording and using the records of the costs of data processing?

XII. External Relations

A. How soon after the decision to conduct a feasibility study was made was an announcement made to the employees?

    1. Through what medium?

    2. Under what authority?

    3. What was included in this announcement?

    4. Did employee gossip and/or fears cause any difficulties?

    5. Were any announcements made to the general public?

B. During the conduct of the feasibility and applications studies:

    1. Were periodic reports made to the employees?

    2. What was reported?

    3. Through what medium?

    4. Under what authority?

    5. Were any announcements made to the general public?

C. When the decision was made to install a computer:

    1. How soon was an announcement made to the employees?

    2. Through what medium?

    3. Under what authority?

    4. What was included in this announcement?

    5. Was any announcement made to the general public?

D. Was there any real effort to fill data processing positions from within?

    1. What was done?

    2. How successful was it (by types of position)?

    3. Were people already in the company given any preference over outsiders ?

E. What efforts were made to publicize the advantages of data processing throughout the company? How successful were they?

F. What methods were used to influence potential "customers" to make more extensive use of data processing?

G. Are records kept on incoming data (dates and times received) and when reports are sent to "customers"?

H. What has been especially advantageous or disadvantageous concerning the manner in which external relations were handled?

XIII. Training

A. Were executive-orientation courses offered?

    1. For whom? By whom? When?

    2. How successful were they?

B. Were orientation courses offered for employees who would have no direct contact with data processing?

    1. For whom? By whom? When?

    2. How successful were they?

C. Were orientation courses offered for employees who will furnish input to data processing?

    1. By whom?

    2. How successful were they?

D. Were employees who will furnish input data to data processing trained in such data preparation?

    1. By whom?

    2. How successful were they?

E. Were employees who will use the output of data processing given orientation in computers?

    1. By whom?

    2. How successfully?

F. Were orientation courses offered for employees who will be, or think they will be, affected by the computer?

    1. By whom?

    2. How successfully?

G. Were retraining courses offered to those whose positions will be affected by the computer?

    1. What percentage of these employees will enter directly into the data processing effort?

    2. For those who will enter directly into the data processing effort:
       a. What kind of training were they given?
       b. By whom?
       c. How successful was it?

    3. For those who will work outside data processing:
       a. What kind of training were they given?
       b. By whom?
       c. How successful was it?

H. Did the head of data processing receive any formal training?

    1. By whom?

    2. What type of training?

    3. How successful was it?

I. What training courses were offered for systems analysts?

    1. By whom?

    2. What were they taught?

    3. How successful were they?

J. What training courses were offered for programmers?

    1. By whom?

    2. What were they taught?

    3. How successful were they?

K. What training courses were offered for console operators?

    1. By whom?

    2. How successful were they?

L. What training courses were offered for maintenance personnel?

    1. By whom?

    2. How successful were they?

M. What training courses were offered for control personnel?

    1. What was taught?

    2. By whom?

    3. How successful were they?

N. What training courses were offered for tape handlers?

    1. By whom?

    2. How successful were they?

O. What training courses were offered for tape librarians?

    1. What was taught?

    2. By whom?

    3. How successfully?

P. What training courses were offered for operators of peripheral equipment?

    1. By whom?

    2. How successful were they?

Q. What training courses were offered for other operating personnel?

       1. By whom?

       2. How successful were they?

R. Has attendance at users' meetings been used as a training device?

       1. For whom?

       2. How successfully?

S. Has attendance at professional conferences been used as a training device?

       1. For whom?

       2. How successfully?

T. Have visits to other computer installations been used as training devices?

       1. For whom?

       2. How successfully?

U. Has published material been used as a training device?

       1. What material?

       2. For whom?

       3. How successfully?

V. Is there a formal education program for data processing employees?

       1. If so, is there a full-time educational program?
          a. For whom?
          b. How successful was it?

       2. Is there a part-time educational program?
          a. For whom?
          b. How successful?

◀ BIBLIOGRAPHY

Accounting

Canadian Institute of Chartered Accountants. *Computer Control Guidelines.* Princeton, N.J.: Auerbach Publications, Inc., 1971.

Clark, Frank James. *Accounting Programs and Business Systems.* Palisades, Calif.: Goodyear Publishing Co., Inc., 1971.

Cunitz, Jonathan A. *Computer Cases in Accounting.* Englewood Cliffs, N.J.: Prentice-Hall, Inc., 1972.

Pillsbury, William F. *Computer Augmented Accounting.* Dallas, Texas: South-Western Publishing Co., 1971.

Sweeney, Robert B. *The Use of Computers in Accounting.* Englewood Cliffs, N.J.: Prentice-Hall, Inc., 1971.

Applications

Abrams, Michael Ellis, ed. *Medical Computing.* New York: American Elsevier Publishing Co., Inc., 1970.

Alford, B. G., and F. E. Colvin. *Hospital Electronic Data Processing Journal Articles.* Flushing, N.Y.: Medical Examination Publishing Co., 1970.

Amstutz, Arnold Everett. *Computer Simulation of Competitive Market Response.* Cambridge, Mass.: MIT Press, 1970.

Anderson, J., and J. Forsythe, eds. *Information Processing of Medical Records.* Amsterdam: North-Holland Publishing Co., 1970.

Andrews, Harry C. *Computer Techniques in Image Processing.* New York: Academic Press, Inc., 1970.

Apter, Michael John. *The Computer Simulation of Behaviour.* London: Hutchinson Publishing Group, Ltd., 1970.

Baillie, Ann, and R. J. Gilbert, eds. *Automation Mechanization and Data Handling in Microbiology.* New York: Academic Press, Inc., 1970.

Barrodale, Ian, et al. *Elementary Computer Applications in Science, Engineering, and Business.* New York: John Wiley & Sons, Inc., 1971.

Bellman, Richard Ernest, et al. *Algorithms, Graphs and Computers.* New York: Academic Press, Inc., 1970.

Bisco, Ralph L., ed. *Data Bases, Computers, and the Social Sciencs.* New York: John Wiley & Sons, Inc., 1970.

Blackman, Sheldon, and K. M. Goldstein. *An Introduction to Data Management in the Behavioral and Social Sciences.* New York: John Wiley & Sons, Inc., 1971.

Bongard, Mikhail Moiseevich. *Pattern Recognition.* Washington, D.C.: Spartan Books, 1971.

Brittin, Geoffrey M., and M. Werner, eds. *Automation and Data Processing in the Clinical Laboratory.* Springfield, Ill.: Charles C. Thomas, Publishers, 1970.

Chartrand, Robert Lee, ed. *Systems Technology Applied to Social and Community Problems.* Washington, D.C.: Spartan Books, 1970.

Clynes, Manfred, and J. H. Milsum, eds. *Biomedical Engineering Systems.* New York: McGraw-Hill Books Co., Inc., 1970.

Davis, Sidney, *Computer Data Displays.* Englewood Cliffs, N.J.: Prentice-Hall, Inc., 1971.

Davisson, William Ira. *Information Processing: Applications in Social and Behavioral Sciences.* New York: Appleton-Century-Crofts, 1970.

Eisele, James E. *Computer Assisted Planning of Curriculum and Instruction.* Englewood Cliffs, N.J.: Educational Technology Publications, Inc., 1971.

Enrick, Norbert Lloyd. *Creative Graphic Communication.* Princeton, N.J.: Auerbach Publications, Inc., 1972.

Fraser, Alex, and Donald Burnell. *Computer Models in Genetics.* New York: McGraw-Hill Book Co., Inc., 1970.

Fu, King-Sun, ed. *Pattern Recognition and Machine Learning.* New York: Plenum Press, Inc., 1970.

Hayes, Robert M., and J. Becker. *Handbook of Data Processing for Libraries.* New York: John Wiley & Sons, Inc., 1970.

Hemming, R. *Computers and Society.* New York: McGraw-Hill Book Co., Inc., 1972.

Hobbs, L. C., et al, eds. *Parallel Processor Systems, Technologies and Applications*. Washington, D.C.: Spartan Books, 1970.

Holtzman, Wayne Harold, ed. *Computer-Assisted Instruction, Testing and Guidance*. New York: Harper & Row, Publishers, 1971.

Konrad, Evelyn, et al. *Computer Innovating in Marketing Analysis*. New York: American Management Association, Inc., 1970.

Krieg, Arthur F., et al. *Clinical Laboratory Computerization*. Baltimore: University Park Press, 1971.

Lewis, Richard J. *A Logistical Information System for Marketing Analysis*. Dallas, Texas: South-Western Publishing Co., 1970.

Lincoln, Harry B., ed. *The Computer and Music*. Ithaca, N.Y.: Cornell University Press, 1970.

McDaniel, Herman, ed. *Applications of Decision Tables*. Princeton, N.J.: Brandon/Systems Press, Inc., 1970.

Margolin, J. B., and M. R. Misch. *Computers in the Classroom*. Washington, D.C.: Spartan Books, 1970.

Meltzer, Bernard Nathan, and D. Michie, eds. *Machine Intelligence 5*. New York: American Elsevier Publishing Co., 1970.

Meridith, J. C. *The CAI Author/Instructor*. Englewood Cliffs, N.J.: Educational Technology Publications, Inc., 1971.

Merritt, Frederick S. *Modern Mathematical Methods in Engineering*. Englewood Cliffs, N.J.: Prentice-Hall, Inc., 1970.

Middleton, Robert Gordon. *Computers and Artificial Intelligence*. Indianapolis: Howard W. Sams & Co., Inc., Publishers, 1970.

Miller, Arthur Raphael. *The Assault on Privacy*. Ann Arbor: University of Michigan Press, 1971.

Myers, Charles Andrew. *Computers in Knowledge-Based Fields*. Cambridge, Mass.: MIT Press, 1970.

Orr, Charles Henry, and J. A. Norris, eds. *Computers in Analytical Chemistry*. New York: Plenum Press, Inc., 1970.

Pescoe, J. K., ed. *Efficient Production Control, Loading, and Scheduling on the Computer*. Englewood Cliffs, N.J.: Prentice-Hall, Inc., 1971.

Prince, M. D. *Interactive Graphics for Computer-Aided Design*. Reading, Mass.: Addison-Wesley Publishing Co., Inc., 1971.

Rothman, Stanley, and Charles Mosmann. *Computers and Society*. Chicago, Ill.: Science Research Associates, 1972.

Sachman, H., and N. Nie, eds. *The Information Utility and Social Choice*. Montvale, N. J.: AFIPS Press, 1970.

Schade, J. P., and J. Smith, eds. *Computers and Brains*. New York: American Elsevier Publishing Co., 1970.

Schriber, Thomas J., and L. A. Madeo. *FORTRAN Applications in Business Administration* (Vol. II). Ann Arbor: University of Michigan Press, 1970.

Seely, Samuel, et al. *Digital Computers in Engineering*. New York: Holt, Rinehart & Winston, Inc., 1971.

Sheldon, Alan, et al, eds. *Systems and Medical Care*. Cambridge, Mass.: MIT Press, 1970.

Spindel, Paul D. *Computer Applications in Civil Engineering*. New York: Van Nostrand-Reinhold Company, 1971.

Tobler, W. R., ed. *Selected Computer Programs*. Ann Arbor: University of Michigan Press, 1970.

Weiss, Eric Alan, ed. *Computer Usage; Applications*. New York: McGraw-Hill Book Co., Inc., 1970.

Whisenand, Paul M., and T. T. Tamaru. *Automated Police Information Systems*. New York: John Wiley & Sons, Inc., 1970.

Whiteside, Conan Doyle. *EDP Systems for Credit Management*. New York: John Wiley & Sons, Inc., 1971.

Wolberg, J. R. *Application of Computers to Engineering Analysis*. New York: McGraw-Hill Book Co., 1971.

General

Alt, Franz Leopold, et al., eds. *Advances in Computers* (Vol. 1). New York: Academic Press, Inc., 1971.

ANSI Standard Vocabulary for Information Processing. Montvale, N.J.: AFIPS Press, 1970.

Awad, Elias Michael. *Business Data Processing* (3rd ed.) Englewood Cliffs, N.J.: Prentice-Hall, Inc., 1971.

Awad, Elias Michael, and the DPMA. *Automatic Data Processing* (2d ed.) Englewood Cliffs, N.J.: Prentice-Hall, Inc., 1970.

Bartee, Thomas C. *Digital Computer Fundamentals* (3d ed.) New York: McGraw Hill Book Co., Inc., 1972.

Benice, Daniel D. *Computer Selections*. New York: McGraw-Hill Book Co., Inc., 1971.

Benice, Daniel D. *Introduction to Computers and Data Processing*. Englewood Cliffs, N.J.: Prentice-Hall, Inc., 1970.

Bohl, Marilyn. *Information Processing*. Chicago, Ill.: Science Research Associates, 1971.

Boyes, R. L., et al. *Introduction to Electronic Computing: A Management Approach*. New York: John Wiley & Sons, Inc., 1971.

Cashman, Thomas J. *Review Manual for Certificate in Data Processing*. Anaheim, Calif.: Anaheim Publishing Co., 1970.

Cashman, Thomas J., and W. I. Keys. *Data Processing and Computer Programming*. New York: Harper & Row, Publishers, 1971.

Chapin, Ned. *Computers: A Systems Approach*. New York: Van Nostrand Reinhold Company, 1971.

Clark, Frank James. *Information Processing*. Palisades, Calif.: Goodyear Publishing Co., Inc., 1970.

Davis, Gordon B. *Introduction to Electronic Computers* (2d ed.) New York: McGraw-Hill Book Co., Inc., 1971.

Dawson, Clive B., and T. C. Wool. *From Bits to If's*. New York: Harper & Row, Publishers, 1971.

Desmonde, William Herbert. *Computers and Their Uses* (2d ed.) Englewood Cliffs, N.J.: Prentice-Hall, Inc., 1971.

Diebold, John. *Business Decisions and Technological Change*. New York: Frederick A. Praeger, Inc., 1970.

Dun & Bradstreet, Inc. *What the Manager Should Know About the Computer*. New York: Thomas Y. Crowell Co., 1970.

Elliott, Clarence Orville. *Plan for Introduction to Data Processing*. Homewood, Ill.: Richard D. Irwin, Inc., 1970.

Elliott, Clarence Orville, and R. S. Wasley. *Business Information Processing Systems* (3d ed.) Homewood, Ill.: Richard D. Irwin, Inc., 1971.

Feingold, C. *Introduction to Data Processing*. Dubuque, Iowa: Wm. C. Brown Company, Publishers, 1971.

Fuchs, Walter Robert. *Cybernetics for the Modern Mind.* New York: The Macmillan Co., Publishers, 1971.

Gleim, George A. *Electronic Data Processing Systems and Procedures.* Englewood Cliffs, N.J.: Prentice-Hall, Inc., 1971.

Gould, I. H. *IFIPS Guide to Concepts and Terms in Data Processing.* Montvale, N.J.: AFIPS Press, 1971.

Greenberger, Martin, ed. *Computers, Communications, and the Public Interest.* Baltimore: The Johns Hopkins Press, 1971.

Gruenberger, Fred Joseph, ed. *Expanded Use of Computers in the 70's.* Englewood Cliffs, N.J.: Prentice-Hall, Inc., 1971.

Gruenberger, Fred Joseph, ed. *Fourth Generation Computers.* Englewood Cliffs, N.J.: Prentice-Hall, Inc., 1970.

Gupta, Roger. *Electronic Information Processing.* New York: The Macmillan Co., Publishers, 1971.

Harman, Alvin J. *The International Computer Industry: Innovation and Comparative Advantage.* Cambridge, Mass.: Harvard University Press, 1971.

Holmes, J. D. J., and E. M. Awad. *Perspectives on Electronic Data Processing.* Englewood Cliffs, N.J.: Prentice-Hall, Inc., 1972.

Hull, Thomas Edward, and D. D. F. Day. *Computers and Problem Solving.* Reading, Mass.: Addison-Wesley Publishing Co., 1970.

Laurie, Edward J. *Modern Computer Concepts.* Dallas, Texas: South-Western Publishing Co., 1970.

Lorin, H. *Parallelism in Hardware and Software.* Englewood Cliffs, N.J.: Prentice-Hall, Inc., 1971.

Lott, Richard W. *Basic Data Processing* (2d ed.) Englewood Cliffs, N.J.: Prentice-Hall, Inc., 1971.

Luskin, Bernard J., and R. L. Howe. *Problems in Data Processing.* New York: The Macmillan Co., Publishers, 1971.

MacGowan, Roger A., and R. Henderson, eds. *CDP Review Manual: A Data Processing Handbook.* Princeton, N.J.: Auerbach Publications, Inc., 1972.

Martin, James Thomas, and A. R. D. Norman. *The Computerized Society.* Englewood Cliffs, N.J.: Prentice-Hall, Inc., 1971.

Meadow, Charles Troub. *The Story of Computers*. Irvington-on-Hudson, N.Y.: Harvey House Inc., Publishers, 1970.

Murphy, John Stewart. *Basics of Digital Computers* (Rev., 3 vols.) New York: Hayden Book Company, Inc., 1970.

Price, Wilson Titus. *Introduction to Data Processing*. San Francisco, Calif.: Rinehart Press, 1972.

Pylyshin, Zenon W. *Perspectives on the Computer Revolution*. Englewood Cliffs, N.J.: Prentice-Hall, Inc., 1971.

Sanders, Donald Howard. *Computers and Management*. New York: Mc-Graw-Hill Book Co., Inc., 1970.

Sanders, Donald Howard. *Computers in Business* (2d ed.) New York: Mc-Graw-Hill Book Co., Inc., 1972.

Saxon, James Anthony, and W. W. Steyer. *Basic Principles of Data Processing*. Englewood Cliffs, N.J.: Prentice-Hall, Inc., 1970.

Taviss, Irene, ed. *The Computer Impact*. Englewood Cliffs, N.J.: Prentice-Hall, Inc., 1970.

Wainous, S. J., et al. *Introduction to Automatic Data Processing*. Dallas, Texas: South-Western Publishing Co., 1971.

Withington, F. G. *The Use of Computers in Business Organizations*. Reading, Mass.: Addison-Wesley Publishing Co., 1971.

Information Storage and Retrieval

Henley, John Patrick. *Computer-Based Library and Information Systems*. New York: American Elsevier Publishing Co., 1970.

Jones, K. S. *Automatic Keyword Classifications for Information Retrieval*. London: Butterworth & Co., Ltd., 1971.

Kent, Allen. *Information Analysis and Retrieval*. New York: John Wiley & Sons, Inc., 1971.

Calton, G., ed. *The SMART Retrieval System*. Englewood Cliffs, N.J.: Prentice-Hall, Inc., 1971.

Vickery, Brian Campbell. *Techniques of Information Retrieval*. Hamden, Conn.: Archon Books, 1970.

Management

Benjamin, Robert I. *Control of the Information Systems Development Cycle*. New York: John Wiley & Sons, Inc., 1971.

Brandon, Dick H. *Management Planning for Data Processing.* Princeton, N.J.: Brandon/Systems Press, Inc., 1970.

Brandon, Dick H., and M. Gray. *Project Control Standards.* Princeton, N.J.: Brandon/Systems Press, Inc., 1970.

Brink, Victor Zinn. *Computers and Management, the Executive Viewpoint.* Englewood Cliffs, N.J.: Prentice-Hall, Inc., 1971.

Dickmann, Robert A. *Personnel Implications for Business Data Processing.* New York: John Wiley & Sons., Inc., 1971.

Ditri, Arnold E., et al. *Managing the EDP Function.* New York: McGraw-Hill Book Co., Inc., 1971.

Fowler, Gus. *Management's Decisions in Computer Equipment Selection.* New York: Vantage Press, Inc., 1971.

Freed, Roy N. *Materials and Cases on Computers and Law.* Boston: Boston University Press, 1970.

Harold, F. G. *A Handbook for Orienting the Manager to the Computer.* Princeton, N.J.: Auerbach Publications, Inc., 1971.

Head, Robert V. *A Guide to Packaged Systems.* New York: John Wiley and Sons, Inc., 1971.

Hemphill, Charles F., Jr. *Security for Business and Industry.* Homewood, Ill.: Dow Jones-Irwin, Inc., 1971.

Joslin, Edward O., ed. *Analysis, Design and Selection of Systems.* Arlington, Va.: College Readings, Inc., 1971.

Kanter, Jerome. *Management Guide to Computer Selection and Use.* Englewood Cliffs, N.J.: Prentice-Hall, Inc., 1970.

Rauseo, Michael J. *Management Controls for Computer Processing.* New York: American Management Association, Inc., 1970.

Rothery, Brian. *Installing and Managing a Computer.* Princeton, N.J.: Brandon/Systems Press, Inc., 1970.

Rubin, Martin L., and P. Zuckerman. *Handbook of Data Processing Management.* Princeton, N.J.: Brandon/Systems Press, Inc., 1970.

Shaw, J. C., and W. Atkins. *Managing Computer System Projects.* New York: McGraw-Hill Book Co., Inc., 1970.

Sibson, R. E. *Managing Professional Enterprises.* New York: Pitman Publishing Corp., 1971.

Stuart, H., and R. Yearsley. *Computers and Management*. New York: American Elsevier Publishing Co., 1970.

Szweda, Ralph A. *Information Processing Management*. Princeton, N. J.: Auerbach Publications, Inc., 1972.

Tatham, Laura Esther. *The Use of Computers for Profit*. New York: McGraw-Hill Book Co., Inc., 1970.

Tomlin, Roger. *Managing the Introduction of Computer Systems*. New York: McGraw-Hill Book Co., Inc., 1970.

Weinberg, Gerald Marvin. *The Psychology of Computer Programming*. New York: Van Nostrand Reinhold Company, 1971.

Whisler, Thomas. L. *The Impact of Computers on Organization*. New York: Frederick A. Praeger, Inc., 1970.

Operations Research

Dallenback, H. F., and E. J. Bell. *User's Guide to Linear Programming*. Englewood Cliffs, N.J.: Prentice-Hall, Inc., 1970.

Emshoff, James R., and R. L. Sisson. *Design and Use of Computer Simulation Models*. New York: The Macmillan Co., 1970.

Gass, Saul Irving. *An Illustrated Guide to Linear Programming*. New York: McGraw-Hill Book Co., Inc., 1970.

House, William C., ed. *Operations Research—An Introduction for Modern Applications*. Princeton, N.J.: Auerbach Publications, Inc., 1971.

Howell, J. E., and D. Teichroew. *Mathematical Analysis for Business Decisions* (Rev. ed.) Homewood, Ill.: Richard D. Irwin, Inc., 1971.

McGarlan, F. W. et al. *The Management Game*. New York: The Macmillan Co., 1970.

McMillan, Claude, Jr. *Mathematical Programming*. New York: John Wiley & Sons, Inc., 1970.

Maisel, Herbert, and G. Gnugnoli. *Simulation*. Chicago, Ill.: Science Research Associates, 1972.

Naylor, Thomas H. *Computer Simulation Experiments with Models of Economic Systems*. New York: John Wiley & Sons, Inc., 1971.

Orchard-Hays, W. *Advanced Linear Programming Computer Techniques*. New York: McGraw-Hill Book Co., Inc., 1970.

Schmidt, Joseph William, and R. E. Taylor. *Simulation and Analysis of Industrial Systems.* Homewood, Ill.: Richard D. Irwin, Inc., 1970.

Steinetz, C., and P. Rogers. *A Systems Analysis Model of Urbanization and Change.* Cambridge, Mass.: MIT Press, 1971.

Wagner, Harvey Maurice. *Principles of Operations Research.* Englewood Cliffs, N.J.: Prentice-Hall, Inc., 1970.

Programming

Breckner, David, and Peter Abel. *Principles of Business Computer Programming.* Englewood Cliffs, N.J.: Prentice-Hall, Inc., 1970.

Chapin, Ned. *Flowcharts.* Princeton, N.J.: Auerbach Publications, Inc., 1971.

Cohen, L. J. *Operating System Analysis and Design.* Washington, D. C.: Spartan Press, 1970.

Cuttle, Geoffrey, and P. B. Robinson, eds. *Executive Programs and Operating Systems.* New York: American Elsevier Publishing Co., 1970.

Emerick, Paul L., and J. W. Wilkinson. *Computer Programming for Business and Social Service.* Homewood, Ill.: Richard D. Irwin, Inc., 1970.

Farina, Mario Victor. *Flowcharting.* Englewood Cliffs, N. J.: Prentice-Hall, Inc., 1970.

Flores, Ivan. *Data Structure and Management.* Englewood Cliffs, N. J.: Prentice-Hall, 1970.

Galler, Bernard A., and A. J. Perlis. *A View of Programming Languages.* Reading, Mass.: Addison-Wesley Publishing Co., Inc., 1970.

Gauthier, Richard L., and S. D. Ponto. *Designing Systems Programs.* Englewood Cliffs, N. J.: Prentice-Hall, Inc., 1970.

Gildersleeve, Thomas Robert. *Computer Data Processing and Programming.* Englewood Cliffs, N. J.: Prentice-Hall, Inc., 1970.

Gleim, George A. *Program Flowcharting.* New York: Holt, Rinehart and Winston, Inc., 1970.

Gross, J. L., and Walter S. Brainerd. *Fundamental Programming Concepts.* New York: Harper & Row, Publishers, 1972.

Gruenberger, Fred Joseph. *Computing: A Second Course.* New York: Harper & Row, Publishers, 1971.

Husson, Samir S. *Microprogramming: Principles and Practices.* Englewood Cliffs, N. J.: Prentice-Hall, Inc., 1970.

Joslin, Edward O., ed., and R. C. McAdams. *Software for Computer Systems.* Arlington, Va.: College Readings, Inc., 1970.

Katzan, Harry, Jr. *Advanced Programming: Programming and Operating Systems.* New York: Van Nostrand Reinhold Company, 1970.

Lenher, J. K. *Flowcharting Workbook.* Princeton, N. J.: Auerbach Publishers Inc., 1972.

McDaniel, Herman. *Decision Table Software.* Princeton, N. J.: Brandon/ Systems Press, Inc., 1970.

Maginnis, J. B. *Elements of Compiler Construction.* New York: Appleton-Century-Crofts, 1971.

Pollock, B. W., ed. *Compiler Techniques.* Princeton, N. J.: Auerbach Publications, Inc., 1971.

Rustin, R. *Debugging Techniques in Large Systems.* Englewood Cliffs, N. J.: Prentice-Hall, Inc., 1971.

Sanderson, Peter Crenshaw. *Computer Languages: A Practical Guide to the Chief Programming Languages.* New York: Philosophical Library, Inc., 1970.

Sayers, A., ed. *Operation Systems Survey.* Princeton, N. J.: Auerbach Publications, Inc., 1971.

Sterling, Theodore David, and S. V. Pollack. *Computing and Computer Science.* New York: The Macmillan Co., Publishers, 1970.

Systems

Beckett, John A. *Management Dynamics.* New York: McGraw-Hill Book Co., Inc., 1971.

Benton, William King. *The Use of the Computer in Planning.* Reading, Mass.: Addison-Wesley Publishing Co., Inc., 1971.

Bocchino, William A. *Management Information Systems: Tools and Techniques.* Englewood Cliffs, N. J.: Prentice-Hall, Inc., 1972.

Brightman, Richard W. *Information Systems for Modern Management.* New York: The Macmillan Co., Publishers, 1971.

Brightman, Richard W., et al. *Data Processing for Decision Making* (2d ed.) New York: The Macmillan Co., Publishers, 1971.

Caruth, D. L., and F. M. Rachel. *Business Systems: Articles, Analyses, and Cases*. San Francisco, Calif.: Canfield Press, 1972.

Clifton, Harold Dennis. *Data Processing Systems Design*. Princeton, N. J.: Auerbach Publications, Inc., 1972.

CODASYL Systems Committee. *Feature Analysis of Generalized Data Base Management Systems*. New York: Association for Computing Machinery, 1971.

Daniels, Alan, and D. Yeates. *Systems Analysis*. Chicago. Ill.: Science Research Associates, 1971.

Dearden, John, et al. *Managing Computer-Based Information Systems* (Rev.) Homewood, Ill.: Richard D. Irwin, Inc., 1971.

Fuchs, Walter Robert. *Cybernetics for the Modern Mind*. New York: The Macmillan Co., Publishers, 1971.

Gildersleeve, Thomas Robert. *Decision Tables and Their Practical Application in Data Processing*. Englewood Cliffs, N. J.: Prentice-Hall, Inc., 1970.

Gildersleeve, Thomas Robert. *Design of Sequential File Systems*. New York: John Wiley & Sons, Inc.; 1971.

Head, Robert V. *Manager's Guide to Management Information Systems*. Englewood Cliffs, N. J.: Prentice-Hall, Inc., 1972.

Helvey, T. C. *The Age of Information*. Englewood Cliffs, N. J.: Educational Technology Publications, Inc., 1971.

House, William C., ed. *The Impact of Information Technology on Management Operation*. Princeton, N. J.s Auerbach Publishers Inc., 1971

House, William C., ed., *Information Systems: Current Developments and Future Expansions*. Montvale, N. J.: AFIPS Press, 1970.

Kelly, Joseph F. *Computerized Management Information Systems*. New York: The Macmillan Co., Publishers, 1970.

Krauss, Leonard I. *Computer-Based Management Information Systems*. New York: American Management Association, Inc., 1970.

Kriebel, Charles H., et al., eds. *Management Information Systems: Progress and Perspectives*. Pittsburgh, Penna.: Carnegie-Mellon University, 1971.

Li, D. H. *Design and Management of Information Systems*. Chicago, Ill.: Science Research Associates, 1972.

Lott, Richard W. *Basic Systems Analysis.* New York: Harper & Row, Publishers, 1971.

Lyon, John K. *An Introduction to Data Base Design.* New York: John Wiley & Sons, Inc., 1971.

McKeever, J. M., and B. Kruse. *Management Reporting Systems.* New York: John Wiley & Sons, Inc., 1971.

McRae, Thomas Watson, ed. *Management Information Systems.* Middlesex, Eng.: Penquin Books, Ltd., 1971.

Martin, James Thomas. *Future Developments in Telecommunications.* Englewood Cliffs, N. J.: Prentice-Hall, Inc., 1970.

Martin, James Thomas. *Introduction to Teleprocessing.* Englewood Cliffs, N. J.: Prentice-Hall, Inc., 1972.

Martin, James Thomas. *Systems Analysis for Data Transmission.* Englewood Cliffs, N. J.: Prentice-Hall, Inc., 1972.

Martin, James Thomas. *Teleprocessing Network Organizations.* Englewood Cliffs, N. J.: Prentice-Hall, Inc., 1971.

Martin, M. S. S. *Management Decision Systems.* Cambridge, Mass.: Harvard University Press, 1971.

Meadow, Charles Troub. *Man-Machine Communication.* New York: John Wiley & Sons, Inc., 1970.

Murdick, Robert Gordon, and J. E. Ross. *Information Systems for Modern Management.* Englewood Cliffs, N. J.: Prentice-Hall, Inc., 1971.

O'Brien, James Jerome. *Management Information Systems.* New York: Van Nostrand Reinhold Company, 1971.

Pollack, S. L. *Decision Tables: Theory and Practice.* New York: John Wiley & Sons, Inc., 1971.

Prince, Thomas Richard, *Information Systems for Management Planning and Control* (Rev.). Homewood, Ill.: Richard D. Irwin, Inc., 1970.

Ross, Joel E. *Management by Information System.* Englewood Cliffs, N. J.: Prentice-Hall, Inc., 1970.

Rothstein, Michael F. *Guide to the Design of Real-Time Systems.* New York: John Wiley & Sons, Inc., 1970.

Sachman, Harold, and R. Citrenbaum. *On-Line Planning: Toward Creative Problem Solving.* Englewood Cliffs, N. J.: Prentice-Hall, Inc., 1972.

Schoderbek, Peter Paul, ed. *Management Systems* (2d ed.). New York: John Wiley & Sons, Inc., 1971.

Wanous, S. J., et al. *Fundamentals of Data Processing*. Dallas, Texas.: South-Western Publishing Co., 1971.

Watson, Richard W. *Time Sharing System Design Concepts*. Montvale, N. J.: AFIPS Press, 1971.

Yourdon, E. *Design of On-Line Computer Systems*. Englewood Cliffs, N. J.: Prentice-Hall, Inc., 1972.

◀ INDEX